BM195 .N40

W9-AEX-156

Department of Religious Studies
Moore Reading Room
University of Kansas

Death and Birth of Judaism

DEATH AND BIRTH OF JUDAISM

The Impact of Christianity,

Secularism, and the Holocaust

on Jewish Faith

JACOB NEUSNER

Basic Books, Inc., Publisher   *New York*

The following publishers have generously given permission to use extended quotations from copyrighted works: From *Return to Judaism: Religious Renewal in Israel*, by Janet Aviad. Copyright © 1983 by the University of Chicago. All rights reserved. Published in 1983. Paperback edition 1985. Printed in the United States of America. Reprinted by permission of the publisher and the author. From *The Golden Tradition: Jewish Life and Thought in Eastern Europe*, by Lucy S. Dawidowicz. Copyright © 1967 by Lucy S. Dawidowicz. Reprinted by permission of Henry Holt and Company. From *The Israelis: Founders and Sons*, by Amos Elon. Copyright © 1971 by Amos Elon and renewed 1981 by Amos Elon and Adam Publishers. Reprinted by permission of the author. The poem "We believe," quoted in *Profiles of Eleven Men Who Guided the Destiny of an Immigrant Society and Stimulated Social Consciousness among the American People*, by Melech Epstein. Copyright © 1965 by Wayne State University Press. Reprint edition (with new introduction) by arrangement with Wayne State University Press in *Brown Classics in Judaica* (Washington, D.C.: University Press of America, 1987). From *The People of the Book: Drama, Fellowship, and Religion*, by Samuel Heilman. Copyright © 1983 by the University of Chicago. All rights reserved. Published 1983. Printed in the United States of America. Reprinted by permission of the publisher. From *The Zionist Idea: A Historical Analysis and Reader*, by Arthur Hertzberg, ed. Copyright © 1959 by Herzl Press, Inc. Reprinted by permission of the publisher. From *The Collected Writings*, vols. 1 and 3, by Samson Raphael Hirsch. Copyright © 1984 by Philipp Feldheim, Inc.

Art credit: pp. 31, 73, 187, 293—Suzanne R. Neusner

Library of Congress Cataloging-in-Publication Data

Neusner, Jacob, 1932–
    Death and birth of Judaism.

    References: p. 367
    Includes index.
    1. Judaism—History—Modern period, 1750–
2. Judaism—20th century.   3. Judaism—United States.
I. Title.
BM195.N48   1987   296'.09'03   86-47733
ISBN   0-465-01577-8

Copyright © 1987 by Basic Books, Inc.
Printed in the United States of America
Designed by Vincent Torre
87 88 89 90 RRD 9 8 7 6 5 4 3 2 1

For
Francis S. M. Hodsoll, Chairman
of the National Endowment for the Arts

for
the entire staff
of the National Endowment for the Arts

In tribute to excellence of leadership and professionalism in
administration

in the service
of those acts of the soul and spirit that cannot be administered
but only cherished and appreciated

and for
my colleagues on the National Council on the Arts

In tribute to the sagacity of friends and co-workers
who have taught me the wisdom of contributing
through acts of commission
in consultation, warning, and encouragement
and acts of omission
in restraint and forbearance

It is a privilege to join in public service with such as these.

CONTENTS

CONTENTS

ix

PREFACE

This book forms the final component of a trilogy in which I present a general theory of the history of Judaism—a trilogy that arose out of an earlier work, *Foundations of Judaism: Method, Teleology, Doctrine.*[1] In my researches for this latter book, I found myself drawn over and over to the pages of the Talmud of the Land of Israel, a document that reached closure late in the fourth century of the common, or Christian, era. Gradually I was led to the thesis that it was in that century, with the establishment of Christianity as the state church in the West, that Judaism took the form that became normative over the next fifteen centuries. (I have had the pleasure of finding the same thesis, on the basis of other evidence, announced by Rosemary Radford Ruether.[2])

In the first volume of my trilogy, *Judaism in the Matrix of Christianity,*[3] I set forth the thesis that Judaism in its received and classical form took shape in the fourth century; and in the second volume, *Judaism and Christianity in the Age of Constantine,*[4] I compare the treatment of important topics confronting the two fourth-century heirs of ancient Israel's heritage, in order to place into a larger context the initial results of the two earlier books. Also, in this second volume, I focus on the political crisis that led to that normative Judaism—the Judaism of the dual Torah—and thus lay the foundations for this third, and final, volume.

Parallel to this book is a separate study, *Self-Fulfilling Prophecy: Exile and Return in the History of Judaism,* which presents a single field theory for the entire history of Judaism.[5] This theory links the theory behind the trilogy to the larger paradigm of the Judaism that came to expression in the Torah of Moses, which was set forth in the aftermath of the destruction of the First Temple in 586 and the return to Zion in the fifth century B.C.E. (before the common era, or B.C.). In this work, I maintain that a single generative pattern served as paradigm for all Judaisms from the fifth century B.C.E. to the present, inclusive of those Judaisms of the twentieth century that in no way draw upon the Judaism of the dual Torah.

In the book at hand, I place into the context of the Christian West what I call the "death and birth of Judaism." For my view is that when, in the late eighteenth century with the French and American revolutions, Christianity lost its status as self-evident truth to Christians in parts of the West, the Judaism framed centuries before in the encounter with that claim likewise lost its self-evidence to Jews in those same areas, and died. And after the end of self-evidence—looking back, we call it innocence—came self-consciousness. Then, for Jews, began the modern age in the history of Judaism, with the birth of not just one new Judaism but of several Judaisms or Judaic systems. It is these systems and their great predecessor, the Judaism of the dual Torah, that I propose to examine here.

Now that I have presented my thesis, let me briefly introduce myself. First, I do not claim to have found my way alone through the byways of the several major contemporary Judaisms but have relied on road maps supplied by others. I bear responsibility only for selecting as my sources of facts and description—and, in some measure also, of analysis—the particular specialists I cite in each chapter in the shank of my book. However heavily I have drawn on the research of these authors, I have known precisely what I wanted to find out in it. That definition of the inquiry constitutes, in my judgment, my principal contribution to this theory of the history of Judaism: that is, the question properly asked.

This question has two parts: one descriptive, one interpretive. In describing the history of Judaism, I ask whether each Judaism continues in a linear and incremental way the preceding systems, or whether each is essentially new and inventive. And, in interpreting the history of Judaism, I ask a three-part question: First of all, why did Judaism work when it worked? Second, why did it stop working? Third— here as a believing Jew I want to know—what can we do to make it work again?

I care about the answers to these questions of interpretation because I value all of the Judaisms—religious and mythic alike—that I analyze here, and have found a comfortable niche in most of them; to me, none lacks in human interest. As a Jew myself, I am mostly the fish, not much the ichthyologist. For my own deepest conviction is that the Judaism that accords with the human situation of the Jewish people is the Judaism of the dual Torah, the one that came to literary expression in the political situation of the fourth century and found its competition in the political situation of the nineteenth and mainly the twentieth. And I think that the fourth century, for all its urgent problems of state and creed, provided for humanity a better life than has the twentieth—humanly better, if not quite so interesting, there having been then less murder of nations as a whole. But that personal judgment plays no role in this book, except as it imparts to my vision a certain astigmatism.

My scholarly ambition has always extended to the framing of a general, or field, theory for the entire history of Judaism—ancient, medieval, and modern. I wrote this book at the point at which, after thirty years of work, my approaches to the study of the period in which I specialize had yielded questions pertinent as much to the analysis of the Judaisms of our own day as to those of the third and fourth centuries. My interest in framing a field theory to encompass the history of Judaisms in modern times, on the one side, and the entire history of Judaism, on the other, therefore made it inevitable that the present experiment in interpretation would be undertaken.

In closing I wish to acknowledge the valuable work of my editors at Basic Books, Steven Fraser and Phoebe Hoss. They taught me much. If this book proves persuasive and engaging, they should get the credit. My deepest conviction has always been that my editor is everywhere right. These gifted partners of mine once more validate that faith.

For many years I have discussed with a number of colleagues the theoretical ideas that finally reach formulation in this book. The profound influence of Jonathan Z. Smith makes itself felt on every page. Everyday discourse with Ernest S. Frerichs, Wendell S. Dietrich, and William Scott Green and the fresh and stimulating perspective of Calvin Goldscheider and Alan Zuckerman draw my attention upward from late antiquity, where I live most of the time, to the twentieth century.

—JACOB NEUSNER
Program in Judaic Studies
Brown University
Providence, Rhode Island

28 July 1986
My fifty-fourth birthday

Death and Birth of Judaism

RELIGION, THEOLOGY, AND POLITICAL CHANGE

The Judaism that died and in new expressions came to re-birth in modern times addressed a set of urgent questions, and, for its followers, who included most Jews in the world, answered those questions with truths deemed self-evident. The birth of the Judaism that died in modern times had taken place fourteen hundred years earlier, in the year 312—that is, the year of Constantine's victory and acces-sion to the throne of Rome after a vision of a cross and the words, "By this sign you will conquer." That moment

3

marked the beginning of Western civilization, for in it was born the Christian polity, which until nearly our own day has defined the civilization of the West. With Constantine, Christianity became the definitive power in the politics of the West. It died in 1787, with the American Constitution (as we Americans would see matters) or with the French Revolution (as Europeans might prefer). Then Christianity began its journey out of its dominant position in the center of the political arena. The Judaism that flourished in Christendom and in Islam addressed the questions of Judaic polity in a subordinated but tolerated status—that is, the polity that came into being in 312. That same Judaism passed away in 1787 (as we would see it) or in 1789 (as Europeans would prefer), when a new and different set of questions impressed large numbers of Jews as urgent. Those questions concerned not a Judaic polity but the Jewish citizen, not the collectivity but the individual. Answers to these questions constituted the Judaisms aborning in modern times.

This book, which deals with eight Judaisms, tells the story of the death, in consequence of political change, of one of them, the Judaism that had flourished throughout the history of the Christian West; and it further surveys the birth of seven, each a new Judaism responding to the questions precipitated by those same changes. In fact, three powerful forces, all of them realized in wholly political forms, successively defined the questions Jews identified as urgent. These were Christianity, down into the nineteenth century; secularism, through the nineteenth and into the twentieth century; and the Holocaust, from the last third of the twentieth century—it would now appear—into deep into the twenty-first. Beyond that time no one can now imagine.

Christianity defines the starting point; and, its demise, the death of that Judaism. For the Judaic system at hand, the one that flourished through the history of the West as Christendom, took up the challenge of Christianity and therefore explained to Jews the context and meaning of Israel, political and supernatural alike. Christianity (and, in its time and place, Islam as well) took for granted the fundamental facticity of Israel's claim to form not only a distinct, but a distinctive and special, nation in God's commonwealth. According special status to Israel, Christendom and Islam affirmed the biblical picture, though, of course, modifying it in light of what each deemed further chapters in the sacred history. True, Christianity would further maintain that the Church formed the new Israel; that along with the Hebrew Scriptures, a further set of holy books, the New Testament, contained the word of God. Along these same lines, Islam held that, beyond Moses, then Jesus, Muhammed formed the seal of prophecy, the Quran, God's last and perfect word. But both Christianity and Islam saw Israel, the Jewish people, within the same supernatural view of a world created and governed by one God, who had revealed Himself to Israel (if also through Jesus Christ and the prophet Muhammed), a view contained within the Hebrew Scriptures revered, also, by Israel, the Jewish people. For its part, a defeated and disappointed people, Israel in those same Scriptures read an account of itself that contradicted its present condition. The scriptural story of a contract between Israel and God, confirmed in the experience of exile and return from 586 B.C., with the destruction of the First Temple of Jerusalem, to 450 B.C., with the building of the Second, pointed toward rules governing Israel's history that, for the moment, had not been kept. The advent of Christianity as the religion of the Roman empire made acute a long-standing chronic crisis in the divine economy, and thus determined the agenda of the Judaism that reached written expression at the end of the fourth century. This, the Judaism of the dual Torah, mediated between the expectation and the reality. Answering all of the questions then and, for the history of the Christian West, afterward pressing upon Israel, this Judaism explained the Jews' distinctive way of life in the here and now as a medium of sanctification and promised in response to acceptance of its subordinated political position and adherence to its way-of-life salvation in the end of days.

Challenging Israel to explain itself, Christendom and Islam therefore received from the Judaism of the dual Torah those answers that, for Israel, constituted self-evident truth: the way of life, the world view, formed by a concrete Israel, that in that time and place constituted a Judaism. Specifically, the urgent and inescapable question answered by the Judaism that first took shape in response to the rise of Christianity addressed the standing and status of Israel in a world in the charge of others than Israel. That Judaism had to explain the meaning of a history that produced the Christian empire, Rome (and later would yield the Islamic nation as well). Identifying, within its theory of Israel, Christendom and Islam with the family of Israel, that Judaism saw Rome as Esau, as against Jacob, and later would identify Islam as Ishmael, as against Isaac. The Judaism of the dual Torah further answered the question, Who is Israel? by showing that Israel, living the holy way of life prescribed by the Torah as interpreted by Israel's sages, would humbly accept God's will now and, in time, would receive that salvation that is coming to God's first love. The defeated nation therefore learned from its political subordination the lesson of correct service to its true lord and master, God alone. The politics of the defeated and subordinated nation bore within itself confirmation of the supernatural standing of that same nation: nothing was what it seemed; everything pointed toward a deeper truth, beneath appearances. So long as Christianity, in its diverse forms, defined that intellectual and political structure that accorded to Israel, the Jewish people, a role of supernatural consequence, the Judaism that took up the challenge of Christianity retained its standing, among Jews, as a complete and ample reply to the urgent questions of the world. The world view of Judaism in its classic statement furthermore corresponded to the way of life lived by Jews in accord with that same statement; and both accounted for the condition of Israel, the Jewish people. The whole fit together and, moreover, proved coherent with the political context in which Israel endured.

A measure of the remarkable success of that Judaism (which, as I shall explain, we call the Judaism of the dual Torah because of its insistence that God at Sinai had revealed God's will, the Torah, in two media, written and oral) is readily at hand. Two hundred years later, Islam swept across the Middle East and North Africa, by that time Christian for half a millennium; and Christianity, which had triumphed by the sword of Constantine, fell before the sword of Muhammed. The Christian ocean evaporated, as vast once-Christian populations accepted Islam. Yet the small, deep pools of Judaism scarcely receded. That Judaic system that accounted for and made tolerable Judaic subordination in the here and now explained this new event. And the same Judaic system, into the nineteenth century in eastern Europe, and down to the middle of the twentieth century for the great Judaic communities in Muslim countries, flourished—which is to say, remained the self-evident answer to the urgent question.* In chapter 1, I tell the story

---

* Because no equivalent process revised the politics of the Islamic world, in general the issues facing the Jews there remained constant. Where a process of secularization of politics did get under way, as in Algeria and the other parts of Islam subject to European rule, the received Judaic system met competition within Jewry. But, for the bulk of the Jews in Islam in the mid-twentieth century, the creation of the State of Israel and (for a great many) emigration from the Muslim to the Western nations, including the State of Israel, marked the beginning of the same processes that, for European and American Judaic systems, began with the American

of that Judaism of the dual Torah, oral and written, as it lived and died in the Christian West.

Redefining the political civilization of the West, a vast process of secularization removed Christianity—first in the Protestant West, then in the Roman Catholic center and south, and finally in the Christian Orthodox (Greek, Russian) east, of Europe—from its established position as the definitive force.* Throughout the nineteenth century, far-reaching political movements—appealing to the nation-state and to man as the measure of all things, rather than to the kingdom of God and to heaven's will—set forth a new politics. That program of secularization raised a fresh set of questions also for Israel, the Jewish people. In the nature of things, these had nothing whatever to do with Israel's supernatural standing in God's plan for creation and the history of humanity. Posed by political changes—as much as the original questions had taken political form—the new set of urgent concerns engaged many Jews, at first particularly in western European countries, later on in the eastern European ones and in their extension in America, in a new set of inquiries. These inquiries produced a fresh program of self-evident answers, and those answers in the nineteenth century constituted a new set of Judaisms.

Constitution and the French Revolution. And, we must notice, those same processes of secularization and political change took place in a very different world from the one that defined the setting for the birth of the Judaic systems of Europe and America in the nineteenth and twentieth centuries. That is why the study of the Judaisms of the Jewries of North Africa and the Middle East, who now form the majority of the population of the State of Israel, today forms the single most interesting topic for a study of the history of Judaism. But that subject falls well outside the framework of this book, for the simple reason that, for the larger part of the Jewries of the Islamic world, the Judaism of the dual Torah never died, as it progressively did for the bulk of the Jewries of Christendom from the eighteenth century on.

* Why the mythic structure and ritual construction of the dual Torah served the Jews equally successfully in Islamic countries represents a separate set of questions, of no interest here. Whether the same political considerations apply has no bearing on my case in this book.

Continuous with the received system of the dual Torah, these new Judaisms broke from that system because they took up a critical issue wholly outside the imagination of the received Judaism: the Jew as individual and citizen, not Israel as supernatural social entity. Indeed, all of them took as their principal concern the definition and justification of permissible change. For two hundred years, all new Judaisms began by defining the character and meaning of their departure from the old, received system. The generative issue faced by each new Judaic system had to do with the secular standing and status of Jews, seen as individuals and (at least ideally) as citizens like all other citizens. "To the Jews as citizens, everything, to the Jews as a nation, nothing" found in the Jewish Enlightenment the counterpart slogan: "A Jew at home, a man outside."* That formulation violated the language rules of the Judaism of the dual Torah, for the appropriate subject of any verb was not *a* Jew but *Israel*, understood always to refer to the holy people. The received Judaism of the dual Torah did not (and did not have to) deal with the possibility that Jews could ever be individual, let alone secular—that is to say, anything other than holy Israel, all together, all at once. It made no provision for Jews to be something else, unless they ceased, of course, to be Jews at all. The Judaism of the Torah surely could not imagine the Jews ever to be something in addition, over and above Israel. But all Judaisms of the nineteenth century explained that *something else* that Jews could and should become.

Taking that same political form that the received system

---

* The role and standing of women in the history of the formation of Judaic systems in modern times forms a subject awaiting systematic study. In general, the new Judaisms also redefined the theory of the woman. Reform Judaism was first to ordain women as rabbis, but did so only in the 1970s. Much earlier, by contrast, both Jewish socialism and Zionism in theory, and sometimes even in practice, accorded to women equal responsibilities and rights.

had adopted, the new Judaisms explained where, how, and why Jews could find, in addition to the category *Israel*, a place in a new classification: namely, the classification of citizens of diverse countries, not solely (or not mainly) members of a holy, supernatural nation of their own. In exploring the premise that Jews could be also German or American or British or French, the Judaisms of the nineteenth century—first Reform, then Orthodox, finally Conservative—provided self-evidently valid answers to their communicants. Concurring that Jews would continue to be Israel, all three Judaisms redefined the category *Israel* that formed the centerpiece of any Judaism. All three moreover reworked the world view contained within the canon of the Judaism of the dual Torah, and reconsidered the way of life required by it. And, finally, addressing the condition of secularity in which, Jews imagined, they would find for themselves a place within the nation-state then coming into existence, the three Judaisms of continuation of the Judaism of the dual Torah further adopted the premise of the secular as distinct from the religious and—in answering the question of how to be both Israel and something in addition—posited that Judaism is, therefore always had been, a religion. In part II of this book, comprising chapters 2, 3, and 4, I describe and interpret the self-evident answers produced by three Judaisms that presented, as the ineluctable question, the issue of political change joined to the secularization of the politics of the West.

Unhappily for Israel, the Jewish people, the political changes that framed the urgent question for nineteenth-century Judaisms generated quite different issues from those that had been anticipated. Jews (and not they alone) imagined that they had to find a way of being both Jewish and something else. But their enemies wanted to find a way for Jews to stop *being* altogether—and very nearly succeeded. These anti-Semites began their work in the late nineteenth century, writing a chapter on the Jews in the larger history of imperialism and racism that encompasses in a single history most of Europe, Africa, and Asia, as well as the Western hemisphere. Part of the long and dismal story of anti-Semitism, culminating in the Holocaust (but, alas, still a powerful force in today's world), forced upon the Jews a question they had never before had to answer. The generally benign, but sometimes malign, settlement of Christendom and Islam* ordinarily promised the Jews (at least) their lives, so the critical question facing them involved merely their dignity and self-respect, of which they themselves could take charge. The new issue, by contrast, changed the circumstances of Jews' existence no less drastically than had the destruction of the Second Temple in Jerusalem, in the year 70, and far more decisively than had the rise of Christianity to political dominance in the fourth century.

The impact of the Holocaust on Judaism began long before the advent of Hitler. Anti-Semitism from the late nineteenth century identified the Jews as the source of all misfortune. Economic changes at the same time dislocated those long-term structures that for centuries had sustained the peoples of eastern Europe, including the Jews. While Jews identified as the critical issue the question of change— political, but also religious—the world, as it happened, changed in other ways. The stakes proved those of life or death, in both politics and economics. When large numbers of Jews faced underemployment and near-starvation, as they did in eastern Europe during the general changes accompanying modernization of the region's economy, political and even religious change seemed trivial. For the Judaisms of the twentieth century, the new age began

---

* To Islam, Judaism represented a trivial matter, not the obsession that, for theological reasons, it involved in Christendom.

in 1897, when two great systems were founded: Zionism, which did not become popular until the Holocaust and the creation of the State of Israel; and Jewish socialism (in the form of the Jewish union, the Bund), the most powerful Judaism of the first half of the twentieth century.

While both fell into the classification of secular and political movements, concentrating on organizing powerful institutions of political and economic change, each in its way framed a Judaic system. For the requirements of such a system—a world view that answered the critical question, a way of life that expressed in concrete ways the elements of the world view, the two components coherent and explicitly addressed to a clearly defined Israel—were met by both. Zionism answered the political question with the (to its devotees) self-evidently true answer that the Jews constitute "a people, one people," and should found the Jews' state. Jewish socialism answered the economic question (also a political one) with the (to its adherents) obviously true answer that the Jews had to form their own union and undertake economic action as the Jewish sector of the working class of the entire world, united effectively to reform the economic foundations of the West. Jewish socialism further identified itself with the Yiddish language, and the ideology of yiddishism joined Jewish socialism, so that yiddishism formed the cultural and ideological statement—the world view, in terms of the analytical categories used here—for that Judaism for which Jewish socialism dictated the way of life. Part III of this book, in chapters 5 and 6, describes and analyzes the Judaisms that maintained, as self-evident truths, the positions that the Jews form a political entity like other polities (Zionism) or constitute part of the international working class and must organize themselves as a distinct ethnic entity with its own language (yiddishism) into effective unions for class interest (Jewish socialism).

The twentieth century produced one further Judaism of note, like the others stressing political questions, but framing its own set of urgent questions and producing its distinctive, self-evident answers. It is what I call here *American* Judaism: that is, a Judaic system particular to the American setting (though with counterparts in other parts of the Judaic world, including the State of Israel).* American Judaism is the Judaism of Holocaust and Redemption, which takes as its ineluctable question the meaning of Jewish existence after the systematic murder of most of the Jews of Europe, and offers as its self-evident reply the proposition that the redemption constituted by the creation of the State of Israel serves as the other half of the whole story of the meaning of what has happened. The way of life of that distinctive Judaic system—flourishing side by side with the way of life of the continuator Judaisms of the nineteenth century—lays emphasis upon activities in support of the State of Israel and of other political causes closely related to Israeli concerns—for example, the liberation of Soviet Jewry. The world view of the Judaism of Holocaust and Redemption, a set of self-evidently valid truths identified or discovered (not merely formed) in response to this essentially political agenda, sees the Jews as beleaguered, without choices or alliances, facing a world of unremitting hostility, which, however, Jews can through political action change to their own taste.

That distinctively American Judaism, separate in all im-

* The Israeli counterpart, also a Judaism of Holocaust and Redemption, bears its own points of stress. It answers Israeli questions—for example, Why should I live here? It provides its own way of life. While it corresponds to the American Judaism of Holocaust and Redemption, it is in no important way cogent with it—despite the fact that it appeals to the same symbolic vocabulary. Its way of life, for one thing, lays entirely different demands on the devotee from those placed upon the devotee of American Judaism. The Israeli who frames the world view and way of life presented by the Israeli Judaism of Holocaust and Redemption lives in the State of Israel, and the American counterpart not only does not do so but also does not imagine why he or she should have to do so.

portant ways from the Judaism of the dual Torah, should not be confused with the nineteenth-century Judaisms of continuation, which carried forward the system of the dual Torah. Reform, Orthodoxy, and Conservative Judaisms formed Judaisms *in America*, adapting to the American circumstance Judaisms that had taken shape elsewhere and answering a set of questions essentially distinct from the concerns that would prove particular to the American context. American Judaism, by contrast, in no important way carried forward the received Judaism of the dual Torah, but created institutions distinct from the institutions that gave social and concrete form to that received Judaism in its American version, and drew not at all from the inherited canon, except for proof-texts. These proof-texts—quotations of Scripture, for instance—were assembled after the fact, to prove propositions already adopted for reasons unrelated to the proof-texts' canonical authority. In part III, chapter 7, I describe the American Judaism, a Judaic system of Holocaust and Redemption.

The seventh of the new-born Judaisms of modern times treated here differs from the first six. It is the Judaism of reversion, a style characteristic of several Judaisms more than of a singular system, and uses the language of "return" (in Hebrew, *teshuvah*, which bears the further resonance of repentance for sin) to advocate fresh encounter with the Judaism of the dual Torah as both way of life and world view addressed to an Israel made up of the saving remnant: the Jews who will survive (whatever survival means). What that group of Judaic systems, all of them seen as Judaisms of reversion, has sought is the opposite of what the others found it necessary to explain and justify. Where the six Judaisms of the nineteenth and twentieth centuries all took for granted the death of the received system of the dual Torah, devotees of Judaisms of reversion have tried to remember what the earlier Judaisms wanted, in one way or an-

14

other, either to forget or to transcend. The self-evident fact of life addressed by the six Judaisms of the nineteenth and twentieth centuries derived from political change and explained how people should interpret and, in concrete terms, respond to facts of politics. All six Judaisms took for granted that the received system of the dual Torah had lost its standing as the given, the definitive structure that set the terms and categories of Jews' lives and of the life of Jews as a group. Each Judaism therefore provided a program pointing outward from that received system and specifying how one might legitimately change the received system or why Jews should abandon it altogether.

But by the end of the twentieth century, a Judaism was beginning to take shape that adopted as its premise a different question altogether: How to get back? We have to regard the Judaisms of reversion, or return, as a set of distinct systems because of the diverse forms they have taken. Reversionary Judaism in America may bring secular Jews to Reform, Orthodox, or Conservative synagogues and their respective schools. It may bring many to the circles of Hasidic followers of holy men (*rebbes*), and it brings some to what many call "traditional yeshivas"—that is, study centers for Torah learning, institutions of the Judaism of the dual Torah unaffected by the political changes that created the Judaisms under discussion here. Reversionary Judaism in the State of Israel brings secular Jews to yeshivas, also monastic centers for the study of the Torah, and leads secular collective communities, kibbutzim, to experiment with the texts and practices of the received and canonical systems of the dual Torah. In chapter 8, I spell out what I understand as the Judaisms of reversion and provide a description of the world view and way of life, as well as of the definition of the Israel under discussion, of those Judaisms.

This brings us to the startling gap of seventy-five years between the birth of Jewish socialism and Zionism in 1897

15

and that of American Judaism and the Judaisms of reversion late in the twentieth century—both of these being the most derivative and the least inventive of the Judaisms of rebirth after the death of the received system. In chapter 9, I argue that the failure of "systemopoeia"—the creation of systems—in Jewry constitutes one of the as yet immeasurable costs of the Holocaust. Furthermore, in my view, the desiccated conditions, in the twentieth century, of the inner life of the Jews' polity correspond to the bureaucratization of the corporate life of society, whether in government, academy, industry, economy, or culture.

That, briefly, forms the tale of the death and birth of Judaism as I propose to tell it and make sense of it. I suggest a general, or field, theory of Judaism in modern times, to explain what has happened and why. My question is a simple one but I wish to state it with emphasis: *Why did the Judaism of the dual Torah—called also "classical," "traditional," "rabbinic," or "talmudic" Judaism—work when it worked, and why did it stop working where and when it did?*

My basic account goes over familiar facts, but frames them in what I believe is a fresh and suggestive way. In modern times, that Judaic system for many Jews, particularly in the West and in contexts of political change and modernization, ceased to function as a Judaism of self-evident truth. For those Jews who determined both that they would remain Jews and that they would do so in ways not dictated by the received system, the received system lost not credibility but relevance (and therefore, of course, credibility too). Those Jews responded to the questions they found inescapable and answered them with truths they regarded as unavoidable and self-evident. In doing so, they worked out new meanings to what it meant in the conditions of modernization to be human within their particular idiom. The Judaisms of continuity, in the nineteenth cen-

16

tury, and the Judaisms of renewed self-evidence, in the twentieth, show us how inventive and brave people faced up to what was—we now know—change beyond measure, danger beyond endurance.

The reader, by this point, surely will want definitions of the somewhat special meanings I attach to words to convey my interpretation of the death and birth of Judaism: first, *system* (including *religious system*); second, *Judaism*. A religious system comprises a world view, explaining who people are, where they come from, what they must do; a way of life, expressing in concrete deeds that world view and linking the life of the individual to the polity; and a particular social group—in the case of a Judaic system, an "Israel," to whom the world view and the way of life refer. A Judaic system—or simply, a Judaism—comprises a world view, a way of life, and a group of Jews who hold the one and live by the other. When we speak of the birth of a Judaism, therefore, we point to the time and circumstance in which a given world view, way of life, and social group have coalesced in a definitive way. How do we discern that moment of coalescence? We look for the resort to a striking and also distinctive symbol, something that expresses the whole all together and all at once. For the symbol—whether visual or verbal, whether in gesture or in song or in dance or in, even, the definition of the role of woman—will capture the whole and proclaim its special message: its way of life, its world view, its definition of who is Israel.

Throughout the history of the Jewish people, diverse Judaisms have won the allegiance of groups of Jews here and there, each system specifying the things it regards as urgent both in belief and in behavior. All systems in common allege that they represent the true and authentic Judaism, or torah, or will of God for Israel, and that their devotees are Israel. Each ordinarily situates itself in a single historical line—hence, a linear history—from the entirety of the

17

past. Commonly a Judaism sees itself as the natural out-growth, the increment of time and change. These traits of historical or even supernatural origin characterize nearly all Judaisms. How, then, do we know one Judaism from an-other? When we can identify the principal symbol to which a given system on its own appeals, we realize that we have a wholly distinct and distinctive system.

Now that I have defined the categories of inquiry at hand, let me turn to the larger implications of my field theory for the interpretation of the modern history of religion. For my discipline is the history of religions, and I see the Judaisms of modern times as a set of interesting examples of proposi-tions of general intelligibility in the study not of religions but of religion.*

I see the Jews as a paradigm for what has happened to humanity at large. This, a further burden of the final chap-ter, is the point of the book as a whole and explains why I address here anyone interested in religion. I also regard the Jews as exemplary of certain propositions of interest in the analysis both of the nature of religion in general and of the history of religion in modern times. While therefore I offer a description, analysis, and interpretation of the Jews' power to create Judaic systems in response to Christianity, secularism, and the Holocaust, I mean in this book to sug-gest theses of general intelligibility and broad relevance. My intent is to treat the Jews as exemplary and suggestive, a lesson (among other lessons) in what it means to be human in our times. I have in mind, in particular, three theses: one on the history of Judaism; the other two on the nature of religion as exemplified by the history of Judaism, with spe-cial interest in the modern and contemporary period.

The first thesis is as follows: Judaism as it flourished in

---

* My debt to Jonathan Z. Smith, the principal (and sole important) theo-rist in the study of the history of religion today, is self-evident but gladly acknowledged.

the West was born in the encounter with Christianity as it defined the civilization of the West, and that same Judaism lost its power to persuade Jews of its self-evident truth when Christianity ceased to enjoy self-evidence among Christians. I shall spell out this thesis presently and offer evidence and argument for it in chapter 1.*

The second, on what we learn about religion from the history of Judaism, is unrelated to the first. It addresses the position, widely held, that there is such a thing as a religious tradition, which is continuous, has a history, and unfolds in a linear continuity. In the case of Judaism, the same premise maintains that there is such a thing as Judaism (not a Judaism, not a Judaic system) and that it develops in incremental steps, yielding in the end, at the zenith, Judaism as "we" know "it." The we is that group of Jews that identifies it—its particular system—not as a choice but as the choice: Judaism pure and simple. Many theologians argue precisely that position, whether Reform or Orthodox or Conservative. But, as I shall show, in the context of modern times, no single Judaism—hence, as a matter of hypothesis, no religious system—recapitulates any other of its species let alone the genus religion. Each Judaism—that is, each system—begins on its own and then—only then—goes back to the received documents in search of texts and proof-texts.†

* In my *Judaism and Christianity in the Age of Constantine* and *Judaism in the Matrix of Christianity*, I work out these propositions in great detail. The latter work, moreover, rests on the results of my earlier *Foundations of Judaism*.[1]

† This point, which I argue in *Self-Fulfilling Prophecy: Exile and Return in the History of Judaism*,[2] places me in the tradition of Max Weber. The study of Judaism in light of the debate precipitated by Weber has yet to begin. His feeble effort was in no way up to the standard of his analytical work on other special topics; and what has been done in the recent past is, in my judgment, ignorant and heavy-handed. The comparative study of Judaisms cannot, after all, take place among people who without study or analysis know that there was, and is, only a single Judaism (whichever one or group they identify as such), and that that Judaism had no history and

True, all Judaisms see themselves as incremental developments, the final and logical outcome of *the* (inevitable, necessary) history of Judaism. It is in the nature of theology to take precisely that position; and, from the perspective of the theologian, I can imagine no other. Every Judaism commences in the definition (to believers, the *discovery*) of its canon, whether of relevant historical facts or of holy books. All Judaisms therefore testify to humanity's power of creative genius: making something out of nothing. For, as we shall see, while each Judaism among the seven (inclusive of the reversionary Judaisms of our own day) claims to form the "tradition" or the "natural and historically necessary next step," in fact all pick and choose. Each creates and defines itself. I shall repeatedly emphasize that every Judaism in modern times alleges that it is the natural, or historical, Judaism but that that allegation always denies the obvious fact. Each Judaism begins in its own time and place and then goes in search of a useful past. Every system serves to suit a purpose, to solve a problem—in our context, to answer through a self-evidently right doctrine a question that none can escape or ignore. Orthodoxy, no less than Reform, takes up fresh positions and presents stunningly original and relevant innovations. The Judaism of the dual Torah in its day did no less. This is the burden of chapters 2 through 8, and the focus of my description of the six Judaisms treated in those chapters. Readers may find somewhat repetitious my interest in what was new, as well as in what was continuous, in the new Judaisms born after the death of the received system. But the polemic and apologetic of all Judaisms require us to test each against the same standard and criterion. The linear, incremental theory of Judaism (whichever one) so pervades Judaic discourse that it has, also, to define what for us is the urgent question. And, alas,

---

made no history. Weber scholarship, in its application to the study of religion in general, has yet to meet the standard of Weber himself.

the repetitious results in the end will form a self-evident answer.

The third thesis concerns the nature of religion in a time of change, such as the modern age of the death of Judaism and the birth of Judaisms has been, and proposes to account for the ongoing formation of new religious systems—in the language of this book, the new Judaisms that take up inescapable questions and produce ineluctable answers. The thesis is as follows: religion recapitulates resentment. I mean two things: one psychological, the other political. In psychological terms, a generation that reaches the decision to change (or to accept or to recognize the legitimacy of change) expresses resentment of its immediate setting and therefore of its past, its parents, as much as it proposes to commit itself to something better, the future it proposes to manufacture. In political change, each Judaism addresses a political problem not taken up by any other, and proposes to solve that problem. So when, in the second of the three theses, I say that the urgent question yields its self-evidently true answer, my meaning is this: resentment— whether at home or in the public polity—produces resolution. The two, when joined, form a religious system—in this book, a Judaism. That is the thesis of chapter 9.

Let me spell out the theses at hand and what I wish to explain in framing them. It is a simple proposition. In the tradition of Max Weber (not to mention of all religious believers in all religions all over the world), I maintain that religion forms one of the powerful forces in the life of humanity. It is not contingent, not secondary, not a function of some other, deeper reality, whether psychological or economic or sociological or political, as many people imagine; but is itself an autonomous power in the definition of history, society, culture, mind. In the language of social science, I argue that religion forms an independent variable. In particular, I propose to contribute to the study of religion a theory on the impact of political change on theological ideas. At issue is how particular ideas relate to the political circumstances of the people who hold those ideas. Religion as a fact of politics constitutes a principal force in the shaping of society and imagination alike; while politics, for its part, profoundly affects the conditions of religious belief and behavior. So I want to know how a stunning shift in the political circumstance of a religion affected that religion's thought about perennial questions. In fact, I deal with two moments of fundamental and radical change—one at the beginning, the other at the end—of the history of a religious system.*

All that has been said indicates my fundamental premise about what, in connection with the study of any religion, we wish to know. It is not theology or doctrine or belief but the interplay of religion and society: that is, the relationship between contents and context, conviction and circumstance, each viewed as distinct and autonomous, an independent variable. I regard religion as a decisive fact of social reality, and not merely as a set of beliefs on questions viewed in an abstract and ahistorical setting. Hence in this book I pursue one critical issue. I want to know the relationship between religious ideas and the circumstances, in particular in politics, of the society that holds them: the interplay, therefore, of religious contents and political and social context. So, in the great tradition, I treat the human being as a political animal, engaged in symbolic transactions of a collective—that is, a political—character. Thus I insist that religion, too, is something people do together. Not only so, but—to continue the idiom just used—a Judaism is something Jews do not by themselves but in the context of a larger world: in the West, Jews "do Judaism"

---

* The proposition of this paragraph and the preceding one is worked out in my *Self-Fulfilling Prophecy.*[3]

among Christians "doing Christianity," and in response to that circumstance and setting.

Let me give one concrete example of the consequence, in this book, of that conviction about the historical power of Judaism not only to respond to, but also to make, a world. When we ask about the relationship between context and contents, we adopt as our premise the view that Judaisms respond to the questions of the religious world around them but also shape that world. The argument here, for example, is that Judaisms answer questions forced upon Israel, the Jewish people, by important shifts in political facts. Historians of Judaism, both the Orthodox and the Zionist ones, for example, however, take as dogma the view that (because God revealed the Torah, which is beyond the control of man, or because the Jews are a distinct nation, utterly separate from all other nations) Christianity never made any difference to Judaism (any more than did Islam, a totally distinct set of problems). Faith of a "people that dwells apart" (these historians hold), Judaism went its splendid, solitary way, exploring paths untouched (for instance) by Christians. Christianity (the theory goes) was born in the matrix of Judaism; but Judaism, from then to now, officially ignored the new "daughter" religion and followed its majestic course in aristocratic isolation. Since, moreover, Judaism (in any form) is supposed always to have ignored, and never to have been affected by, Christianity in any form (the implicit argument), the future security of the faith of Judaism requires continuing this same policy, pretending that Christianity simply never made, and does not now make, any difference at all to Israel, the Jewish people. Here I treat that dogma as irrelevant. In my view—as I demonstrate in chapter 1—the Jews' world view and way of life began by taking full account of the political situation of Israel, the Jewish people, as a subordinated but tolerated polity. Then in chapters 2 through 8, we see the same pro-

23

Introduction

cess working itself out. Hence I argue that Judaisms form
social statements to political situations, as much as do other
religions. But religion—in context, a Judaic system—also
endures beyond the circumstance of its origination and so
bears within itself the power to shape and define the Jews'
polity.

That premise, as is now clear, accounts for the starting
point of this field theory of Judaisms in modern times, beginning in the fourth century. My stress on what has happened in modern times—the period of the death of one Judaism and the birth of other Judaisms—should not obscure
the importance, in the theory of modernization of Judaic
systems presented here, of the point of origin of the Judaism that I claimed at the outset was born in 312 and died in
1787. For when I allege, as I do, that a Judaism takes shape
to provide self-evidently valid answers to absolutely inescapable questions, I speak not of modern times alone but of
all times and all Judaisms. When I allege that the Judaism
of the dual Torah worked, when it worked, because it answered the questions posed to Israel by Christianity (and
later, Islam) and ceased to serve very well when other questions struck Jews as urgent and the original questions were
no longer critical, I am drawn to the fourth century. That
is when the Christian challenge took shape; and that, as it
happens, also is when the Judaism of the dual Torah came
into existence.

At this point, readers will want a clearer picture of that
Judaism of the dual Torah. The term *dual Torah* refers to
the generative conviction of the Judaism at hand, that when
God gave the Torah to Moses at Mount Sinai, the Torah
came to Moses and thence to Israel in two media, written
and oral. The written Torah, the five Books of Moses, as
well as the oral Torah, written down in the books produced
by the ancient rabbis, together constitute the canon of the
Judaism of the dual Torah. What is unique in the symbolic

24

system of the Judaism of the dual Torah is not appeal to the Torah in general—far from it. The Torah of Moses—that is, the Pentateuch, or the Five Books of Moses: Genesis, Exodus, Leviticus, Numbers, and Deuteronomy; or, indeed the entirety of the Hebrew Scriptures the world knows as the Old Testament—clearly occupied a critical place in all systems of Judaism from the closure of the Torah book, the Pentateuch, in the time of Ezra, about 450 B.C., onward. But in late antiquity, for one group alone the book developed into an abstract and encompassing symbol: specifically, in the Judaism that took shape in the formative age, the first seven centuries of the common era, but reached its characteristic symbolic expression only at the end of the fourth century, everything was contained in that one thing.

When we speak of *torah*, in the rabbinical literature of late antiquity, the word loses the capital T required when it refers to a single document, for *torah* does not denote a particular book, on the one side, or the contents of such a book, on the other. Instead, it connotes a broad range of clearly distinct categories of noun and verb, concrete fact and abstract relationship alike. *Torah* stands for a kind of human being. It connotes a social status and a sort of social group. It refers to a type of social relationship. It further denotes a legal status and differentiates among legal norms. As symbolic abstraction, the word encompasses things and persons, actions and status, points of social differentiation and legal and normative standing, as well as "revealed truth." In all, the main points of insistence of the whole of Israel's life and history come to full symbolic expression in that single word. If people wanted to explain how they would be saved, they would use the word *torah*. If they wished to sort out their parlous relationships with gentiles, they would use the word *torah*. *Torah* stood for salvation and accounted for Israel's this-worldly condition and the hope, for individual and nation alike, of life in the world to come. For the Judaism under discussion, therefore, the word *torah* stood for everything. The *torah* symbolized the whole, at once and entire. When, therefore, we wish to describe the unfolding of the definitive doctrine of Judaism in its formative period, the first exercise consists in paying close attention to the meanings imputed to a single word.

The Judaism of the dual Torah, which came to full expression in the writings of the sages of the Land of Israel, ("the Holy Land," "Palestine") of the later fourth and fifth centuries, takes a position separate from all of the prior Judaisms, as well as from those that would follow in modern times. What distinguishes the Judaism at hand is its doctrine of the dual media by which God's will for Israel, contained in the Torah revealed at Sinai, came down from ancient times. Specifically, this Judaism maintains that when God revealed the Torah at Sinai, it was transmitted in two media: one in writing, now contained in the written Torah (which the Christian world calls the "Old Testament"); the other through memory: that is, the other Torah was transmitted orally and memorized by great prophets, then sages, down to the time of the sages of the fourth century.

This other, orally formulated and orally transmitted Torah—this memorized Torah—derives from this Judaism and no other. We find the substance of the memorized, or oral, Torah in the writings of the ancient rabbis of late antiquity. While referring to an oral tradition that began at Sinai, these rabbis wrote their books from about 200 to 600. The first document of this oral Torah was the Mishnah, a philosophical law code closed at about the year 200. Further writings that fall into the classification of oral Torah include the Tosefta, a collection of supplements to the Mishnah's laws; a commentary on the Mishnah accomplished in the Land of Israel and called the Talmud of the Land of Israel, of about the year 400; a second such commentary, done in the Jewish communities of Babylonia and called the

Talmud of Babylonia, of about the year 600; as well as commentaries to the written Torah by the sages of the age—such as Sifra on Leviticus, Sifré on Numbers, another Sifré on Deuteronomy, Genesis Rabbah, Leviticus Rabbah, and the like. All of these other documents, but especially the Mishnah and its two great Talmuds, contain the teachings of sages in late antiquity, from the first through the sixth centuries of the common era. All together they form that other, that oral Torah, that God revealed to Moses at Sinai.

While, as I shall explain in chapter 1, the Judaism that reached its first formulation in writing began in the year 200 with the Mishnah (itself drawing upon statements formulated over the preceding century or so), it is only in the Talmud of the Land of Israel, about 400, and its closely allied documents, Genesis Rabbah and Leviticus Rabbah, that that Judaism's principal and indicative doctrines, symbols, and beliefs came to full and complete expression. The Mishnah shows us, therefore, a version of the Judaism of the dual Torah that reached writing before Christianity made an impact on the Judaic sages, while the Talmud of the Land of Israel and its associates show us the changes that were made in the encounter with Christianity as the triumphant religion of the Roman state. The first full statement of that Judaism of the dual Torah is contained in the Talmud of the Land of Israel, with complementary materials in other documents of the same age—namely, the end of that critical century that began with Constantine's declaring Christianity licit, then favored, religion, and ended with the Roman empire's declaring Christianity the religion of the state. Precisely how the Judaism of the dual Torah responded to the crisis at hand remains to be seen.

The Judaism that took shape in the Land of Israel in the fourth century, attested by documents brought to closure in the fifth, responded to that Christianity and in particular to its challenge to the Israel of that place and time and

27

flourished in Israel, the Jewish people, so long as the West was Christian. The reason, I hold, that Judaism, for Israel, dealt effectively with the urgent issues deriving from the world defined by now-regnant Christianity arises from that very point of definition. Before that time, Christian and Judaic thinkers had not accomplished the feat of framing a single program for debate. Judaic sages had earlier talked about their issues to their audience; Christian theologians had, for three centuries, pursued their arguments on their distinctive agenda. The former had long pretended the latter did not exist. Afterward, the principal intellectual structures of a distinctive Judaism—the definition of the teleology, method, and doctrine of that Judaism—reached definition and ample articulation. Each of these components of the system, as I show in chapter 1, met head on and in a fundamental way the challenge of politically regnant Christianity.

To conclude, let me state the thesis of the book in one brief paragraph.

The Judaic answer to the Christian *défi* remained valid, for believing Israel, as a matter of self-evidence for so long as Christianity dictated the politics in which Judaism and Christianity confronted one another. A Judaism of a particular sort was born in the matrix of Christianity (chapter 1); died with the death of the Christian world into which it had been born; and, in the West, yielded place to new Judaisms in response to three new worlds (chapters 2 through 8). These were: first, the post-Christian world of the nineteenth century; then, the non-Christian (indeed, anti-Christian) and secular world of the earlier twentieth century; and, finally, the era formed in the aftermath of mass annihilation in the later twentieth century. Those three worlds in modern times—respectively, the Christian, the secular, the *annihilative**—dictated the terms in which, as

* The Holocaust continues to generate its own new language.

28

well as it could, Israel, the Jewish people, made its life. In answering the urgent questions of the age of Christianity, secularity, and Holocaust, Israel, the Jewish people, framed those truths that, in their splendid power to answer questions to which, in truth, there can be no answers, provided sustenance in this age of suffering. So much for my premises, thesis, and argument.

Let me close with my judgment of the truth of the Judaisms before us. We may take the full measure of the power and the truth of those Judaisms—all of them—in a simple fact. When we realize that—despite it all, and in the face of it all, and against it all—in the aftermath of the Holocaust, Israel, the Jewish people, did not give up but did will to endure, we recognize the power of Judaic truth. To persuade Jewry to want to go on, to build even with the memory of entire destruction that had taken place, attests to that enduring self-evidence with which, even now, Jews invest these, their Judaisms. For each, in its acutely contemporary way, teaches that eternal truth of the Torah of Moses at Sinai, composed (to be sure) in the aftermath of the destruction of the First Temple and the building of the Second, 586–450 B.C., that for a Jew it is a sin to despair.

So, too, is it for us all; for, in the end, all that any of us can decide is solely to endure: to live to death—and beyond.

PART I
The Age of
Self-Evidence

CHAPTER 1

THE JUDAISM OF
THE DUAL TORAH

The Challenge of Christianity

We begin the story of the Christian impact on Judaism in the fourth, not the first, Christian century, because that is when Christianity as it would shape the West began; and because it was at the end of the age of Constantine that the Talmud of the Land of Israel and associated writings came forth with their initial formulations of the Judaism of the dual Torah. This Judaism reached its first clear and complete canonical expression between 400 and 450 in the Talmud and also in exegeses of the pentateuchal books of Genesis, on the origins of the world and of the holy people, Israel, and of Leviticus, on the holy way of life of that people. In these documents, the Judaism of the dual Torah, oral and written, first laid out its basic propositions on who is Israel.

33

Because of a political event that Israel could not ignore and the Church deemed probative, discourse between Judaism and Christianity in the fourth century found different people talking to different people about some of the same things. For the prior three hundred years, these same people had not debated a common issue; and for the next fourteen hundred years, they would not do so again. At the end of the eighteenth century a new politics presented to Israel, the Jewish people, a new set of questions and, by the way, called into question the self-evident truth of the enduring answers to the questions of the old agenda. These facts present a simple proposition: Judaism, as it flourished in the Christian West, was born in the age of Constantine and died in the beginning of the American experiment, when, in 1787, an other-than-Christian politics, and specifically secular, began with the Constitution of the United States of America and the French Revolution. Thus, Constantine inaugurated the politics in which Christianity defined the civilization of the West; and the American Constitution and the French Revolution brought to a conclusion the age in which a politically paramount Christianity had set the norm for the West.

Why did the advent of Christian rule in the Roman empire produce a Judaism? To Jews, the empire's move from reverence for Zeus to adoration of Mithra had meant nothing: the pagan gods were all alike, lacking any differentiation. Christianity was something else *because it was like Judaism*. Christians claimed that theirs was a Judaism—in fact, *the* Judaism—now fulfilled in Christ. Christians read the Torah and claimed to declare its meaning. They furthermore alleged, like Israel, that they alone worshiped the one true God. And they challenged Israel's claim to know that God—and even to be Israel, continuator of the Israel of the promises and grace of ancient Scripture. Accordingly, for their part, Israel's sages cannot have avoided the issue of

34

the place, within the Torah's messianic pattern, of the remarkable turn in world history represented by the triumph of Christianity. Since the Christians celebrated confirmation of their faith in Christ's messiahship and Jews were hardly prepared to concur, Constantine's conversion must have seemed to be the dark before the dawning of the messianic age.

At that time, through the fourth and into the fifth century, important Judaic documents were completed: particularly the Talmud of the Land of Israel, brought to a conclusion around C.E. 400; Genesis Rabbah, a systematic expansion of the story of Creation in line with Israel's later history; and Leviticus Rabbah, a search for the laws of history and society undertaken in passages of the book of Leviticus. These writings undertook to deal with agenda arising from the political triumph of Christianity: first, the meaning of history; second, the coming of the Messiah; third, the definition of who is Israel. The triumph of Christianity called all three, for Israel, into question. Christian thinkers for their part reflected on issues presented by the political revolution in the status of Christianity. Issues of the interpretation of history from Creation to the present, the restatement of the challenge and claim of Christ the King as Messiah against the continuing expectation of Israel that the Messiah is yet to come, and the definition of who is Israel—these made their appearance in Judaic and Christian writings of the day. Issues of Judaism as laid forth in documents redacted in the fourth and early fifth centuries exhibit remarkable congruence to the contours of the intellectual program presented by Christian thinkers.

The Judaic and Christian systems of the first century had prepared their respective peoples for worlds that would never exist. The Judaism of the day addressed a self-governing people, secure within its own political institutions; and the Christianity that emerged never envisioned

35

a Christian state. In the fourth century, the two systems traded places: the one prepared for politics lost its political system; the one unprepared inherited the world. In many ways, therefore, the fourth century marks the point of intersection of the histories of the two groups of religious systems, Judaic and Christian. For the histories of Judaism and Christianity in late antiquity mirror one another. When Christianity began, Judaism was the dominant tradition in the Holy Land and framed its ideas within a political framework until the early fifth century. Christianity there was subordinate and, from the beginning, had to work out against the background of that politically definitive Judaism. Judaism pondered deeply on political issues; but Christianity, never anticipating that it would inherit an empire and rule the world, scarcely made itself ready for its coming political power. The roles reversed themselves when the politically well-framed Judaism lost all access to an effective polity, while a politically mute Christianity entered onto responsibilities scarcely imagined a decade before they came into being.

True, Christians confronted a world for which nothing had prepared them. But they did not choose to complain. For the political triumph of Christ, now ruler of the world in dimensions wholly unimagined, brought its own lessons. All of human history required fresh consideration, from the first Adam to the last. The writings of churches now asked to be sorted out, so that the canon, Old and New, might correspond to the standing and clarity of the new Christian situation. So, too, one powerful symbol, that selected by Constantine for his army and the one by which he won— the cross—took a position of dominance and declared its distinctive message of a Christianity in charge of things. Symbol, canon, systemic teleology—all three responded to the unprecedented and hitherto not-to-be-predicted circumstance of Christ on the throne of the nations.

Just after that century of turnabouts, in the year 429, Israel in the Land of Israel lost its institution of autonomous government. The Jews of the Land of Israel then confronted a situation without precedent. That year marked the end of the patriarchal government that had ruled the Jews of the Land of Israel for the preceding three centuries, as the Roman government no longer accorded it recognition. It was the end of the Jews' political entity, their instrument of self-administration and government in their own land. Tracing its roots back for centuries and claiming to originate in the family of David, the Jewish government of the patriarchs had succeeded the regime of the priests in the Temple and the kings, first allies, then agents, of Rome on their throne. Israel's tradition of government, of course, went back to Sinai. No one had ever imagined that the Jews would define their lives other than together, as a people, a political society, with collective authority and shared destiny and a public interest. The revelation of Sinai addressed a nation; the Torah gave laws to be kept and enforced; and, as is clear, Israel found definition in comparison to other nations. It would have rulers—subject to God's authority, to be sure; and it would have a king now, and a king-Messiah at the end of time.

So the dawn of the fifth century brought a hitherto unimagined circumstance: an Israel lacking the authority to rule itself under its own government, even the ethnic and patriarchal one that had held things together on the other side of the end of long centuries of priestly rule in the Temple and of royal rule in Jerusalem. In effect, the two systems had from the first century to the eve of the fourth prepared for worlds that neither would inhabit: the one for the status of governed, not governor; the other, for the opposite. Christianity in politics would define not the fringes but the very fabric of society and culture. Judaism, out of politics altogether, would find its power in the donated obedience of people in no way to be coerced, except from within or from on high. Whatever "Christianity" and "Judaism" would choose as their definition beyond the time of turning, therefore, would constitute mediating systems, with the task, for the systems to emerge, of responding to a new world out of an inappropriate old. The Judaism that would take shape beyond the fourth century, beginning in writings generally thought to have come to closure at the end of that momentous age, would use writings produced in one religious ecological system to address a quite different one; and so, too, would the Christianity that would rule, both in its Western and in its Eastern expressions.

The confrontation (there never was a dialogue) between Christianity in all its forms and Judaism in the form imparted by sages, who were masters of the Torah and often employees of the Patriarch, continued for centuries because the conditions that precipitated it—specifically the rise to political dominance of Christianity and the subordination of Judaism—remained constant for fifteen hundred years. It seems to me self-evident, therefore, that—so far as ideas bearing political implications matter in bonding a group—the success among the people of Israel in Europe, western and eastern alike, of the Judaism defined in the fourth-century writings of the sages of the Land of Israel derives from the power and persuasive effect of the ideas of that Judaism. Coming to the surface in the writings of the age, that Judaism secured for despairing Israel a long future of hope and confident endurance.

For Israel did endure in the Christian West, secure in the conviction of constituting that Israel after the flesh to which the Torah continued to speak. How do we know the sages' Judaism won? Because when, in turn, Islam gained its victory some four centuries later, Christianity throughout the Middle East and North Africa gave way; but the sages' Judaism in those same vast territories retained the loyalty and conviction of the people of the Torah. The cross would rule only where the crescent and its sword did not. But the Torah of Sinai everywhere and always sanctified Israel in time and promised secure salvation for eternity. So Israel believed, and so does Israel believe today.

Issues in the Initial Confrontation

In the fourth century, two groups of intellectuals—Judaic sages, Christian theologians—argued about the same matters: the meaning of history, the identification of the Messiah, and the definition of who is Israel. They appealed to the same facts (those supplied by Scripture) and employed essentially the same mode of argument (historical facts indicate social laws that reveal God's plan and purpose for society). Two facts account for Judaic sages' and Christian theologians' sharing such a common program.

First is the inherited and shared Scripture of ancient Israel; and second is the political cataclysm of the advent of the age of Constantine. The Christianization of the Roman empire in the fourth century and the entry of Christianity into the world of politics and government in that same age defined the issues confronting both parties. Scripture told both parties that political change matters. For example, the rise and prosperity of a king was seen as a direct result of the people's obedience to the requirements of the Torah or the will of God. In Leviticus, chapter 26, the entire fate of the Israelite state was joined to obedience to the covenant, and the same viewpoint characterized nearly the whole of the prophetic literature. The upshot was that political change was taken to represent God's will—and God's judgment on the moral character of the people. The events of the day demonstrably affected Christians' conceptions of the meaning and end of history, vindicating their belief in Jesus as Christ, validating their claim to form the community of the saved, and constituting, for some believers, an Israel. And those same facts demanded from the sages a vivid and (for Israel, at any rate) persuasive response.

Christianity's explicit claims, now validated in world-shaking events of the age, demanded a reply. The sages of the Talmud provided it. At those specific points at which the Christian challenge met head on old Israel's world view, the sages' doctrines responded. What did Israel's sages have to present as the Torah's answer to the cross? It was the Torah. This took three forms. The Torah was defined in the doctrine, first, of the status, as oral and memorized revelation, of the Mishnah and, by implication, of other rabbinical writings. The Torah, moreover, was presented as the encompassing symbol of Israel's salvation. The Torah, finally, was embodied in the person of the Messiah who, of course, would be a rabbi. The Torah in all three modes confronted the cross, with its doctrine of the triumphant Christ, Messiah and king, ruler now of earth as of heaven.

The symbolic system of Christianity, with Christ triumphant, with the cross as the now-regnant symbol, with the canon of Christianity now defined and recognized as authoritative, called forth from the sages of the Land of Israel a symbolic system strikingly responsive to the crisis. The Messiah served, for example, to explain the purpose of the Judaic way of life: keep the rules of the Torah as sages teach them, and the Messiah will come. So the coming of the Messiah was set as the teleology of the system of Judaism as sages defined that system. The symbol of the Torah expanded to encompass the whole of human existence as the system laid forth the outlines of that existence. So the distinctive Judaic way of life derived, the system taught, from God's will. As for the importance of the doctrine that when

God revealed the Torah to Moses at Sinai, it was in two media, written (the Hebrew Scriptures) and oral (the teaching of the sages, beginning with the Mishnah), the canon of Sinai was broadened to take account of the entirety of the sages' teachings, as much as of the written Torah everyone acknowledged as authoritative. So the doctrine of the dual Torah told the Jews that their sages understood God's will, and that others did not. The challenge was met: Jesus, now king-Messiah, is not what the Christians say. God will yet send Israel's Messiah—when Israel does what has to be done to hasten the day. And Israel must keep the faith with the holy way of life taught as Torah—God's revelation—by the sages at hand. Thus, the Torah and not the cross stood as the principal symbol.

All we can do is point to the contrast between the sages' system as revealed in writings closed in the later second and third centuries, in particular the Mishnah and its closely allied documents, and the system that emerged in the writings of the later fourth and fifth centuries. The contrast tells the tale.

True, we do not know that in the books they produced at the end of the fourth century—the Talmud of the Land of Israel, the Genesis Rabbah, and the Leviticus Rabbah—Israel's sages said what they said specifically in order to meet the Christian challenge. Nor can we demonstrate that Jews for fifteen hundred years found self-evidently true the system of the sages because that system dealt with the political and intellectual challenge of Christianity. All we have is what the people said, in documents they edited, at that time. The topics that they chose to consider may be seen as a point-by-point response to the concerns that shaped the Christians' agenda. Thus, there really was an encounter, a confrontation, a kind of argument, upon the foundations of shared premises and a common core of facts agreed upon by both parties: not a dialogue, but at least an argument.

Judaism without Christianity: The Mishnah

Before the crisis of Constantine's age, we find a Judaism without Christianity. If Christianity presented an urgent problem to the sages behind the Mishnah—for example, giving systemic prominence to a given category rather than some other—we cannot point to a single line of the document that says so: that Judaism, for one thing, had no richly developed doctrine of the Messiah; for another thing, that Judaism worked out issues of sanctification, rather than those of salvation made urgent by Christian emphasis on that category. The Mishnah, a philosophical law code brought to closure at about the year 200, shows us a Judaism framed in response to issues of the destruction of the Temple and the subsequent defeat in the failed war for the restoration. The two issues that defined the setting of the Mishnah—therefore, its concerns—were, first, the destruction of the Temple in 70 and, second, the defeat of Bar Kokhba in 135. But the catastrophe of Bar Kokhba's war discredited this picture of the salvation of Israel that had enjoyed prominence for so long. For it was clear that whatever might happen, what would not occur is what had happened before. So Israel found itself cut off from the moorings of many centuries' endurance.

When, in the aftermath of the destruction of the Second Temple in the year 70 C.E. and the still more disheartening defeat of 135, sages worked out a Judaism without a Temple and a cult, they produced in the Mishnah a system of sanctification focused on the holiness of the priesthood, the cultic festivals, the Temple and its sacrifices, as well as on the rules for protecting that holiness from levitical uncleanness—four of the six divisions of the Mishnah on a single theme. When, in the aftermath of the conversion of the Roman empire to Christianity and the triumph of Christianity in the generation beyond Julian "the apostate," sages worked out, in the pages of the Talmud of the Land of Israel and in the exegetical compilations of the age, a Judaism intersecting with the Mishnah's but essentially asymmetrical with it, it was a system for salvation, focused on the salvific power of the sanctification of the holy people. Judaism as a whole, with its equal emphases on sanctification in the here and now and salvation at the end of time, would come to full and classic expression only in the Talmud of Babylonia, two hundred years after the Talmud of the Land of Israel. But the first of the two Talmuds set the compass and locked it into place.

The system portrayed in the Mishnah emerged in a world in which there was no effective Christianity. First, we find in the Mishnah no explicit and systematic theory of scriptural authority. We now know how much stress the Judaism in confrontation with Christianity laid on Scripture, with important commentaries produced in the age of Constantine. The framers of the Mishnah did not find necessary either a doctrine of the authority of Scripture or a systematic exegetical effort at the linking of the principal document, the Mishnah, to Scripture. Only Christianity made pressing the question of the standing and status of the Mishnah in relationship to Scripture, through the claim that the Mishnah was man-made and a forgery of God's will, which was contained only in Scripture.

Second, in the Mishnah we look in vain for a teleology focused on the coming of the Messiah as the end and purpose of the system as a whole. The Mishnah's teleology in no way invokes an eschatological dimension, as I shall discuss.

Third, the same Judaism laid no particular stress on the symbol of the Torah, though, of course, the Torah enjoyed prominence as a scroll, as a matter of status, and as the revelation of God's will at Sinai. Indeed, the Mishnah was so independent of Scripture that when the authors wished to say what Scripture said, they did so in their own words and in their own way. Whatever the intent of the Mishnah's authors, therefore, it clearly did not include explaining to a competing Israel, heirs of the same Scriptures of Sinai, just what authority validated the document and how the document related to Scripture.

When we listen to the silences of the Mishnah, as much as to its points of emphasis, we hear a single message—a message of a Judaism that answered a single encompassing question concerning the enduring sanctification of Israel, the people, the land, the way of life. What, in the aftermath of the destruction of the holy place and holy cult, remained of the sanctity of the holy caste, the priesthood, the holy land, and, above all, the holy people and its holy way of life? The answer: sanctity would persist, indelibly, in *Israel, the people*, in its way of life, in its land, in its priesthood, in its food, in its mode of sustaining life, in its manner of procreating and so sustaining the nation. That holiness would endure. And the Mishnah then laid out the structures of sanctification: What does it mean to live a holy life? But that answer found itself absorbed, in time to come, within a successor system, with its own points of stress and emphasis. That successor system, both continuous and asymmetrical with the Mishnah, would take over the Mishnah and turn it into the one whole Torah of Moses, our rabbi, that became Judaism.

Christianity and the Indicative Traits of the Judaism of the Dual Torah

When Rome became Christian, and when Christianity became first licit, then established, and finally triumphant, the condition of Israel changed in some ways but not in others. First, the politics and social context of a defeated nation remained the same. Israel in the Land of Israel/Palestine/ the Holy Land had long ago lost its major war as an autonomous political unit of the Roman empire. In the year 70 C.E., the Romans had conquered the capital and destroyed the Temple there. In 132, the Jews rebelled under the leadership of Bar Kokhba ("son of a star"), with the evident expectation that after three generations God would call an end to the punishment, as God had done in the time of the destruction of the First Temple in 586 B.C.E. and its restoration some three generations later. But history did not repeat itself. Israel again suffered defeat, this time worse than before. Jerusalem now transformed into a forbidden city to Jews, the Temple now in permanent ruins, Israel, the Jewish people, took up the task of finding an accommodation with enduring defeat. So whether Rome accepted pagan or Christian rule had no bearing on the fundamental fact of Israel's life: it was a beaten nation.

But while Israelites in the Land of Israel persisted as a subject people—that is what they had been, that is what they remained—Judaism now confronted a world in which its principal components—hermeneutic, teleology, symbol—were being challenged by the corresponding components of the now triumphant faith in Christ. The Judaism that emerged dealt with that challenge in a way particular to Christianity. The doctrines that assumed central significance—those concerning the Messiah, on the one side, and

45

the character of God's revelation in the Torah to Moses at Sinai, on the other—took up questions addressed to Judaism by Christianity and only by Christianity. So what changed did so because of the distinctive claims of Christianity, and what remained intact out of the antecedent heritage did so because Israel continued as a subjugated people—a condition to which prior heritage had already proved its congruence.

In the Christian view, as we know, the Hebrew Scriptures, the written Torah, demanded to be read as the Old Testament, predicting the New. History now proved that Scripture's prophetic promises of a king-Messiah had, to begin with, pointed toward Jesus, now Christ enthroned. Concomitantly, the teleology of the Israelite system of old, focused as it was on the coming of the Messiah, now found confirmation and realization in the rule of Jesus, again Christ enthroned. And the symbol of the whole—hermeneutics and teleology alike—rose in heaven's heights: the cross that had triumphed at the Milvian Bridge. In more secular language, Constantine had had a vision of the cross, "In this sign you will conquer," and had won the battle. No wonder, then, that the critical components of the prior system of Judaism now came under sharp revision. To be concrete, let me specify the changes I think significant.

1. The written Torah found completion in the oral one. So Judaism's extrascriptural traditions found legitimacy as God's revelation to Moses at Sinai.

2. The system as a whole now was made to point toward an eschatological teleology, to be realized in the coming of the Mishnah when Israel's condition, defined by the one whole Torah of Sinai, was itself warranted.

3. It would necessarily follow, that the symbol of the Torah would expand to encompass the teleology and hermeneutic at hand. Salvation comes from the Torah, not from the cross.

If we inquire what exactly the sages did at that time—
what books they wrote and what they said in them that they
had not said earlier—the answer is clear. They composed
the Talmud of the Land of Israel as we know it. They collected exegeses of Scripture and made them into systematic
and sustained accounts of, initially, the meaning of the Pentateuch (probably during the late third through early fifth
centuries, for sifra, the two sifrés, Genesis Rabbah and Leviticus Rabbah). At the same time, Christians were working
out their collections of exegesis of the Hebrew Scriptures.
In looking at what Christians had to say to Israel, we may
find entirely reasonable the view that compiling scriptural
exegeses constituted part of a Jewish apologetic response.
For one Christian message was that Israel "after the flesh"
had distorted and continually misunderstood the meaning
of its own Scripture. Failing to read the Old Testament in
the light of the New—the prophetic promises in the perspective of Christ's fulfillment of those promises—Israel
"after the flesh" had lost access to God's revelation to
Moses at Sinai. To this challenge a suitably powerful, yet
appropriately proud, response would have two qualities.
First, it would supply a complete account of what Scripture
had meant, and always must mean, as Israel read it. Second,
it would do so in such a way as not to dignify the position
of the other side with the grace of an explicit reply.

The compilations of exegeses and the Talmud of the Land
of Israel—accomplished at this time by the sages in a systematic and thorough way—assuredly take up the challenge of restating the meaning of the Torah revealed by God
to Moses at Mount Sinai. At the same time, these collections in no way suggest that the charges of the other side
had precipitated this work of compilation and composition. The issues of the documents are made always to
emerge from the inner life not of Israel in general, but of
the sages' estate in particular. Scripture was thoroughly rab-

47

binized, as earlier it had been Christianized. None of this suggests that the other side had won a response for itself. Only the net effect—a complete picture of the whole, as Israel must perceive the whole of revelation—suggests the extraordinary utility for apologetics, outside as much as inside the faith, served by these same compilations.

It follows, I think, that the changes at the surface, in articulated doctrines of teleology, hermeneutics, and symbolism, respond to changes in the political condition of Israel as well as in the religious foundations of the politics of the day. Paganism had presented a different and simpler problem to sages. Christianity's explicit claims, validated in the world-shaking events of the age, demanded a reply. The sages of the Talmud of the Land of Israel provided it. So it was at those very specific points at which the Christian challenge met head on old Israel's world view that sages' doctrines changed from what they had been. What did Israel have to present to the cross? The Torah, in the doctrine, first, of the status, as oral and memorized revelation, of the Mishnah, and, by implication, of other rabbinical writings. The Torah, moreover, in the encompassing symbol of Israel's salvation. The Torah, finally, in the person of the Messiah who, of course, would be a rabbi. The Torah in all three modes confronted the cross, with its doctrine of the triumphant Christ, Messiah, and king, ruler now of earth as of heaven. What had changed were those components of the sages' world view that now stood in direct confrontation with counterparts on the Christian side. What would remain the same were the doctrines governing fundamental categories of Israel's social life to which the triumph of Christianity made no material difference.

Christianity and the Symbol of the Torah

As I explained at the outset, every detail of the religious system of the dual Torah exhibits essentially the same point of insistence, captured in the simple notion of the Torah as the generative symbol, the total, exhaustive expression of the system as a whole. Hence the definitive ritual of studying the Torah as the generative symbol, the total, exhaustive expression of the system as a whole. Hence the definitive myth explaining that one who studies Torah will become holy, like Moses "our rabbi," and like God, in whose image humanity was made and whose Torah provides the plan and the model for what God wants of a humanity created in His image.

The clerks who knew and applied the law of the Mishnah had to explain the standing of that law, meaning its relationship to the law of the Torah. But the Mishnah provided no account of itself. Unlike biblical law codes, the Mishnah begins with no myth of its own origin. It ends with no thanksgiving. Discourse commences in the middle of things and ends abruptly. As a result of such laconic mumbling, the exact status of the document required definition entirely outside its own framework. The framers of the Mishnah having given no hint of the nature of their book, the Mishnah reached the political world of Israel without a trace of self-conscious explanation or any theory of validation.

The one thing that is clear, alas, is negative. The framers of the Mishnah nowhere claim, implicitly or explicitly, that what they have written forms part of the Torah, enjoys the status of God's revelation to Moses at Sinai, or even systematically carries forward secondary exposition and application of what Moses wrote down in the wilderness. Later—

49

two hundred years, I think, after the closure of the Mishnah—the need to explain its standing and origin led to two hypotheses: first, God's revelation of the Torah at Sinai encompassed the Mishnah as much as Scripture; second, the Mishnah was handed on through oral formulation and oral transmission from Sinai to the framers of the document as we have it.

These twin explanations for the status of the Mishnah first surfaced in the Talmud of the Land of Israel, which contains clear allusions to the dual Torah—one part in writing; the other, oral, and now in the Mishnah. That doctrine contains an ample response to those who questioned the standing and authority of both the Mishnah and the sages who applied the Mishnah in the Jewish government.

But for the two hundred years prior to the Talmud of the Land of Israel—that is, through the span of time in which the Judaic sages scarcely accorded recognition to Christianity and its challenge—that apologia for the Mishnah did not come to articulation. As for the Mishnah itself, its Judaism without Christianity contains not a hint that anyone has heard any such tale. The earliest apologists for the Mishnah knew nothing of the fully realized myth of the dual Torah of Sinai. They never referred to the Mishnah as something out there, nor did they speak of the document as autonomous and complete. Only the two Talmuds, beginning with the Talmud of the Land of Israel about the year 400, reveal that conception—alongside their mythic explanation of where the document came from and why it should be obeyed. So the first of the two Talmuds marks the change.

Still, the absence of even an implicit claim demands explanation. For when ancient Jews wanted to gain for their writings the status of revelation, of torah, or at least to link what they thought to what the Torah had said, they could do one of four things: They could sign the name of a holy man of old—for instance, Adam, Enoch, Ezra; they could

50

imitate the Hebrew style of Scripture; they could claim that God had spoken to them; and they could, at the very least, cite a verse of Scripture and impute to the cited passage their own opinion. These four methods—pseudepigraphy, stylistic imitation (hence, forgery), claim of direct revelation from God, and eisegesis—found no favor with the Mishnah's framers; to the contrary, they signed no name to their book. Their Hebrew was new in its syntax and morphology, completely unlike that of the Mosaic writings of the Pentateuch. They never claimed that God had anything to do with their opinions. They rarely cited a verse of Scripture as authority. It follows that, whatever the authors of the Mishnah said about their document, the implicit character of the book tells us that they did not claim God had dictated or even approved what they had to say. The framers simply ignored all the validating conventions of the world in which they lived. And, as I said, they failed to make explicit use of any others.

The issue is clearly drawn. It is not whether we find in the Mishnah exaggerated claims about the priority of the disciple of a sage: We do find such claims. The issue is whether we find in the Mishnah the vivid assertion that whatever a sage has on the authority of his master in fact goes back to Sinai. We seek a definitive view that what the sage says falls into the classification of Torah, just as what Scripture says constitutes Torah from God to Moses.

About a generation after the formation of the Mishnah, around 250, a distinct tractate came to closure: the Sayings of the Founders; in Hebrew, Pirqé Abot. This tractate, which contained an elaborate set of sayings assigned to sages from Moses and Joshua to names occurring even in the Mishnah itself, formed the first apologetic for the Mishnah. In tractate Abot, Torah as status is instrumental: The figure of the sage, his ideals and conduct, forms the goal, focus, and center. And the sage appears in the Mishnah and supplies the authority for the Mishnah. So the Mishnah is taught by sages, and what sages teach is Torah, and, it follows, the Mishnah is Torah—too. That is the syllogism of Abot. Let me unravel it.

Abot regards study of the Torah as what a sage does. The substance of the Torah to be studied is what a sage says— whether or not the saying relates to scriptural revelation. The content of the sayings attributed to sages endows those sayings with status as part of the Torah of Sinai. In tractate Abot, the sages usually do not quote verses of Scripture and explain them, nor do they speak in God's name. Yet, it is clear, sages talk Torah. It follows that if a sage says something, what he says is Torah. More accurately, what he says falls into the classification of Torah. Accordingly, as I said, Abot treats Torah learning as symptomatic, an indicator of the status of the sage; hence as merely instrumental. But then the Mishnah, which is taught by sages, forms part of the Torah, for sages teach it! But the tractate at hand does not say so explicitly, and the doctrine of a dual Torah scarcely emerges. Only at the end of the fourth century, in the Talmud of the Land of Israel, do we find clear evidence that people were speculating about a dual Torah or, at least, about teachings transmitted orally and through memory, as against those transmitted in writing.

So once more we come to the end of the fourth century, specifically, to the Talmud of the Land of Israel. As we shall now see, it is there in particular that the doctrine of the dual Torah emerges for the first time in the unfolding canonical writings of contemporary Judaism. The Mishnah is held in the Talmud of the Land of Israel to be equivalent to Scripture (Yerushalmi Horayot 3:5). But the Mishnah is not called Torah or part of the Torah. Still, once the Mishnah has entered the status of Scripture, it is but a short step to a theory of the Mishnah as part of the revelation at Sinai— hence, oral Torah. In the first Talmud we find the first glimmerings of an effort to theorize in general, not merely in detail, about how specific teachings of the Mishnah relate to specific teachings of Scripture. The citing of scriptural proof-texts for Mishnah propositions would not, after all, have much surprised the framers of the Mishnah; they themselves included such passages (though not often).

A particular abstract from the Talmud of the Land of Israel can illustrate in a concrete way precisely the doctrine at hand. While the following passage does not make use of the language, Torah-in-writing and Torah-by-memory, it does refer to the "written" and the "oral." I believe myself fully justified in supplying the word *Torah* in brackets in VD and F, but not in K or L. So the fully articulated theory of two Torahs (not merely one Torah in two forms) does not reach final expression in this passage. But, short of explicit allusion to Torah-in-writing and Torah-by-memory, which (so far as I am able to discern) we find mainly in the Talmud of Babylonia, the basic theory is contained here:

[VD] R. Zeirah in the name of R. Eleazar: " 'Were I to write for him my laws by ten thousands, they would be regarded as a strange thing' (Hos. 8:12). Now is the greater part of the Torah written down? [Surely not. The oral part is much greater.] But more abundant are the matters which are derived by exegesis from the written [Torah] than those derived by exegesis from the oral [Torah]."

[E] And is that so?

[F] But more cherished are those matters which rest upon the written [Torah] than those which rest upon the oral [Torah]. . . .

[J] R. Haggai in the name of R. Samuel bar Nahman, "Some teachings were handed on orally, and some things were handed on in writing, and we do not know which of them is the more precious. But on the basis of that which is written, 'And the Lord said to Moses, Write these words; in accordance with these words I have made a covenant with you and with Israel' (Ex. 34:27), [we conclude] that

[K]   the ones which are handed on orally are the more precious."

[K]   R. Yohanan and R. Yudan b. R. Simeon: One said, "If you have kept what is preserved orally and also kept what is in writing, I shall make a covenant with you, and if not, I shall not make a covenant with you."

[L]   The other said, "If you have kept what is preserved orally and you have kept what is preserved in writing, you shall receive a reward, and if not, you shall not receive a reward."

(Yerushalmi Hagigah 1:7. Translated by the author.)

Here we have absolutely explicit evidence that people believed that part of the Torah had been preserved not in writing but orally. Linking that part to the Mishnah remains a matter of implication. But the link surely comes fairly close to the surface when we are told that the Mishnah contains Torah traditions revealed at Sinai. From that view, it requires only a small step to the allegation that the Mishnah is part of the Torah, the oral part. So—treating this story as a small part of the evidence on the issue in the Talmud of the Land of Israel—we conclude that the age of Constantine marks the point where the Mishnah takes up its position as part of the Torah.

The fresh definition of the Torah required that all things receive a new definition as well. From our viewpoint, the most important transformation affected the Messiah, who, learned in the Torah, would be a sage, just as David in the rabbis' writings had taken his place in the sages' academy and taught Torah. While none of this had any bearing on the relationship with Christianity, one thing did come to make a difference: the status of the Mishnah, on the one side; the standing of the sages, on the other. The one enjoyed the status of the Jews' law code but found no place in the Scripture that the Christians revered in common with the Jews. The other enjoyed authority and standing in Jewry, but on what basis? That question demanded an answer as part of the legitimation of the Judaism that flourished side by side with Christianity: the Judaism that invoked not only Scripture, which Christians acknowledged, but the writings of sages, which Christians did not recognize as God's will.

The Messianization of the Judaism of the Dual Torah

When constructing a systematic account of Judaism—that is, the world view and the way of life for Israel presented in the Mishnah—the philosophers of the Mishnah did not make use of the Messiah myth but found it possible to present a statement of goals for their projected life of Israel which was entirely separate from appeals to history and eschatology. Since they certainly knew, and even alluded to, long-standing and widely held convictions on eschatological subjects, beginning with those in Scripture, the framers thereby testified that they made choices different from others before and after them. Their document accurately and ubiquitously expresses these choices, both affirmative and negative.

The appearance of a messianic eschatology fully consonant with the larger characteristic of the system of the dual Torah—with its stress on the viewpoints and proof-texts of Scripture, its interest in what was happening to Israel, its focus upon the national-historical dimension of the life of the group—indicates that the encompassing rabbinic system stood essentially autonomous of the prior, mishnaic system. True, what had gone before was absorbed and fully assimilated. But the rabbinic system, first appearing in the Talmud of the Land of Israel, is different in the aggregate

55

from the mishnaic system. It represents more, however, than a negative response to its predecessor. The rabbinic system of the two Talmuds, emerging in the first of the two at the end of the fourth century, took over the fundamental convictions of the mishnaic world view about the importance of Israel's constructing for itself a life beyond time. The rabbinic system then transformed the Messiah myth in its totality into an essentially ahistorical force: if people wanted to reach the end of time, they had to rise above time—that is, history—and stand off at the side of great movements of political and military character.

That is the message of the Messiah myth as it reaches full exposure in the rabbinic system of the two Talmuds. At its foundation it is precisely the message of teleology without eschatology expressed by the Mishnah and its associated documents. Accordingly, we cannot claim that the rabbinic or talmudic system in this regard constitutes a reaction against the mishnaic one, but must conclude, quite to the contrary, that the Talmuds and their associated documents restate in classical mythic form the ontological convictions that had informed the minds of the second-century philosophers. The new medium contained the old and enduring message: Israel must turn away from time and change, submit to whatever happens, so as to win for itself the only government worth having; that is, God's rule, accomplished through God's anointed agent, the Messiah.

Within the Judaism born in the centuries after 70, the distinct traditions of priest, sage, and messianist were joined in a new way. In the person of the sage—that is, rabbi, holy man, Torah incarnate, avatar, and model of the son of David—rabbinic Judaism found its hero and symbol. So the diverse varieties of Judaic piety present in Israel before 70 came to be bonded over the next several centuries in a wholly unprecedented way, with each party to the union imposing its logic upon the other constituents of the whole.

The ancient categories remained. But they were so profoundly revised and transformed that nothing was preserved intact. Through the person and figure of the rabbi, the whole burden of Israel's heritage was taken up, renewed, and handed on from late antiquity to the present day.

The character of the Israelite Scriptures, with their emphasis upon historical narrative as a mode of theological explanation, leads us to expect all Judaisms to evolve as eschatological in their definition of their goals, and therefore to anticipate that all Judaisms will be deeply messianic religions, since it is the nature of the eschatological focus to draw in its wake some sort of messianic doctrine, at least among Judaisms (and all the more so Christianities). With all prescribed actions pointed toward the coming of the Messiah at the end of time, and all interest focused upon answering the historical-salvific questions ("How long?"), the Judaism of the dual Torah presents no surprises. Its liturgy evokes historical events to prefigure salvation; prayers of petition repeatedly turn to the speedy coming of the Messiah; and the experience of worship invariably leaves the devotee expectant and hopeful. Just as rabbinic Judaism is a deeply messianic religion, secular extensions of Judaism, as we shall see in part III, have commonly proposed secularized versions of the focus upon history and have shown interest in the purpose and dénouement of events. Teleology again appears as an eschatology embodied in messianic symbols. The eschatological character of Zionism and socialism in their symbolic, especially rhetorical, expression, leaves no doubt on the matter.

Yet, for a brief moment, the Mishnah—again, our "sages' Judaism without Christianity"—presented a Judaism in which history did not define the main framework of teleology. In the Mishnah, therefore, the issue of teleology took a form other than the familiar eschatological one; and—as

57

I shall explain presently—historical events were absorbed into an ahistorical system through their trivialization within encompassing, ahistorical taxonomic structures. In the Judaism in this document, messiahs, to be sure, played a part. But these were mere "anointed men"—for example, a priest of a certain classification, an "anointed priest"—and had no distinctive historical role. The figures classified as anointed undertook a task quite different from that assigned to Jesus by the framers of the Gospels: they were merely a species of priest, falling into one classification rather than another.

So let us ask the Mishnah the questions at hand: What of the Messiah? When will he come? To whom, in Israel, will he come? And what must, or can, we do while we wait to hasten his coming? If we now reframe these questions and divest them of their mythic cloak, we ask about the Mishnah's theory of the history and destiny of Israel and the purpose of the Mishnah's own system in relationship to Israel's present and end: the implicit teleology of the philosophical law at hand. Answering these questions out of the resources of the Mishnah is not possible. The Mishnah presents no large view of history. It contains no reflection whatever on the nature and meaning of the destruction of the Temple in the year 70, an event that surfaces only in connection with some changes in the law explained as resulting from the end of the cult. The Mishnah pays no attention to the matter of the end of time. The word *salvation* is rare; *sanctification*, commonplace. More strikingly, the framers of the Mishnah are virtually silent on the teleology of the system; they never tell us why we should do what the Mishnah tells us, let alone explain what will happen if we do. Incidents in the Mishnah are preserved either as narrative settings for the statement of the law or, occasionally, as precedents. Historical events are classified and turned into entries on lists. But incidents, in any case, come few and far between. True, events do make an impact—but always for the Mishnah's own purpose and within its own taxonomic system and rule-seeking mode of thought. To be sure, the framers of the Mishnah may also have had a theory of the Messiah and of the meaning of Israel's history and destiny; but, if so, they kept it hidden, and their document manages to provide an immense account of Israel's life without explicitly telling us about such matters.

The Messiah in the Mishnah does not stand at the forefront of the framers' consciousness. The issues encapsulated in the myth and person of the Messiah are scarcely addressed. The framers of the Mishnah do not resort to speculation about the Messiah as a historical-supernatural figure. So far as that kind of speculation provides the vehicle for reflection on salvific issues, or, in mythic terms, narratives on the meaning of history and the destiny of Israel, we cannot say that the Mishnah's philosophers take up those encompassing categories of being: Where are we heading? What can we do about it? It is not that questions found urgent in the aftermath of the destruction of the Temple and the disaster of Bar Kokhba failed to attract the attention of the Mishnah's sages. But they treated history in a different way, offering their own answers to its questions. To these I now turn. Indeed, given the stress, in the Judaisms of the nineteenth and twentieth centuries, on history as the source of proof-texts for Jewish belief, we had best examine with some care the view of history defined at the beginning.

For one of the stunning differences between the Judaism of the dual Torah and the Judaisms of the nineteenth and twentieth centuries lies in the resort, by the latter, to proofs from "historical facts." To the framers of the Mishnah and the Talmud of the Land of Israel (as well as of the other writings of the age), historical facts by themselves proved nothing and added up to nothing.

By *historical* I mean not merely events, but how events serve to teach lessons, reveal patterns, tell us what we must do and what will happen to us tomorrow. But what lessons, in that sense, can history teach? In that context, some events contain richer lessons than others; the destruction of the Temple of Jerusalem teaches more than does a crop failure; being kidnaped into slavery, more than stubbing one's toe. Furthermore, lessons taught by events—"history" in the didactic sense—follow a progression from trivial and private to consequential and public. The framers of the Mishnah refer to very few events, focusing on those they do mention for their own purposes and quite apart from any connection with outer reality. They rarely create narratives; historical events do not supply organizing categories or taxonomic classifications. We find no tractate devoted to the destruction of the Temple, no complete chapter detailing Bar Kokhba's rebellion, or even a sustained celebration of the events of the sages' own historical lives.

How then does the Mishnah treat historical events? The Mishnah absorbs into its encompassing system all events, small and large. With them the sages accomplish what they accomplish in everything else: a vast labor of taxonomy, an immense construction of the order and rules governing the classification of everything on earth and in heaven. The disruptive character of history—one-time events of ineluctable significance—scarcely impresses these philosophers. They find no difficulty in showing that what appears unique and beyond classification has in fact happened before and so falls within the range of trustworthy rules and known procedures. Once history's components, one-time events, lose their distinctiveness, then history as a didactic intellectual construct, as a source of lessons and rules, also loses all pertinence. History becomes cyclical, an exercise in the re-enactment of what was at the beginning—or is to come at the end.

60

So lessons and rules come from sorting things out and classifying them, hence derive from the procedures and modes of thought of the philosopher or the social scientist seeking regularity. To this labor of taxonomy, the historian's way of selecting data and arranging them into patterns of meaning to teach lessons proves inconsequential. One-time events are not important. The world is composed of nature and supernature. The laws that count are those to be discovered in heaven and, in heaven's creation and counterpart, on earth. Keep those laws, and things will work out. Break them, and the result is predictable: Calamity of whatever sort will supervene in accordance with the rules. But just because it is predictable a catastrophic happening testifies to what has always been and must always be, in accordance with reliable rules and within categories already discovered and well explained. That is why the lawyer-philosophers of the mid-second century produced the Mishnah—to explain how things are. Within the framework of well-classified rules, there could be messiahs, but no single Messiah.

If the end of time and the coming of the Messiah do not serve to explain, for the Mishnah's system, why people should do what the Mishnah says, then what alternative teleology does the Mishnah's first apologetic, Abot, provide? Only when we appreciate the clear answers given in that document of about the year 250 will we grasp how remarkable the shift, which took place in later documents of the rabbinic canon, was to a messianic framing of the issues of the Torah's ultimate purpose and value. Let us see how the framers of Abot, in the aftermath of the creation of the Mishnah, explain the purpose and goal of the Mishnah: an ahistorical, nonmessianic teleology. Whatever teleology the Mishnah as such would ever acquire would derive from Abot which, in presenting statements to express the ethos and ethic of the Mishnah, provides a kind of theory.

61

Abot agreed with the Mishnah's other sixty-two tractates: history proved no more important here than it had been before. With scarcely a word about history and no account of events at all, Abot manages to provide an ample account of how the Torah—written and oral; thus, in later eyes, Scripture and Mishnah—came down to its own day. Accordingly, the passage of time as such plays no role in the explanation of the origins of the document, nor is the Mishnah presented as eschatological. Occurrences of great weight ("history") are never invoked. How then does the tractate tell the story of Torah, narrate the history of God's revelation to Israel, encompassing both Scripture and Mishnah? The answer is that Abot's framers manage to do their work of explanation without telling a story or invoking history at all. They pursue a different way of answering the question, exploiting a nonhistorical mode of thought and method of legitimation. And that is the main point: teleology serves the purpose of legitimation and hence is accomplished in ways other than explaining how things originated or assuming that historical fact explains anything.

Disorderly historical events entered the system of the Mishnah and found their place within the larger framework of the Mishnah's orderly world. The Mishnah's framers did not ignore what was happening but worked out their own way of dealing with historical events, whose disruptive power they not only conceded but freely recognized. Further, they did not intend to compose a history book or a work of prophecy or apocalypse. Even if they had wanted to narrate the course of events, they could hardly have done so through the medium of the Mishnah. Yet the Mishnah presents its philosophy in full awareness of the issues of historical calamity confronting the Jewish nation. So far as the philosophy of the document confronts the totality of Israel's existence, the Mishnah, by definition, also presents a philosophy of history. So much for Judaism framed in majestic indifference to the "daughter" religion, Christianity: Historical questions, asking about the meaning of large patterns of events—each standing in line as a unique happening, bearing a heavy burden of meaning—scarcely demand attention.

The Mishnah's subordination of historical events contradicts the emphasis of a thousand years of Israelite thought. The biblical histories, the ancient prophets, the apocalyptic visionaries all had testified that events themselves were important. Events carried the message of the living God. Events constituted history, pointed toward, and so explained, Israel's destiny. An essentially ahistorical system of timeless sanctification, worked out through the construction of an eternal rhythm that centered on the movement of moon and stars and seasons, represented a life chosen by few outside the priesthood. Furthermore, it expresses the pretense that what happens matters less than what is. That view testified against palpable and memorable reality. Israel had suffered enormous loss of life. The Talmud of the Land of Israel takes these events seriously and treats them as unique and remarkable. The memories proved real. The hopes evoked by the Mishnah's promise of sanctification of a world in static perfection did not. For they had to compete with the grief of an entire century of mourning.

Thus we come to the doctrines that reached expression in writings at the end of the fourth century. The most important change is the shift in historical thinking adumbrated in the pages of the Talmud of the Land of Israel, a shift from focus upon the Temple and its supernatural history to close attention to the people Israel and its natural, this-worldly history. Once Israel, holy Israel, had come to form the counterpart to the Temple and its supernatural life, that other history—Israel's—would stand at the center of things. Accordingly, a new sort of memorable event came to the fore in the Talmud of the Land of Israel. Let me give this new history appropriate emphasis: *it was the story of Israel's suffering, remembrance of that suffering, on the one side, and an effort to explain events of such tragedy, on the other.*

So a composite "history" constructed out of the Talmud of the Land of Israel's units of discourse that were pertinent to consequential events would contain long chapters on what happened to Israel, the Jewish people, and not only, or not mainly, what had earlier occurred in the Temple. The components of the historical theory of Israel's sufferings were manifold. First and foremost, history taught moral lessons. Historical events entered into the construction of a teleology for the Talmud of the Land of Israel's system of Judaism as a whole. What the law demanded reflected the consequences of wrongful action on the part of Israel. So, again, Israel's own deeds defined the events of history. Rome's role, like Assyria's and Babylonia's, depended upon Israel's provoking divine wrath as it was executed by the great empire. Israel had to learn the lesson of its history to also take command of its own destiny.

But this notion of determining one's own destiny should not be misunderstood. The framers of the Talmud of the Land of Israel were not telling the Jews to please God by doing commandments in order to gain control of their own destiny. To the contrary, the paradox of the Talmud of the Land of Israel's system lies in the fact that only by humbly agreeing to accept God's rule can Israel free itself of control by other nations. The nations—Rome, in the present instance—rest on one side of the balance, while God rests on the other. Israel must then choose between them. There is no such thing for Israel as freedom from both God and the nations, total autonomy and independence. There is only a choice of masters, a ruler on earth or a ruler in heaven.

With propositions such as these, the framers of the

Mishnah certainly concurred. For the fundamental affirmations of the Mishnah about the centrality of Israel's perfection in stasis—sanctification—prove readily congruent to the attitudes at hand. Once the Messiah's coming had become dependent upon Israel's condition—hence Israel's sanctification—and not upon Israel's actions in historical time aimed at bringing salvation, then the Mishnah's system imposed its fundamental and definitive character upon the Messiah myth. An eschatological teleology framed through that myth then would prove wholly appropriate to the method of the larger system of the Mishnah. The Messiah then enters the system in the Talmud of the Land of Israel, but he does so as a sage. And what characterizes the true Messiah is his message: submission to God's will. There is nothing to do, but Israel has a task of *being:* of becoming holy. The mark of sanctification is submission to God's will as revealed in the Torah.

One can know that the Messiah doctrine I have outlined is paramount by asking, What makes a messiah a false messiah? In this Talmud, it is not his claim to save Israel, but his claim to save Israel without the help of God. The meaning of the true Messiah is Israel's total submission, through the Messiah's gentle rule, to God's yoke and service. So God is not to be manipulated through Israel's humoring of heaven in rite and cult. The notion of keeping the commandments so as to please heaven and get God to do what Israel wants is totally incongruent with the text at hand. Keeping the commandments as a mark of submission, loyalty, humility before God is the rabbinic system of salvation. So Israel does not "save itself." Israel never controls its own destiny, either on earth or in heaven. The only choice is whether to cast one's fate into the hands of cruel, deceitful men or to trust in the living God of mercy and love. We shall now see how this critical position is spelled

65

out in the setting of discourse about the Messiah in the Talmud of the Land of Israel.

Bar Kokhba's war, above all, exemplifies arrogance against God. He lost the war because of that arrogance. In particular, he ignored the authority of sages:

[X J]   Said R. Yohanan, "Upon orders of Caesar Hadrian, they killed eight hundred thousand in Betar."

[K]   Said R. Yohanan, "There were eighty thousand pairs of trumpeteers surrounding Betar [Bar Kokhba's capital]. Each one was in charge of a number of troops. Ben Kozeba [that is, Bar Kokhba] was there and he had two hundred thousand troops who, as a sign of loyalty, had cut off their little fingers.

[L]   "Sages sent word to him, 'How long are you going to turn Israel into a maimed people?'

[M]   "He said to them, 'How otherwise is it possible to test them?'

[N]   "They replied to him, 'Whoever cannot uproot a cedar of Lebanon while riding on his horse will not be inscribed on your military rolls.'

[O]   "So there were two hundred thousand who qualified in one way, and another two hundred thousand who qualified in another way."

[P]   When he would go forth to battle, he would say, "Lord of the world! Do not help and do not hinder us! 'Hast thou not rejected us, O God? Thou dost not go forth, O God, with our armies' " [Ps. 60:10].

[Q]   Three and a half years did Hadrian besiege Betar.

[R]   R. Eleazar of Modiin would sit on sackcloth and ashes and pray every day, saying "Lord of the ages! Do not judge in accord with strict judgment this day! Do not judge in accord with strict judgment this day!"

[S]   Hadrian wanted to go to him. A Samaritan said to him, "Do not go to him until I see what he is doing, and so hand over the city [of Betar] to you. [Make peace . . . for you.]"

[T]   [The Samaritan] got into the city through a drain pipe. He went and found R. Eleazar of Modiin standing and

66

praying. [The Samaritan] pretended to whisper something in his ear.

[U] The townspeople saw [the Samaritan] do this and brought him to Ben Kozeba. They told him, "We saw this man having dealings with your friend."

[V] [Ben Kozeba] said to him, "What did you say to him, and what did he say to you?"

[W] He said to [the Samaritan], "If I tell you, then the king will kill me, and if I do not tell you, then you will kill me. It is better that the king kill me, and not you.

[X] "[Eleazar] said to me, 'I should hand over my city.' ['I shall make peace.']"

[Y] He [Ben Kozeba] turned to R. Eleazar of Modiin. He said to him, "What did this Samaritan say to you?"

[Z] He replied, "Nothing."

[AA] He said to him, "What did you say to him?"

[BB] He said to him, "Nothing."

[CC] [Ben Kozeba] gave [Eleazar] one good kick and killed him.

[DD] Forthwith an echo came forth and proclaimed the following verse:

[EE] "Woe to my worthless shepherd, who deserts the flock! May the sword smite his arm and his right eye! Let his arm be wholly withered, his right eye utterly blinded! [Zech. 11:17].

[FF] "You have murdered R. Eleazar of Modiin, the right arm of all Israel, and their right eye. Therefore may the right arm of that man wither, may his right eye be utterly blinded!"

[GG] Forthwith Betar was taken, and Ben Kozeba was killed.

(Yerushalmi Taanit 4:5)

We notice two complementary themes. First, Bar Kokhba (or Ben Kozeba, as in this passage) treats heaven with arrogance, asking God merely to keep out of the way. Second, he treats an especially revered sage with a parallel arrogance. The sage had the power to preserve Israel. Bar Kokhba destroyed Israel's one protection. The result was inevitable. The Messiah, the centerpiece of salvation history and hero of the tale, emerged as a critical figure. The historical theory of this Talmud of the Land of Israel passage is stated very simply. In their view, Israel had to choose between wars, either the war fought by Bar Kokhba or the "war for Torah." "Why had they been punished? It was because of the weight of the war, for they had not wanted to engage in the struggles over the meaning of the Torah" (Yerushalmi Taanit 3:9 XVI I). Those struggles, which were ritual arguments about ritual matters, promised the only victory worth winning. Then Israel's history would be written in terms of wars over the meaning of the Torah and the decision of the law.

Gentile kings are boastful; Israelite kings are humble. So, in all, the Messiah myth deals with a concrete and limited consideration of the national life and character. The theory of Israel's history and destiny as it was expressed within that myth interprets matters in terms of a single criterion: what others within the Israelite world had done or in the future would do with the conviction that, at the end of time, God would send a (or the) Messiah to "save" Israel; it was a single idea for the sages of the Mishnah and the Talmuds and collections of scriptural exegesis. And that conception stands at the center of their system; it shapes and is shaped by their system. In context, the Messiah expresses the system's meaning and so makes it work.

True, the skins are new, but the wine is very old. For while we speak of sages and learning, the message is the familiar one. It is Israel's history that works out and expresses Israel's relationship with God. The critical dimension of Israel's life, therefore, is salvation, the definitive trait, a movement in time from now to then. It follows that the paramount and organizing category is history and its lessons. In the Talmud of the Land of Israel, we witness, among the Mishnah's heirs, a striking reversion to biblical convictions about the centrality of history in the definition of Israel's reality. The heavy weight of prophecy, apocalyptic and biblical historiography, with their emphasis upon salvation and on history as the indicator of Israel's salvation, stood against the Mishnah's quite separate thesis of what truly mattered. What, from the Mishnah's viewpoint, demanded description and analysis and required interpretation? It was the category of sanctification, for eternity. The true issue framed by history and apocalypse was how to move toward the foreordained end of salvation, how to act in time to reach salvation at the end of time. The Mishnah's teleology beyond time and its capacity to posit an eschatology without a place for a historical Mishnah take a position beyond that of the entire antecedent sacred literature of Israel. Only one strand, the priestly one, had ever taken so extreme a position on the centrality of sanctification and the peripheral nature of salvation. Wisdom had stood between, with its own concerns, drawing attention both to what happened and to what endured. But to wisdom what finally mattered was not nature or supernature, but rather abiding relationships in historical time.

So at the end of the fourth century the system emerges from the Talmud of the Land of Israel complete, each of its parts stating precisely the same message as is revealed in the whole. The issue of the Messiah and the meaning of Israel's history framed through the Messiah myth convey in their terms precisely the same position that we find everywhere else in all other symbolic components of the rabbinic system and canon. The heart of the matter, then, is Israel's subservience to God's will, as expressed in the Torah and embodied in the teachings and lives of the great sages. When Israel fully accepts God's rule, then the Messiah will come. Until Israel subjects itself to God's rule, the Jews will be subjugated to pagan domination. Since the condition of Israel governs, Israel itself holds the key to its own redemption. But this it can achieve only by throwing away the key!

The paradox must be crystal clear: Israel acts to redeem itself through the opposite of self-determination—namely, by subjugating itself to God. Israel's power lies in its negation of power. Its destiny lies in giving up all pretense at deciding its own destiny. So weakness is the ultimate strength; forbearance, the final act of self-assertion; passive resignation, the sure step toward liberation. (The parallel is the crucified Christ.) Israel's freedom is engraved on the tablets of the commandments of God: to be free is freely to obey. That is not the meaning associated with these words in the minds of others who, like the sages of the rabbinical canon, declared their view of what Israel must do to secure the coming of the Messiah.

It remains to ask why there was a shift from the symbolic expression of the Mishnah's teleology in non-eschatological terms, as in tractate Abot, to the profoundly eschatological formulation of the symbol emerging in the Talmud of the Land of Israel. In my judgment, the political triumph of Christ in the Roman Empire made ineluctable the confrontation with the Messiah question. For at issue is not what the sages said. As I have emphasized, I do not think they said a great deal that had not been stated in non-eschatological, nonmessianic terms, by their predecessors. At issue is the mode of symbolic expression selected to convey that enduring message. If I had to explain to despairing Jews what had happened with the Christian takeover of the Roman empire, I do not see how I could avoid confronting the question of the Messiah. Specifically, if not this one, why not? The answer I see before us: because the Messiah is going to be not a king but a sage. And the kings of the gentiles do not qualify, because they are arrogant. The counterpart, the sages of Israel, will qualify, through humility and conciliation and acceptance of God's will. So the upshot is a simple and strikingly relevant message: "Do not despair but hope, do not rebel but accept and humbly submit, do not mistake the present for the end, which, even now, we may attain by fulfilling, by embodying the Torah."

Christianity and the Success of Judaism

The fact that Judaic sages conceived doctrines on a program of issues shared with Christianity would, as I have said, shape the future history of the Judaism formed by those sages. For as Christianity continued to harp on the same points, the Judaic party to the dispute for centuries to come could refer to the generative symbols and determinative myths of the sages' Judaism, which, to begin with, dealt with these very issues. The Christian challenge, delivered through instruments of state and society, demanded a Judaic response, one involving not merely manipulation of power but exercise of intellect. Jews, continuing as a distinct society, took to heart the negative message of Christianity: "The Messiah has already come, you have no hope in the future, you are not Israel anyway, and history proves we are right." Sages produced responses to these questions, with doctrines of the meaning of history, of the conditions in which the Messiah will come to Israel, and of the definition of Israel. The symbolic system of the sages' Judaism, with its stress on Torah; the eschatological teleology of that system, with stress on the Messiah-sage coming to obedient Israel; the insistence on the equivalence of Israel and Rome, Jacob and Esau, with Esau penultimate and Israel at the end of time—these constituted in Israel powerful responses to the Christian question.

In a profound sense, therefore, the Judaism that reached canonical expression in the late fourth century succeeded in Israel because it dealt in a strikingly relevant way with both the issues and the politics of the Christian world within which Jews lived. The issues carried intellectual weight; the politics imparted to those issues, urgency and power. Because of politics the issues demanded attention. Had the doctrines focused on matters not at issue at all, and had the points of direct confrontation not elicited a response within Judaism, then the Judaism at hand would have proved itself simply irrelevant and died of attrition, of sheer lack of interest.

The Judaism of the canon of the later fourth century and beyond, therefore, flourished when the world to which it spoke found persuasive not the answers alone, but the very questions deemed paramount and pressing. And that Judaism ceased to speak to Jews when its message proved incongruent to questions Jews found they had to answer. The critical issue was not truth or self-evidence of answers, but congruence to circumstance: people acting together in an organized way.

PART II

The Death of Judaism and the Birth of Judaisms

THE NINETEENTH CENTURY AND ITS THEOLOGICAL IDEAS

In the nineteenth century sweeping changes in the political circumstances in which Jews made their lives, as well as in the economic conditions in which they made a living, made urgent issues that formerly had drawn slight attention and rendered inconsequential claims that had for so long demanded response. The Jews had formerly constituted a distinct group. Now in the West they formed part of an undifferentiated mass of citizens, all of them equal before the law, all of them subject to the same law. The Judaism of the dual Torah rested on the political premise that the Jews were governed by God's law and formed God's people. The two political premises—the one of the nation-state, the other of the Torah—scarcely permitted reconciliation. The consequent Judaic systems—Reform, Orthodox, Historical (Conservative, in the United States) addressed issues regarded as acute and not merely chronic; and in the nineteenth century each of these Judaisms alleged that it formed the natural next step in the unfolding of the "tradition," meaning the Judaic system of the dual Torah.

From the time of Constantine to the nineteenth century, Jewry in Christendom had sustained itself—first in the East, later in the West—as a recognized and ordinarily tolerated minority, subject to whichever of the contradictory doctrines of Christianity prevailed at a particular time in a particular place: that is, whether the Jews were Christ killers to be punished, or witnesses to be kept alive and ultimately converted at the second coming of Christ. What explains the long-term survival of the Jews in Europe are such factors as the pluralistic character of some societies (for instance, that in Spain before the fourteenth century), the welcome accorded entrepreneurs in opening territories (for instance, Norman England, Poland and Russia, Lithuania, White Russia and the Ukraine, in the early centuries of their development). The Jews, like many other groups, formed not only a tolerated religious minority but something akin to a guild, specializing in certain occupations—for example, crafts and entrepreneurial commerce in the East. After centuries of essentially ordinary existence in the West, the Crusades forced Jewry to migrate to the eastern frontier of Europe.

Before the nineteenth century, the Jews of Europe were subjected to legal restrictions on where they might live and how they might earn a living, and their political and social rights were severely limited. In the East, where most Jews had lived from the late Middle Ages, they governed their own communities through their own administration and law. They spoke their own language, Yiddish; wore distinctive clothing; ate only their own food; controlled their own sector of the larger economy and ventured outside of it only seldom; and, in all, formed a distinct and distinctive group, among other such groups. Commonly, in the villages where they lived, Jews and Christians dwelled side by side; but in many of these villages Jews formed the majority of the population. These facts made for long-term stability and autonomy. In the West, the Jews formed only a tiny proportion of the population but, until modern times, lived equally segregated from the rest of the country, behind the barriers of language, custom, and economic calling. So the Jews for a long time formed a caste, a clearly defined group—but within the hierarchy ordered by the castes of the society at hand.

A process called "emancipation," part of a larger movement of emancipation of serfs, women, slaves, Catholics (in Protestant countries such as England and Ireland), encompassed the Jews as well. Benzion Dinur defines this process of emancipation as follows:

> Jewish emancipation denotes the abolition of disabilities and inequities applied specially to Jews, the recognition of Jews as equal to other citizens, and the formal granting of the rights and duties of citizenship. Essentially the legal act of emancipation should have been simply the expression of the diminution of social hostility and psychological aversion toward Jews in the host nation . . . but the antipathy was not obliterated and constantly hampered the realization of equality even after it had been proclaimed by the state and included in the law.[1]

The political changes that include the Jews' emancipation began in the eighteenth century and, in half a century, had undermined the stability that had characterized the Jews' social and political life since Constantine. These political changes raised questions that previously either had not been found urgent or, it follows, had been neglected.

Dinur traces three periods in the history of the Jews' emancipation: 1740 to 1789, ending with the French Revolution; 1789 to 1878, from the French Revolution to the Congress of Berlin; and 1878 to 1933, from the Congress of Berlin to the rise of the Nazis to power in Germany. In the first period, the emancipation of the Jews first came under discussion; in the second, western and central European states accorded to the Jews the rights of citizenship; and the third saw the rise of a new racism that in the end all but annihilated the Jews of Europe.

In the background of the emancipation of the Jews was a vast movement in European culture that bears the title of "Enlightenment." The Enlightenment, a movement of European intellectuals in the seventeenth and eighteenth centuries, took the view that reason alone was sufficient to produce knowledge and the improvement of society. Opposed to the theological and political claims of Christianity, the new rationalism brought change in philosophy and politics alike, aiming at nothing short of the perfection of humanity through reason. Attention to the Jews, perceived as one of the imperfections of the world, focused upon the matter of their political and economic status. As part of the skepticism and secularism that were taking shape, the received theory of the Jews as a protected but subordinated caste, separate from other groups, came under question. Christianity saw the Jews as special; the Enlightenment did not. The political emancipation of the Jews, turning them from a pariah community into citizens like everyone else, was therefore part of a vast change in the old order in which Christianity defined the culture and politics of the West.

The leaders of Enlightenment shared the prevailing dislike of the Jews. But they regarded the Jews' condition as evidence of the failure of Christianity to accord that status as human beings that would lead the Jews to a (to them) more acceptable mode of life and behavior. The exercise of reason here as elsewhere would therefore remove the imperfections of the world. The impact upon the Jews of the new thinking about the Jews would prove substantial for two reasons. First, in western European countries, the Jews' political status did change. Second, the Jews themselves began to accept the ideals of the Enlightenment, with the result that political modernization found reinforcement in intellectual skepticism and questioning of the received Judaism of the dual Torah.

The appeal to reason in the perfection of the world addressed the issue of the intolerance of religion. To that intolerance—an imperfection in religion—flaws and faults in society were to be attributed. In that setting of secularization, the spokesmen of the Enlightenment invoked the notion that religious intolerance explains the character of the Jews and their low status. To overcome religious intolerance in general, the Jews in particular would have to be liberated. Among the Jews in central Europe, upper-class intellectuals, exposed to the ideas of the Enlightenment, began to shape a theory of religious doctrine and practice in line with the requirements of reason. Their ideas eventually took shape in Reform Judaism. When, at the end of the eighteenth century and the beginning of the nineteenth, Napoleon brought French political ideas of human rights to the conquered parts of Europe—Belgium, the Netherlands, Italy, Germany, and Austria, and even as far east as Russia—Jews saw a new vision of themselves, and some adopted it. They aspired to the rights of citizens and, concomitantly, gave up the status of a protected social entity, living out its life in isolation from the body politic. Toward the middle and later decades of the nineteenth century, as Italy and Germany attained political unification, as Hungary gained independence and then union with Austria, as

The Death of Judaism and the Birth of Judaisms

Rumania achieved the status of a free and independent country, no longer a dependency of the Ottoman empire, the Jews in those countries found their political status changing. Only in Poland, ruled by tsarist Russia, and in the other provinces of Russia in which the Jews were permitted to live—the Ukraine and White Russia, for example—did the original and enduring pattern persist. There the Jews lived as a distinct social entity. But in western and central Europe, the Jews gained the rights and duties of citizenship.

Dinur explains: "It was stressed that keeping the Jews in a politically limited and socially inferior status was incompatible with the principle of civic equality. . . . 'It is the objective of every political organization to protect the natural rights of man,' hence, 'all citizens have the right to all the liberties and advantages of citizens, without exception.' "[2] The adoption of the Constitution of the United States in 1787 confirmed that nation's position on the matter: Jewish males, along with all other white males, enjoyed citizenship. Jews in the nineteenth century entered the political and cultural life of the Western nations, including their overseas empires. During this second period, Reform Judaism reached its first stage of development, beginning in Germany (chapter 2). This Judaism made it possible for Jews to hold together the two things they deemed inseparable: their desire to remain Jewish, and their wish also to be one with their fellow citizens. By the middle of the nineteenth century, Reform had reached full expression and had won the support of a sizable part of German Jewry. At the same time, in reaction against Reform, Orthodoxy came into existence (chapter 3): this Judaism, no less than Reform, asked how "Judaism" could coexist with "Germanness," meaning citizenship in an undifferentiated republic of citizens. Then, mediating between Reform and Orthodoxy, a centrist position was worked out by theologians in what was then, in Germany, called the Historical School

80

and, in twentieth-century America, took the name of Conservative Judaism (chapter 4). The century from the French Revolution saw the full efflorescence of all the Judaisms of political modernization.

In the years after 1880, Europe took a different turn, and anti-Semitism as a political and social movement came into being. The movement away from the process of political rationalization reached expression in several ways. First, the new nation-states began that process of local rivalry that culminated in the European civil strife of the First and Second World Wars. Nationalism brought with it intolerance of difference; and, in some ways (if only religious ones) the Jews remained different. Second, the forces of imperialism, which brought Europe deep into the life of Africa, Asia, Latin America, and the South Pacific, carried disdain for peoples who were not white, not Christian, and, by the way, for the sector of those peoples that was not male. The representation of the African black as less than human found its counterpart in the treatment of the European Jew as subhuman. Religious reaction saw the formation of religious political parties, from which Jews, of course, were excluded. In these and other ways, Europe in the West turned its back upon the ideals of the Enlightenment and embarked on a path of racism and imperialism, exclusionary nationalism and statism, that in the twentieth century led to wars of mass destruction and the annihilation of whole populations, chief among them the Jews of Europe.

Jews began to realize that, in Dinur's words, "the state's legal recognition of Jewish civic and political equality does not automatically bring social recognition of this equality."[3] The Jews continued to form a separate group and were considered racially inferior. The impact of the new racism would be felt disastrously in the twentieth century.

Clearly, in the nineteenth century, particularly in Western countries, a new order was revising the political settlement that had prevailed for fifteen centuries. Since the time of Constantine, the political questions rising from the Jews' essentially autonomous life as a protected minority had found answers of an essentially supernatural and theological character. But emancipation redefined those questions, which now centered on Jews not as a distinct group but as part of some other polity altogether. Those Jews who simply passed over retain no interest for us: Karl Marx, for example, who converted to Christianity at an early age, produced no ideas important in the study of Judaism(s). But vast numbers of Jews in the West determined to remain Jewish and also to become something else: that is, a citizen of Germany or France or Britain. This issue would not confront the Jews of the Russian empire until the First World War; and these Jews, together with those of the Austro-Hungarian empire, Rumania, and other areas of eastern Europe, formed the vast majority of world Jewry.

While the Jews of the West were only a small minority of the Jews of the world—the Western frontier (extending, to be sure, to California in the farthest west of all) of the Jewish people, their confrontation with political change proved paradigmatic. They were the ones to invent the Judaisms of the nineteenth century. Each of these Judaic systems exhibited three characteristic traits. First, it asked, as I have indicated, how one could be both Jewish and something else—that is, also a citizen, a member of a nation. Second, it defined "Judaism" (that is, its system) as a religion, so leaving ample space for that something else—namely, nationality, whether German (*Deutschtum und Judentum*, "Germanness and Jewishness"), or British, or French, or American. Third, it appealed to history to prove the continuity between its system and the received Judaism of the dual Torah. The resort to historical fact, the claim that the system at hand formed the linear development of the past, the natural increment of the entire history of Israel, the Jewish people, from the beginning to the new day—that essentially factual claim masked a profound conviction concerning self-evidence. The urgent question at hand—the political one—produced a self-evidently correct answer out of the history of politics constituted by historical narrative.

That appeal to history, particularly historical fact, characterizes all three Judaisms. The Reformers stated explicitly that theirs would be a Judaism built on fact. The facts of history, in particular, would guide Jews to the definition of what was essential and what could be dropped. History, then, formed the court of appeal—but also the necessary link, the critical point of continuity. The Historical School took the same position but reached different conclusions: history would show how change could be effected, and the principles of historical change would then govern. Orthodoxy met the issue in a different way, maintaining that Judaism was above history, not an historical fact at all. But the Orthodox position would also appeal most forcefully to the past in its claim to constitute the natural and complete continuation of Judaism in its true form. The importance of history in the theological thought of the nineteenth-century Judaisms derives from the intellectual heritage of the age, with its stress on the nation-state as the definitive unit of society, and on history as the mode of defining the culture and character of the nation-state. History as an instrument of reform, further, had served the Protestant Reformation, with its appeal to Scripture as against (mere) tradition, with its claim that it would restore Christianity to its (historical) purity. Finally and most important, the supernaturalism of the inherited Judaism of the dual Torah, its emphasis upon God's active intervention in history, on miracles, on a perpetual concern for the natural implications of the supernatural will and covenant—that supernaturalism contradicted the rationalism of the age. The one thing the Jewish thinkers wished to accomplish was to show the rationalism, the reason—the normality—of the Judaisms they constructed. The appeal to (mere) facts of history, as against the unbelievable claims of a Scripture, placed upon a positive and this-worldly foundation the religious view of the world that, in the received system of the dual Torah, rested upon a completely supernatural view of reality.

For the three Judaisms of the age, which we see as continuous in important ways, took as their task the demonstration of how they formed out of the received and unwanted old Judaism something new, different, and acceptable. Since the Judaisms of the nineteenth century were born in the matrix of the received system of the dual Torah, among people who themselves grew up in a world in which that Judaism defined what people meant by Judaism, I must address the fact that the framers of the Judaisms of continuation could not evade the issue of continuity. They wished both to continue and also to innovate—and to justify innovation. And this desire affected Orthodoxy as much as Reform. In making changes, the framers of each Judaism appealed to the past for justification. But they pointed to those changes also as proof that they had overcome an unwanted past. The delicate balance between tradition and change attained by each of the Judaisms of continuation marks the genius of its inventors. All worked out the same equation: change but not too much, whatever the proportion a group found excessive.

CHAPTER 2

REFORM JUDAISM: HISTORY AND SELF-EVIDENCE

The Birth of a Judaism

   Reform Judaism began with some modest changes in the liturgy but ended up the single most important and most effective Judaism of the nineteenth century in central Europe and of the later twentieth century in America. The reason is that Reform Judaism forthrightly and articulately faced political changes that redefined the conditions of Jews' lives, and presented a Judaism closely tied to the in-

85

herited system of the dual Torah and fully responsive to those changes. Constructive and intellectually vital in its day, Reform Judaism said what it would do, and did it. Still more interesting, because it was a movement that confronted the issues of the day and the Jews' condition, Reform Judaism found itself able to change itself, its own deepest concerns and values. So the Judaism at hand made itself into an instrument for what Jews wanted and needed it to be—whatever that was. Consequently, Reform Judaism provides the model for the other Judaisms that are continuators of the Judaism of the dual Torah, and furthermore set the issues for debate from then to our own day. No Judaism in the past two hundred years exercised deeper influence in defining the issues Jews would debate; none made a richer or more lasting contribution to the program of answers Jews would find self-evident.

Since I want to examine whether the Judaisms of the nineteenth and twentieth centuries continued the received Judaism of the dual Torah or marked essentially new Judaisms, coming to full creation, each in its own terms and structure and system of viewpoints and practices, I take up Reform Judaism not at its beginning but at its moment of complete exposure and expression. The full and authoritative statement of this system—its world view, with profound implications on its way of life, and its theory of who is Israel—came to expression, in the nineteenth century, not in Europe but in America, in an assembly in Pittsburgh in 1885 of Reform rabbis. At that meeting of the Central Conference of American Rabbis, the Reform Judaism of the age—by now about a century aborning—took up the issues that divided it and made an authoritative statement about them, one that most people could accept.

The very fact that the Judaism before us could conceive of such debate and formulation of a kind of creed indicates that this Judaism found urgent the specification of its systemic structure, testimony to a mature and self-aware frame of mind. We look in vain for equivalent convocations to set public policy, for example, in the antecedent thousand years of the Judaism of the dual Torah. Statements of the world view, as these had emerged in diverse expressions of the received system, had not taken the form of a rabbis' platform, on the one side, and had not come about through democratic debate on public issues, on the other. That world view had percolated upward and represented a rarely articulated and essentially inchoate consensus about how things really are and should be. The received system had come to expression in how things were done, in what people found needless to make articulate at all: the piety of a milieu, not the proposition of a theological gathering. The contrast with Reform Judaism tells us not merely that the latter was a new Judaism, but—of greater interest—that the methods and approaches of this system enjoyed their own self-evident appropriateness. And from that fact we learn how the qualities people found self-evidently right had changed over time.

So we begin our trip in Pittsburgh, Pennsylvania, among rabbis who could point to three or even four generations of Reform antecedents. These were not the founders of the new faith—the Judaism before us came to birth about a generation before anyone recognized it—but the authorities of an established and enduring one. For the end of the nineteenth century found Reform Judaism a major component of the Judaic religious life of America as well as of Germany, and it was making inroads elsewhere as well. The American Reform rabbis, meeting in Pittsburgh in 1885, issued a clear and accessible statement of their Judaism. How did this Judaism formulate the issue of Israel as a political group? For critical to the Judaism of the dual Torah was its view of Israel as God's people, a supernatural polity, living out its social existence under God's Torah. The way of life, one of sanctification, and the world view, one of persistent reference to the Torah for rules of conduct, on the one side, and of the explanation of conduct, on the other, began in the basic conception of who is Israel. Here, too, we find emphasis on who is Israel, with that doctrine exposing for all to see the foundations of the way of life and world view that these rabbis had formed for the Israel they conceived. The Pittsburgh platform declared:

> We recognize in the Mosaic legislation a system of training the Jewish people for its mission during its national life in Palestine, and today we accept as binding only its moral laws and maintain only such ceremonies as elevate and sanctify our lives, but reject all such as are not adapted to the views and habits of modern civilization.... We hold that all such Mosaic and rabbinical laws as regular diet, priestly purity, and dress originated in ages and under the influence of ideas entirely foreign to our present mental and spiritual state.... Their observance in our days is apt rather to obstruct than to further modern spiritual elevation.... We recognize in the modern era of universal culture of heart and intellect the approaching of the realization of Israel's great messianic hope for the establishment of the kingdom of truth, justice, and peace among all men. We consider ourselves no longer a nation but a religious community and therefore expect neither a return to Palestine nor a sacrificial worship under the sons of Aaron nor the restoration of any of the laws concerning the Jewish state.[1]

I cannot imagine a more forthright address to the age. The Pittsburgh platform takes up each component of the system in turn. Who is Israel? What is its way of life? How does it account for its existence as a distinct, and distinctive, group? Israel once was a nation ("during its national life") but today is not a nation. It once had a set of laws regulating diet, clothing, and the like. These no longer apply, because Israel now is not what it was then. Israel forms an integral part of Western civilization. The reason for persisting as a distinctive group is that the group has its work to do:

namely, to realize the messianic hope for the establishment of a kingdom of truth, justice, and peace. For that purpose, Israel no longer constitutes a nation. It now forms a religious community.

What that means is that individual Jews live as citizens in other nations. Difference is acceptable at the level of religion, not of nationality, a position that accords fully with the definition of citizenship of the Western democracies. The world view then lays heavy emphasis on an as-yet unrealized but coming perfect age. The way of life admits to no important traits that distinguish Jews from others, since morality, in the nature of things, forms a universal category, applicable in the same way to everyone. The theory of Israel then forms the heart of matters, and what we learn is that Israel constitutes a "we": that is, the Jews continue to form a group that, by its own indicators, holds together and constitutes a cogent social entity. All this in a simple statement of a handful of rabbis forms a full and encompassing Judaism, one that, to its communicants, presented truth of a self-evident order. But it was also a truth declared, not discovered; and the self-evidence of the truth of the statements competed with the self-awareness characteristic of those who made them. For they could recognize the problem that demanded attention: the reframing of a theory of Israel for that Israel that they themselves constituted; that "we" that required explanation. No more urgent question faced the rabbis, because, after all, they lived in a century of opening horizons, in which people could envision perfection. The First World War would change all that. By 1937 the Reform rabbis, meeting in Columbus, Ohio, would reframe the system, expressing a world view quite different from that of the previous half-century.

Let me briefly summarize the program of urgent issues and self-evident responses that constituted the first of the new Judaisms of the nineteenth century. Questions we find

The Death of Judaism and the Birth of Judaisms

answered fall into two categories: first, why "we" do not keep certain customs and ceremonies but do keep others; second, how "we relate to the nations in which we live." The system of Reform Judaism explained both why and why not: that is, why this, not that—the mark of a fully framed and cogent Judaism. The affirmative side covered why the Jews would persist as a separate group; the negative would account for the limits of difference. These two questions deal with the same urgent problem: namely, working out a mode of Judaic existence compatible with citizenship in (for these rabbis) America. Jews do not propose to eat or dress in distinctive ways. They do seek a place within "modern spiritual elevation . . . universal culture of heart and intellect." They impute to that culture the realization of the "messianic hope"—a considerable stake. And, explicit to the whole, the Jews no longer constitute a nation. They therefore belong to some other nation(s). If I had to specify a single self-evident proposition taken fully into account by Reform Judaism, it is that political change had changed the entirety of Judaism, but the Judaism at hand had the power to accommodate that change. So change in general formed the method for dealing with the immediate problem, which was change in the political and social standing the Jews were now enjoying. So, on the very surface, Reform Judaism formed a Judaic system that confronted immense political change and presented a world view and a way of life to an Israel defined other than as a political entity. Two questions demand attention: How did this Judaism come into being, and how did its intellectuals explain their system?

If I had to specify the single dominant concern of the framers of Reform Judaism, I should point to the Jews' position in the public polity of the several Christian, European countries in which they lived. After the political changes stemming from the American and French revolutions, the received system of the Judaism of the dual Torah answered the wrong questions. A new question, emerging from forces not contained within once-regnant Christianity, demanded attention from Jews affected by those forces. For those Jews, shifts in political circumstances defined the urgent question: change. Historians began to look for evidence of precedents for changing things because their own circumstance had already persuaded them that change mattered: change itself effects change (so to speak). They sought a picture of a world in which they might find a place—and, it went without saying, a picture that would outline a Judaic system—a way of life, a world view, and a definition of the Israel that would live the one and believe the other. The new Judaism was confronted with political change brought about not by Christianity but by forces of nationalism, which conceived of society as the expression not of God's will for the social order under the rule of Christ and his Church or his anointed king (emperor, tsar) but of popular will for the social order under the government of the people and their elected representatives—a considerable shift. When society does not form the aggregate of distinct groups—each with its place and definition, language, and religion—but consists rather of undifferentiated citizens (male, white, wealthy, to be sure), then the Judaism that Jews in such a society have to work out also will account for difference of a different order altogether. That Judaism has to frame a theory of who is Israel consonant with the social situation of Jews who wish to be different, but not so different that they cannot also be citizens.

The original and enduring Judaic system of Reform correctly appealed, for its intellectual foundations, to Moses Mendelssohn, an eighteenth-century Jewish philosopher and follower of the Enlightenment, who (in the words of Michael A. Meyer) called "for a pluralistic society that offered full freedom of conscience to all those who accepted the postulates of natural religion: God, Providence, and a future life.''[2] The initial phrase presents the important component: a pluralistic society which, in the nature of things, constitutes a political category. Issues dominant from Mendelssohn's time on concerned "emancipation"— meaning the provision, for Jews, of the rights of citizens. Reform theologians took the lead in the struggle for such rights. To them it was self-evident that Jews not only should have civil rights and civic equality but also should want them. A Judaism that did not explain why the Jews should want and have full equality as part of a common humanity ignored the issues preoccupying those who found, in Reform Judaism, a corpus of self-evident truths. To those truths, the method—the appeal to historical facts— formed a contingent and secondary consideration.

To the Reform rabbis in Pittsburgh, Christianity presented no urgent problems. The open society of America did. The self-evident definition of the social entity, Israel, therefore had to shift. We recall how the fourth-century rabbis balanced Israel against Rome, Jacob against Esau, the triumphant political messiah, seen as arrogant, against the Messiah of God, humble and sagacious. So Israel formed a supernatural entity and in due course would enter into that final era in God's division of time, in which Israel would reach its blessing. The supernatural entity, Israel, now formed no social presence. Gone was the Christian world, where Christ ruled through popes and emperors, kings claimed divine right, and the will of the Church bore multiform consequences for society; and where, by the way, Israel, too, was perceived in a supernatural framework—if a negative one. So the world at large no longer verified the category of Israel as supernatural entity. Then came the problem of defining what sort of entity Israel did constitute, and what way of life should characterize that Israel, what world view should explain it: that problem produced a new set of urgent and ineluctable questions and inevitably self-evidently true answers, such as those in Pittsburgh later on.

To return to the birth of Reform Judaism, this Judaism dates its beginnings to Germany in the early nineteenth century. The reason for the development in Germany in particular was that German society, after the Napoleonic wars, underwent a process of change and reform. In tearing down the walls of the ghetto in Frankfurt, Napoleon had called into question the centuries-old status of the Jews. That small act formed part of a larger program of political change, and the momentum of that change persisted even after the defeat of Napoleon. For the forces of nationalism that were born in the German victory called into question many aspects of the established political settlement and brought about change on diverse fronts. The Jews, among other groups, now aspired to a position different from the one they had known for centuries. Some of them wished to find a place within the German polity, as citizens equal to other citizens. And, outside their community, forces for change of a political, as well as social and economic, character converged to produce that same result. Over the short term, change yielded dissolution of the Jewish community. For a fair proportion of Jewry simply left the community and adopted the dominant religion of the region in which they lived. This they accepted as the passport to Western civilization, civil rights, and, of course, career advancement. But those Jews who remained within the community determined on another path: that is, to change things in such a way as to accommodate Jewry to the requirements of citizenship. The earliest changes, called reforms and regarded as the antecedents of Reform, concerned trivial aspects of public worship in the synagogue.

These changes derived from the simple fact that many

Jews rejected the received system. People were defecting from the synagogue. Since, it was taken for granted, giving up the faith meant surrendering all ties to the group, the beginning of change required reform and ultimately Reform addressed two issues at one time: (1) making the synagogue more attractive, so that (2) defectors would return, and other Jews would not leave. The reform of Judaism as manifested in synagogue worship—the cutting edge of the faith—therefore took cognizance of something that had already taken place. And that was the loss for the received system—way of life, world view, addressed to a defined Israel—of its standing as self-evident truth. That loss manifested itself in two ways. First, people were simply leaving. Second and more important for the group, the many who were staying looked in a new way on what, for so long, had scarcely demanded examination. But, of course, the real issues involved not the synagogue but society at large. It would take two generations before Reform Judaism found the strength to address that much larger issue, and a generation further for the power of the ideas ultimately formulated in the Pittsburgh platform to be felt.

To begin with, the issue involved not politics but merely the justification for any change at all. But that issue asked the wrong question in the wrong way. The Reformers maintained that change was all right because historical precedent proved that change was all right. But change had long defined the constant in the ongoing life of the Judaism of the dual Torah. Generative causes and modes of effecting change marked the vitality of the system. The Judaism of the dual Torah endured, never intact but always unimpaired, because of its power to absorb and make its own the diverse happenings of culture and society. So long as the structure of politics remained the same, with Israel an autonomous entity, subordinated but recognized as a cogent and legitimate social group in charge of some of its own affairs, the system answered the paramount question. The trivial ones could work their way through and become part of the consensus, to be perceived in the end as tradition, too. A catalogue of changes that took place over fifteen hundred years, from the birth of Judaism to its death, would therefore list many more dramatic and decisive sorts of change than those minor revisions of liturgy—for example, sermons in the vernacular—that attracted attention at the dawn of the age of change-become-Reform.

What, then, made the difference so that change could be perceived as reform and transformed into the reform of Judaism—hence, Reform Judaism? When people could take a stance external to the received mode and effect change as a matter of decision and policy, for them Judaism in its received form had already died. For the received system no longer defined matters but now became subject to definition. And that change marks the move from self-evidence to self-consciousness.

We do not know what had brought about the demise of the received system as definitive and normative beyond all argument. Nothing in the earliest record of liturgical reform tells us. The constructive efforts of the first generation—only later recognized not as people who made changes or even as reformers but as founders of Reform Judaism—focused, as I have said, upon synagogue worship. The services were too long; the speeches were in a language (Hebrew) with which participants were no longer familiar; the singing was not aesthetic; the prayers were in a language no one now understood. Hence, some people recited them as a matter of duty, not in supplication; did not speak the language of the faith; formed other than received opinions on how to sing in synagogue; saw as alien what earlier had marked home and hearth. Those people no longer lived in that same social world that had for so long found right and proper precisely the customs now seen as alien.

The Death of Judaism and the Birth of Judaisms

When the heritage forms an unclaimed, unwanted legacy, out of duty people nonetheless accept it. So the reform that produced Reform Judaism introduced a shortened service, a sermon in the language people spoke, a choir and an organ, prayers in the vernacular. Clearly, much change had taken place prior to the recognition that something had changed. People no longer knew Hebrew; they no longer found pleasing received modes of saying the prayers. We look in vain to the subsequent reforms for answers to the question why people made these changes, and the reasons adduced by historians settle no interesting questions for us. The more interesting question concerns why the persistence of engagement and concern. For people always had the option, which many exercised, of abandoning the received Judaism. Among those for whom these cosmetic changes made a difference, much in the liturgy, and far more beyond, retained its powerful appeal. The premise of change dictated that Jews would say the old prayers in essentially the old formulation. And that premise carried much else: the entire burden of the faith; the total commitment to the group, in some form, defined by some indicators—if not the familiar ones, then some others. So we know that Reform Judaism, in its earliest manifestation in Germany in the early nineteenth century, constituted an essentially conservative, profoundly constructive effort to save for Jews the received Judaism by reforming it in some (to begin with) rather trivial ways.

The theory of the incremental history of a single, linear Judaism played a powerful role in the creative age of Reform Judaism. The ones who made changes (it is too soon to call them Reformers, or the changes Reforms) first appealed to the authoritative texts. Change is legitimate, and these changes in particular were wholly consonant with the law, or the tradition, or the inner dynamics of the faith, or the dictates of history, or whatever out of the past worked

96

that day. The laymen who made the changes tried to demonstrate that the changes fit in with the law of Judaism. They took the trouble because Reform even at the outset claimed to restore, to continue, to persist in, the received pattern. The justification of change always invoked precedent. People who made changes had to show that their guiding principle was not new, even though the specific things they did were. So to lay down a bridge between themselves and their past, they laid out beams resting on deep-set piles. Change was founded on the bedrock of precedent. And more still: change restores, reverts to an unchanging ideal. So the Reformer claimed not to change at all, but only to regain the correct state of affairs, a state that others, in the interval, themselves had changed. That formed the fundamental attitude of mind of the people who made changes and called the changes Reform. The appeal to history, a common mode of justification in the politics and theology of the nineteenth century, therefore defined the principal justification for the new Judaism: it was new because it renewed the old and enduring, the golden Judaism of a mythic age of perfection. Arguments on precedent, as we shall see, drew the Reformers to the work of critical scholarship: they settled all questions by appeal to the facts of history.

We cannot find surprising, therefore, the theory that Reform Judaism stands in a direct line with the prior history of Judaism. Judaism is one. Judaism has a history; that history is single and unitary; and it has always been leading to its present outcome: Reform Judaism. Others would later challenge these convictions: Orthodox Judaism would deny that Judaism has a history at all; Conservative, or Positive Historical Judaism, would discover a different goal for history from that embodied by Reform Judaism. But the mode of argument, appealing to issues of a historical and factual character, and the premises of argument, insisting that history proved or disproved matters of theological conviction,

The Death of Judaism and the Birth of Judaisms

characterized all the Judaisms of the nineteenth century. Not surprisingly, since the Judaisms of the age took shape in the intellectual world of Germany, with its profoundly philosophical and historical mode of thought and argument. So the challenge of political change carried with it its own modes of intellectual response: in the academic, scholarly framework.

In Germany, the method of the Judaism aborning as Reform exhibited a certain congruence to the locale. Whether Luther is demanding reversion to the pure and primitive faith of the Gospels or the earliest generation of Reform leaders are appealing to the Talmud as justification for rejecting what others saw as the Talmud's contemporary requirements, the principle remains the same. Reform renews; recovers the true condition of a faith; selects, out of a diverse past, that age and that moment at which the faith attained its perfect definition and embodiment. Not change, but restoration and renewal of the true modes, the recovery of the way things were in that perfect, paradigmatic time, that age that formed the model for all time: these deeply mythic modes of appeal formed the justification for change, transforming mere modification of this and that into Reform. The leaders of change took on the mantle of Reform, for they revised not only a few lines of a prayer but the entire world view expressed in the accepted liturgy.

The mythic being of the liturgy entailed the longing, in the imagination of the nation, for a return to Zion, for rebuilding of the Temple, for reconstitution of the bloody rites of animal sacrifice. In response to the Christian view that Israel's salvation had occurred in times past and ended with Israel's rejection of the Christhood of Jesus, the dual Torah had insisted on future salvation, at the end of time—which, self-evidently, had not yet arrived. For ages after the original exile, in 586 B.C.E., the Jews had appealed to a Scripture that explained why they had lost their land, their city,

98

their Temple, their cult, and told them what they had to do to get them back. That scriptural message thus, as we have seen, formed a principal plank in the messianic platform of the Judaism of the dual Torah, since sages alleged that if Israel kept the Torah as they taught it, its promises—those of the Pentateuch and prophets alike—would come true. The Messiah-sage stood for exactly that outcome.

To Jews the condition of Israel in exile formed a self-evident fact of politics and culture alike. Speaking their own language, pursuing occupations distinctive to their group, living essentially apart from other peoples of the same time and place (who themselves formed not a uniform nation but a mosaic of equivalent social entities, that is, religion-nations, each with its language and its economy and its distinct society), Jews knew who they were. They were a nation in exile. The early changes, therefore, signaled that much else already had undergone revision and still more would have to change as well. Reform ratified change now a generation old, proposed to cope with it, and so to reframe and revise the received tradition as to mark out new outlines for self-evident truth.

The original changes, in the first decades of the nineteenth century, produced a new generation of rabbis. Some forty years into the century, these rabbis gave to the process of change the name of Reform and created those institutions of Reform Judaism that would endow the inchoate movement with a politics of its own. In the mid-1840s, several rabbinical conferences brought together this new generation. Trained in universities, rabbis who came to these gatherings turned backward, justifying the changes in prayer rites long in place, effecting some further, mostly cosmetic, changes in the observance of the Sabbath and in the laws covering personal status through marriage and divorce. In 1845, a decision to adopt for some purposes German in place of Hebrew led to the departure of conservative

99

Reformers, typified by Zacharias Frankel. But the Reformers found their apologia in the received writings, persisting in their insistence that they formed a natural continuation of the processes of the tradition. Indeed, that point of insistence—that Judaism formed, in the words of the eminent Reform theologian Jacob J. Petuchowski in regard to Abraham Geiger, "a constantly evolving organism"[3]—was the centerpiece of the nascent Judaism at hand.

Reform Theologian: Abraham Geiger

If we want to understand the new Judaisms of the age, we must turn to the leading intellect to show us how people reached their conclusions, not merely what they said or why they found self-evident the positions they took. Abraham Geiger (1810–74) enjoyed the advantage of the finest argumentative mind in Jewry in the nineteenth century, and his life presents facts of less interest than his work. In his work, his way of asking and answering questions tells us what matters in Reform Judaism: what people found self-evident, on the one side, and urgent, on the other. The urgency accounts for the questions, the self-evidence, the mode of discovering the answers. To those two matters, everything else takes second place. The question Geiger found ineluctable takes simple form: How can we explain what has happened to us? The answer: What has taken place—change become Reform—forms the natural and necessary outcome of history. In his emphasis upon the probative status and value of the facts of history, those self-evident principles lead us deep into the consciousness of the man and the Judaism he embodied. What Geiger took for granted—in our terms, held as self-evident—is that history proved propositions of theology. Whatever the particular matter of conviction or custom takes a secondary place. The primary source of verification, therefore, of appropriate and inappropriate traits in Judaism—that is to say, the origin of the reliable definition of Judaism—lies not in revealed records of God's will but in human accounts of humanity's works. To that principle—everywhere taken for granted, occasionally enunciated, but never systematically demonstrated—Geiger's mode of argument and inquiry took second place.

Since the earliest changes changed into reforms, and reforms of Judaism into Reform Judaism, to Geiger we address our principal questions: Old or new? And how did people explain themselves? Abraham Geiger presented in clearest form the argument that Reform carried forward the historical processes of Judaism. He took the position that there was a single, linear Judaism, and that it was affected by history—that is, by change. He appealed to the facts of history, beginning with the critical study of the Bible. Petuchowski summarizes his view as follows:

> Judaism is a constantly evolving organism. Biblical Judaism was not identical with classical rabbinic Judaism. Similarly, the modern age calls for further evolution in consonance with the changed circumstances.... The modern rabbis are entitled to adapt medieval Judaism, as the early rabbis had the right to adapt biblical Judaism.... He found traces of evolution within the Bible itself. Yet for Geiger changes in Judaism had always been organic.... The modern changes must develop out of the past, and not represent a revolutionary break with it.[4]

Geiger, therefore, recognized change as traditional: that is, changing represents the way things always have been and so legitimately now goes forward. The Jews change, having moved from constituting a nation to a different classification of social entity. The Messiah idea now addresses the whole of humanity, speaks not only of national restoration. Revelation then turns out to form a progressive, not a static, fact. In these diverse ways, Geiger—and with him, Reform Judaism through its history—appealed to history to verify its allegations and validate its positions. So facts turn into the evidence for faith.

Geiger grew up in Frankfurt and undertook university studies at Heidelberg, then Bonn, with special interest in philosophy and Semitics.[5] At that time, university study formed the exception, not the rule, for Jews. By definition, therefore, the change Geiger had to explain came about through the decision of the former generation. Geiger explained change; his parents made it. But among the intellectual leaders in Geiger's day, not only he, but his arch-opponent, Samson Raphael Hirsch, founder of Orthodox Judaism, also acquired a university education. So Orthodox Judaism, too, emerged as the result of the decision of the generation prior to the age of the founders (see chapter 3). To both sets of parents, the value of an education in the sciences of the West proved self-evident; the ways of harmonizing that education and its values with the education in the Judaic sciences were considerably less clear. Earlier generations had not sent their sons to universities (and, for a similar right, their daughters would have to wait until nearly our own day). Prior to the generation of the parents of Geiger and Hirsch, most parents found self-evident the value of education in the established institutions of the Judaism of the dual Torah—there alone. Knowledge of another sort, under other auspices, bore no value. Thus, before the advent of the reformer, whether the great intellect of Reform Judaism or the courageous leader of Orthodoxy, change had already affected self-evident truth.

Geiger served a parlous life in synagogue pulpits, not always appreciated for the virtues he brought to them: flawless German and his questioning of routine.[6] He spent most of his time, however, concerned not with the local synagogue community but with the constituency of Judaic learning. He began to produce a periodical, the *Scientific Journal for Jewish Theology*, in 1835. The purpose of scientific knowledge Max Wiener epitomizes in the following statement: "They were convinced that, given the historical facts, it would be possible to draw the correct practical conclusions with regard to the means by which their religion could best be served and elevated to the level of contemporary culture."[7] That is to say, through systematic learning Judaism would undergo reform. Reform Judaism rested on deep foundations of historical scholarship.

It was Geiger's aim to analyze the sources and the evolution of Judaism. If science (used in its German sense of "systematic learning") could uncover the sources of the Jewish "spirit," then, in Wiener's words, "the genius of his people and . . . its vocation" would serve "as a guide to the construction of a living present and future." Geiger's principle of Reform remained fixed. Reform had to emerge from *Wissenschaft*, "a term which he equated with the concept of the understanding of historical evolution." To him, "Judaism in its ideal form was religion per se, nothing but an expression of religious consciousness. Its outer shell was subject to change from one generation to another."[8] All things emerge out of time and of change. But when it comes to tracing the history of time and change, contemporary categories assuredly defined the inquiry. Thus Geiger produced, out of ancient times, portraits suspiciously congruent to the issues of his own day.

For example, in his account of the Sadducees and the Pharisees—the former enjoying a bad press; the latter, in Judaism, a good one—he identified the former with "the strict guardians of traditional institutions, while the latter spoke out in behalf of progress in both religion and

103

politics."[9]* Geiger's principal point was: "What Geiger sought to prove by this demonstration [that the text of Scripture was fluid] is quite obvious. It was not the Bible that created and molded the religious spirit of Judaism; instead, it was the spirit of Judaism that left the stamp of its own form and expression upon the Bible—Life, and its needs and strivings, change from age to age."[11] Wiener and Petuchowski's accounts show what Geiger found to be self-evident: truths beyond all appeal that formed the foundation of his life's work as the first and best historian of Judaism. These premises we identify not in the propositions he proposed to demonstrate, but in the facts concerning change and the constancy of change which he took for granted.

At the outset I raised the question whether the framers of the Judaisms of the nineteenth century claimed to renew the received Judaism of the dual Torah or to invent a Judaism. And if they alleged that they stood as the natural next step in the tradition, does that claim stand? Geiger represents the answer of Reform Judaism in his day, a powerful and one-sided answer. Reform Judaism renews; it does not invent. There was, and is, only a single Judaism. In the current age, Reform undertakes the discovery of that definition. Reform clearly lays its foundations on the basis of history—that is, tradition. Propositions of a theological character, for example, concerning the dual Torah revealed at Sinai, the sanctified and therefore supernatural character of Israel, the holy people, the coming Messiah-sage at the end of time—these take their place in the line of truths to

---

* The Sadducees and Pharisees were sects in the Judaism of the period before the year 70. The Sadducees, who are regarded as upper-class figures, denied the existence of oral tradition. The Pharisees, who are described as influential, affirmed the existence of oral tradition, later called the oral Torah. These matters are placed into their own context in my *Self-Fulfilling Prophecy: Exile and Return in the History of Judaism*.[10]

be investigated through historical method, in historical sources. There may be an incongruity between the propositions at hand and the allegations about the decisive, probative character of historical inquiry in evaluating them. For the facts of history hardly testify, one way or another, concerning the character of revelation at Sinai (though we may know what people recorded in that connection), the status and sanctity of Israel (though the social facts and political issues surely pertained to this-worldly Israel), let alone that event at the end, on the other side, of history altogether—the coming of the Messiah.

The question whether the claim of Reform Judaism finds justification in the "facts" proves beside the point. The facts are what people make of them, whether discovered in history or imputed in revealed and holy writings, in a canon of truth. We can scarcely say that the position of Reform Judaism, as outlined by a brief sketch of Geiger's thought, even intersects or connects with what had gone before. Old or new? Not only new, but out of all relationship to the old. The appeal to the old—to history—turns out to come after the fact, the system, had already come to ample formation. Once the Judaism at hand had come into being, people knew what they wanted to find out from history: that is, whether things change. Geiger followed a far more sophisticated program since, knowing that things do change (to whom would the proposition have brought surprise?), he asked exactly how, in Judaism, change takes place, and in what direction. In his view, it was obvious that the Sadducees looked like the Orthodox of his day, and the Pharisees, like the Reformers.

The point of self-evidence, then, is that the categories defined in Geiger's day pertained a long time ago. That is the mark of the new Judaism called Reform Judaism: its powerful capacity without a trace of self-consciousness to impose anachronistic issues and categories. What changes is the repertoire of self-evident truths.

The Appeal to Historical Precedent: Abraham Cronbach and Jacob R. Marcus

Reform Judaism, once well under way, had to situate itself in relationship to the past. Geiger's powerful appeal to precedent left no choice. For not all precedents sustained contemporary choices—the system as it had already emerged; and some of the more recent choices surely called it into question. So as learning rolled forward, the question arose, Precisely what, in history, serves as a precedent for change-become-Reform? The answer sought the constants in change. To advance our understanding of Reform Judaism, we move once more to America, the country where Reform Judaism enjoyed massive success in the last half of the twentieth century, and where we see in full and articulate formulation the world view of Reform Judaism as it unfolded in a straight line from Geiger's day to our own. Our guide is Abraham Cronbach, a professor at Hebrew Union College during the first half of the twentieth century.

Specifically, in his preface to Abraham Cronbach's *Reform Movements in Judaism*, Jacob Rader Marcus, a principal voice in Reform Judaism in the twentieth century, provides a powerful statement of the Reform view of its place in history. Marcus recognizes that diverse Judaisms have flourished in the history of the Jews. What characterizes them all is that each began as a reform movement but then underwent a process we might characterize as "traditionalization." That is to say, change became not merely reform but tradition, and the only constant in the histories of Judaisms is that process of transformation of the new to the conventional or, in theological language, the traditional. This process Marcus describes as follows: "All [Judaisms] began as rebellions, as great reformations, but after receiving widespread acceptance, developed vested 'priestly' interests, failed their people, and were forced to retreat before the onslaught of new rebellions, new philosophies, new challenges." Nothing in Marcus's picture could have been a surprise to Geiger. So endures the fundamental theological method of Reform Judaism in its initial phase, the appeal to facts of history for the validation of theological propositions. But the claim that everything always changes yields a challenge, which Marcus forthrightly raises: "Is there then nothing but change? Is change the end of all our history and all our striving? No, there is something else, the desire to be free. . . . In the end [the Jew] has always understood that changelessness is spiritual death. The Jew who would live must never completely surrender himself to one truth, but . . . must reach out for the farther and faint horizons of an ever Greater God. . . . This is the meaning of Reform."[12]

Marcus thus treats as self-evident—obvious because it is a fact of history—the persistence of change. And, denying that that is all there is to Reform, at the end he affirms the simple point that change sets the norm. It comes down to the same thing. The something else of Marcus's argument presents its own problems. Appeal to the facts of history fails at the point when a constructive position demands articulation. "The desire to be free" bears a predicate: Free of what? Free to do, to be what? If Marcus fails to accomplish the whole of the theological task, however, he surely conveys the profoundly constructive vision that Reform Judaism afforded to its Israel.

For his part, Cronbach sets forth the five precedents for

the present movement: the Deuteronomic Reformation, the Pentateuchal Reformation, the Pharisaic Reformation, the Karaite Reformation, and the Hasidic Reformation. These reformations include important developments in the history of Judaisms. The Deuteronomic Reformation refers to the writing of the book of Deuteronomy, in two stages—first in 620 B.C., then in 570 B.C. The Pentateuchal Reformation speaks of the creation of the five books of Moses, the written Torah, in the time of Ezra, about 450 B.C. The Pharisaic Reformation draws on the then-established theory of the Pharisees as the founders of the Judaism after the destruction of the Temple in 70 C.E. The Karaite Reformation was a heresy that came to expression in the eighth and ninth centuries and flourished through the Middle Ages. It was a Judaism that rejected the belief in the dual Torah, specifically in the Talmud as the writing down of the oral Torah of Sinai, and maintained that God had revealed only one Torah, the written one. The Hasidic Reformation was a form of the Judaism of the dual Torah that laid great stress on direct encounter with God through prayer and mystical experience. In these reformations, as he called them, Cronbach found precedents for that of his own day and making—and he invoked the theory of a linear and incremental history of Judaism in so doing. His coming reformation appeals to social psychology and aims at tolerance: "Felicitous human relationships can be the goal of social welfare and of economic improvement. . . . Our Judaism of maturity would be dedicated to the ideal of freedom. Corollary of that ideal is what we have just observed about courtesy toward the people whose beliefs and practices we do not share."[13] We have now moved far from the position outlined by Geiger, in which a constant conversation with the received canon of the dual Torah yielded important propositions. But our interest in Reform Judaism hardly requires us to criticize the constructive efforts of its theolo-

108

gians. We want to know two things: First, is it old or new? It is new. Second, if a Judaism turns out to be new, as shown by its essentially distinctive principle of selection, then how does that Judaism establish its claim to form the natural, the necessary next step in the received Judaism? We find the answers to both questions in two further questions. First, does this Judaism ask the questions that for the Judaism of the dual Torah demanded answer, or does it ask other questions? That is a matter of fact. Second, does this Judaism find self-evidently valid the answers of the Judaism of the dual Torah, or do other propositions prove self-evidently true? That, too, is a matter of fact.

Urgent Questions, Self-Evident Answers

Two questions await attention. And the answers to both questions lie right on the surface. Given its intellectual strength, Reform Judaism had no difficulty saying precisely what it wished on classic issues. For this Judaism, the questions of the system of the dual Torah proved no more compelling than its answers. The whole turned from the self-evident statement of God's will to a source of precedents, available for selection and rearrangement. How to pick and choose formed the principal issue of method. The distinction between written and oral Torah provided the answer: choose the written; drop the oral. So the Reform theologians rejected the claim that the oral part of the Torah came from God. It was the work of men, time-bound, contingent, possessed of a merely advisory authority. Whatever precedents and antecedents Reform historians and theologians sought, they would not look in the rabbinic writings that, all together, fall under the name "Talmud," because there

their opposition in orthodoxy found their principal ammu-
nition. The Judaism from which Reform took its leave, the
one that required the changes become reforms yielding Reform—that Judaism found its definition in the dual Torah
of Sinai, as written down from the Mishnah on. So, quite
naturally, when the Reformers addressed the issue of continuity, they leaped over the immediate past, represented by
the Judaism of the dual Torah, and sought their antecedents
in the processes of change instead.

But how did they express their judgment of the particular
Judaism they proposed to revise? It was in clear and explicit
statements that the Talmud at best preserved the wisdom
of ordinary mortals, from which contemporary Jews might,
if they wished, choose to learn.

A sequence of statements among nineteenth-century authorities expressed the entire consensus. So Joshua Heschel
Schorr (1814–95):

> For as long as the Talmud is considered an inherently perfect,
> infallible monument of true divine tradition and is being ac-
> cepted as such, no reform can take place through it. That being
> the case, why do we not get ready to expose the inner imperfec-
> tions and the many irrefutably obvious faults from which the
> work suffers? This would clearly prove that what we possess
> here is a work created by humans, distorted by many errors, and
> that the writing of this volume is not imbued with one wholly
> integrated spirit.[14]

The study of history, therefore, carried a heavy freight of
theological apologetics for Reform Judaism, a fact we have
now confronted time and again. Here the very historical
character of the Talmud made the case. It was the work of
men, not of God. So its authority was no more than that of
other men.

The Talmud will take its place among the works of mortals and lose its position as half of the one whole Torah of

Moses, our rabbi. Michael Creizenach (1789–1842) proposed to distinguish among parts of the Talmud:

> [The Talmud presents] a serviceable means for the interpretation of those ritual commandments which, according to the individual concepts of each man, are binding to this day. . . . We regard those portions of the Talmud which do not elucidate the Mosaic laws as merely humanly instituted decrees. . . . We consider those passages in the Talmud which are not consistent with the principle of the universal love of man, as outbursts of passionate hatred of which unfortunately quite often the best men cannot free themselves when they are oppressed in a disgraceful way and when they see that all considerations to which the dignity of human nature gives them undeniable claims are being violated against themselves.[15]

The upshot was that the changes-become-Reform took a clear and distinct step away from the received Torah. No one, even in the earliest generations of Reform, pretended otherwise. A new program of self-evident truths had taken the place of the old. As a new set of questions demanded responses, an established set of issues no longer mattered very much. So at the end we survey the questions people found they had, as a matter of life or death, to answer—and those answers that gave, and today still give, life.

Self-Evidence and Political Change

The urgent problem was, What is Israel in an age in which individual Jews have become something else, in addition to being Israel? Is Israel a nation? No, Israel does not fall into the same category as the nations. Jews are multiple beings: Israel in one dimension; part of France or Germany or America in a second. But if Israel is not a nation, then what of the way of life that had made the nation different, and what of the world view that had made sense of the way of life? These now formed the questions people could not avoid. The answers constitute Reform Judaism.

To close with the main point: Reform Judaism does not carry forward an unbroken tradition and does not claim to. This Judaism in advance knew as a matter of fact something that in the received Judaism one did not and could not have found out: that is, the simple fact the Jews' political standing could no longer be tolerated. But how to define a politics appropriate both to Jewry and to the hopes and expectations of Jews in nineteenth-century Europe and twentieth-century America? That issue required a fair amount of picking and choosing.

Finding reasonable evidence that Reform Judaism formed a new Judaism hardly challenges our imagination. The Reformers claimed no less. Assessing the claim of continuity presents more of a dilemma. Precedent for change hardly constitutes a chain of continuity, and the particular changes at hand scarcely recapitulate prior ones, either in substance or in social policy. But that is beside the point. Important is not whether the claim may find support in the facts of history, but what we learn about Reform Judaism from the definitive and indicative claim.

Once we know that the system, in all its components and proportions, had attained definition on its own terms, fully defining its program of pressing issues, we realize that the claim of continuity comes long after the fact of innovation. The claim, then, forms part of an apologia, rather than providing the generative force for the new system. That drew its strength elsewhere than from the received Judaism. The new Judaic system as a whole made its own points and, by the way, drew upon the received Judaism in adopting for its own texts held sacred in the established system. And the Judaism that resulted constitutes, therefore, something quite different from a continuous and ongoing tradition. We therefore can identify what the earliest generations of the new Judaism found self-evident: the truths that in their view demanded no articulation, no defense, no argument.

The questions they confronted and could not evade pertained to their understanding of themselves as citizens of a state other than an (imaginary) Jewish one, a polity separate from, and in addition to, Israel. When Petuchowski states simply that Reform Judaism came into existence to deal with political change in the status of Jews, he is leading us to the heart of the matter.[16] But what does that simple, to us self-evident, fact reveal about the incremental theory of Judaism, the notion that things move from point to point step by step? In my view, Reform Judaism presents an insuperable challenge to that theory. For it was not formed by incremental steps out of the received Judaism (the tradition), and it did not move along a path in a straight line from where Jews had been to where they wished to go. The system took shape on its own. Systems relate only in a common genealogy. But they cohere—for all Judaisms do contend with one another and regard one another as (unworthy) opponents within the same arena—because, after all, they address pretty much the same people about the same things.

I end not with analysis of a Judaic system but with recognition of what we learn, from Reform Jews, about the condition of humanity. The human achievement of Reform deserves a simple observation of what these people did and what they were. With acuity, perspicacity, and enormous courage, the Reformers, in the nineteenth and twentieth centuries alike, took the measure of the world and made ample use of the materials they had in hand in manufacturing something to fit it. And Reform did fit those Jews, and they were, and are, very many, to whom the issue of Israel as a supernatural entity has remained vivid. For, after all, the centerpiece of Reform Judaism remained its powerful notion that Israel does have a task and a mission, and thus should endure as Israel. Reform Judaism persuaded generations, from its beginnings to the present, of the worth of human life lived in its Judaic system. More than that we cannot ask of any Judaism.

CHAPTER 3

ORTHODOXY: PERFECT FAITH AND SELECTIVE PIETY

Orthodoxy and the "Tradition"

Orthodox Judaism came into being in Germany in the middle of the nineteenth century among Jews who, in rejecting Reform, were making a self-conscious decision to remain within the way of life and world view they had known and cherished all their lives. This statement will surprise people who reasonably identify all "traditional" or "observant" Judaism with Orthodoxy and who take for granted, furthermore, that all traditional Judaisms are pretty much the same. Here the distinction between those who adhered to the received system of the dual Torah and those who identified with Orthodox Judaism in mid-nineteenth-century Germany concerns such indicators as clothing, language, and, above all, education. When Jews who kept the law of the Torah—for example, as it dictated food choices and use of leisure time (to speak of the Sabbath and festivals in secular terms)—sent their children to secular schools, in addition to or instead of solely Jewish ones, or when, in Jewish schools, they included in the curriculum subjects outside the sciences of the Torah, they crossed the boundary between the received and the new Judaism of Orthodoxy. For the notion that science or German or Latin or philosophy deserved serious study, while not alien to important exemplars of the received system of the dual Torah, in the nineteenth century struck as wrong those for whom the received system remained self-evidently right. Those Jews did not send their children to gentile schools and, in Jewish schools, did not include in the curriculum other than Torah study.

What made Orthodoxy fresh becomes clear in the contrast to Reform Judaism. While the Reformers held that Judaism could change and was a product of history, their Orthodox opponents denied that Judaism could change and insisted that it derived from God's will at Sinai and was eternal and supernatural, not historical and man-made. In these two convictions, of course, the Orthodox were recapitulating the convictions of the received system. But in their appeal to the given, the traditional, they found more persuasive some of its components than others; and, as I have said, in the picking and choosing, in the articulation of the view that Judaism formed a religion to be seen as distinct and autonomous of politics, society, "the rest of life," they entered that same world of self-conscious believing that the Reformers also explored.

116

Let me, then, define Orthodox Judaism in more systematic ways, for mere knowledge of the circumstance, in public disputations with Reform, that gave birth to Orthodoxy does not allow the system its full and autonomous statement. Orthodox Judaism is that Judaic system that mediates between the received Judaism of the dual Torah and the requirements of living a life integrated in modern circumstances. Orthodoxy maintains the world view of the received dual Torah, constantly citing its sayings and adhering with only trivial variations to the bulk of its norms for everyday life. At the same time Orthodoxy holds that Jews adhering to the dual Torah may wear clothing that non-Jews wear and do not have to wear distinctively Jewish clothing; may live within a common economy and not practice distinctively Jewish professions (however, in a given setting, these professions may be defined: for instance, inn-keeping in Russia, commerce in Poland); and may, in diverse ways, take up a life not readily distinguished in important characteristics from the life lived by people in general.

So for Orthodoxy a portion of Israel's life may prove secular, in that the Torah does not dictate and so sanctify all details under all circumstances. Since the Judaism of the dual Torah presupposed not only the supernatural entity Israel but also a way of life that in important ways distinguished that supernatural entity from the social world at large, Orthodoxy proved formidable in finding an accommodation for Jews who valued the received way of life and world view and also planned to make their lives in an essentially integrated social world. The difference between Orthodoxy and the system of the dual Torah was expressed in social policy: integration, however circumscribed, versus the total separation of the holy people.

Many Jews, Orthodox and non-observant alike, see Orthodox Judaism as the same as the tradition, as what is natu-

117

ral and normal, and hold that Orthodoxy now stands for how things always were, for all time. But since the term *Orthodoxy* takes on meaning only in contrast to Reform, Orthodoxy, in a simple sense, owes its life to Reform Judaism. The term first surfaced in 1795[1] and, in general, covers all Jews who believe that God revealed the dual Torah at Sinai, and that Jews must carry out the requirements of Jewish law contained in the Torah as interpreted by the sages through time. This position, of course, had for centuries struck as self-evident the generality of Jewry at large—centuries when Orthodoxy as a distinct and organized Judaism did not exist; it did not have to. Two events changed this situation: first, the recognition of the received system, the tradition as Orthodoxy; second, the specification of the received system as religion. The two go together. So long as the Judaism of the dual Torah enjoyed recognition as a set of self-evident truths, those truths added up to nothing so distinct and special as "religion," but to a general statement of how things are: all of life explained and harmonized in one whole account.

The former of the two events—the view of the received system as traditional—came first. (The matter of the self-aware recognition of Judaism as religion came later.) That identification of truth as tradition occurred when the received system met the challenge of competing Judaisms. Then, in behalf of the received way of life and world view addressed to supernatural Israel, people said that the Judaism of the dual Torah was established of old; was the right, the only way of seeing and doing things; was how things have been and should be naturally and normally: "tradition." But that is a category that contains within itself an alternative—namely, change, as in "tradition and change."

When the system lost its power of self-evidence, it entered, among other apologetic categories, that of the "tradition." And that came about when Orthodoxy met head on

118

the challenge of change-become-Reform. We understand why the category of tradition, the received way of doing things, became critical to the framers of Orthodoxy when we examine the counter claim: that is to say, just as the Reformers justified change, the Orthodox theologians denied that change was ever possible. Thus, so Walter S. Wurzburger: "Orthodoxy looks upon attempts to adjust Judaism to the 'spirit of the time' as utterly incompatible with the entire thrust of normative Judaism which holds that the revealed will of God rather than the values of any given age are the ultimate standard." To begin, the debate was defined by the issue important to the Reformers: that is, the value of what was called "emancipation," or the provision to Jews of civil rights. When the Reform Judaic theologians took a wholly one-sided position affirming emancipation, numerous Orthodox ones adopted the contrary view. The position outlined by these theologians followed the agenda laid forth by the Reformers. If the Reform made minor changes in liturgy and its conduct, the Orthodox rejected even those that, under other circumstances, might have found acceptance. Saying prayers in the vernacular, for example, provoked strong opposition. But everyone knew that some of the prayers, said long ago in Babylonia in Aramaic were, in fact in the vernacular of the earlier age, the third century B.C. to the seventh century A.D. The Orthodox thought that these changes, not reforms at all, represented only the first step of a process leading Jews out of the Judaic world altogether; and, as Wurzburger says, "The slightest tampering with tradition was condemned."[2]

To discover where the received system of the dual Torah prevailed, and where, by contrast, Orthodoxy came to full expression, we have only to follow the spreading out of railway lines; the growth of new industry; the shifts in political status accorded to, among other citizens, Jews; changes in the educational system; in all, the entire process of political change, economic and social, demographic and cultural shifts of a radical and fundamental nature. Where these changes came first, there Reform Judaism met them in its way—and Orthodoxy in its. Where change came later in the century—as in Russian Poland, the eastern provinces of the Austro-Hungarian Empire, and Russia itself—there, in villages contentedly following the old ways, the received system endured. Again, in an age of mass migration from eastern Europe to America and other Western democracies, those who experienced the upheaval of leaving home and country met the challenge of change either by accepting new ways of seeing things or, articulately and in full self-awareness, reaffirming the familiar ones—once more, Reform or Orthodoxy. We may, therefore, characterize the received system as a way of life and world view wedded to an ancient peoples' homelands, the villages and small towns of central and eastern Europe, and Orthodoxy as the heir of that received system as it came to expression in the towns and cities of central and western Europe and America. That rule of thumb allows us to distinguish between the piety of a milieu and the theological conviction of a self-conscious community. Or, we may accept the familiar distinction between tradition and articulate Orthodoxy—a distinction, to be sure, with its own freight of apologetics.

Clearly, the beginnings of Orthodoxy occurred in the areas where Reform made its way—hence in Germany and in southern Hungary. In Germany, where Reform attracted the majority of not a few Jewish communities, the Orthodox faced a challenge indeed. Critical to their conviction was the notion that Israel, all of the Jews, bore responsibility to carry out the law of the Torah. But the community's institutions in the hands of Reform did not obey the law of the Torah as the Orthodox understood it. So, in the end, Orthodoxy took the step that marked it as a self-conscious Judaism, and separated from the established community altogether. The Orthodox set up their own organization and seceded from the community at large. The next step prohibited the Orthodox from participating in non-Orthodox organizations altogether. Isaac Breuer, a leading theologian of Orthodoxy, would ultimately take the position that "refusal to espouse the cause of separation was interpreted as being equivalent to the rejection of the absolute sovereignty of God."[3]

The matter of accommodating to the world at large, of course, did not allow for so easy an answer as mere separation. The specific issue—integration or segregation—concerned preparation for life in the larger politics and economic life of the country, and that meant secular education, involving not only language and science but history and literature, matters of values. Orthodoxy had two distinct wings: one rejected secular learning as well as all dealing with non-Orthodox Jews; the other cooperated with non-Orthodox and secular Jews and accepted the value of secular education. This latter position in no way affected loyalty to the law of Judaism—for example, belief in God's revelation of the one whole Torah at Sinai. The point at which the received system and Orthodox split requires specification. Proponents of the received system never accommodated themselves to secular education, while the Orthodox in Germany and Hungary persistently affirmed it. This affirmation points to a remarkable shift, since central to the received system of the dual Torah is study of Torah— Torah, not philosophy.

Explaining where we find the one and the other, Katzburg works with the distinction I have already made, between an unbroken system and one that has undergone a serious break with the familiar condition of the past:

In Eastern Europe until World War I, Orthodoxy preserved without a break its traditional ways of life and the time-

121

honored educational framework. In general, the mainstream of Jewish life was identified with Orthodoxy, while Haskalah [Jewish Enlightenment, which applied to the Judaic setting the skeptical attitudes of the French Enlightenment] and secularization were regarded as deviations. Hence there was no ground wherein a Western type of Orthodoxy could take root. . . . European Orthodoxy in the 19th and the beginning of the 20th centuries was significantly influenced by the move from small settlements to urban centers . . . as well as by emigration. Within the small German communities there was a kind of popular Orthodoxy, deeply attached to tradition and to local customs, and when it moved to the large cities this element brought with it a vitality and rootedness to Jewish tradition.[4]

These commentators authoritatively define the difference between tradition and Orthodoxy, between the received system accepted as self-evident and an essentially selective—therefore, by definition, new—system, called Orthodoxy. In particular, they tell us where to expect to find the articulated—therefore, self-conscious—affirmation of tradition that characterizes Orthodoxy but does not occur in the world of the dual Torah as it glided in its eternal orbit of the seasons and of unchanging time.

Old and New in Orthodoxy

I find it difficult to imagine what the urban Orthodox might otherwise have done. They experienced change, daily encountered Jews unlike themselves, no longer lived in that stable Judaic society in which the received Torah formed the given of life. The pretense that Jews faced no choices was scarcely a possibility. Nor did the generality of the Jews propose, in the West, to preserve a separate language or to renounce political rights. So Orthodoxy made its peace with change, no less than did Reform. The educational program that led Jews out of the received culture of the dual Torah, the use of the vernacular, the acceptance of political rights, the renunciation of Jewish garments, education for women, abolition of the power of the community to coerce the individual—these and many other originally Reform positions characterized the Orthodoxy that emerged, another new Judaism, in the nineteenth century.[5]

If we wonder how new the Orthodox system was, we find ambiguous answers. In conviction, in way of life, in world view, it was hardly new at all. For the bulk of its substantive positions found ample precedent in the received dual Torah. From its affirmation of God's revelation of a dual Torah to its acceptance of the detailed authority of the law and customs, from its strict observance of the law to its unwillingness to change a detail of public worship, Orthodoxy rightly pointed to its strong links with the chain of tradition. But Orthodoxy constituted a sect within the Jewish group. Its definition of the Israel to whom it wished to speak and the definition characteristic of the dual Torah hardly coincide. The Judaism of the dual Torah addressed all Jews, and Orthodoxy recognized that it could not do so. Orthodoxy acquiesced, however, in a situation that lay beyond the imagination of the framers of the Judaism of the dual Torah.

True, the Orthodox had no choice. Their seceding from the community and forming their own institutions ratified the simple fact that they could not work with the Reformers. But the upshot remains the same. That supernatural entity Israel gave up its place, and a natural Israel, a this-worldly political fact, succeeded to it. Pained though Orthodoxy was by the fact, it nonetheless accommodated the new social reality—and affirmed it by reshaping the sense of Israel in the supernatural dimension. Their Judaism no less than the Judaism of the Reformers stood for something new—a birth not a renewal, a political response to a new politics. True enough, for Orthodoxy the politics was that of the Jewish community, divided as it was among diverse visions of the political standing of Israel, the Jewish people. For the Reform, by contrast, the new politics derived from the establishment of the category of neutral citizenship in an encompassing nation-state. But the political shifts flowed from the same large-scale changes in Israel's consciousness and character; and, it follows, Orthodoxy as much as Reform represented a set of self-evident answers to political questions that none could evade.

Orthodoxy represents the most interesting challenge to the hypothesis I announced at the outset in claiming that no Judaism recapitulates any other. Each began on its own, defining the questions it wished to answer and laying forth the responses it found self-evidently true, and only then going back to the canon of received documents in search of proof-texts. To the proposed rule, then, that every Judaism commences in the definition, or the discovery, of its canon, Orthodoxy surely forms an enormous exception. For its canon recognized the same books, accorded them the same status and authority. Yet that was hardly the case. Orthodoxy produced books to which the received system of the dual Torah could afford no counterpart—and vice versa. Orthodoxy addressed questions not pertinent to the received system or to the world that that system had constructed, and found answers that violated important givens of that system. The single most significant trait of Orthodoxy, we shall now see, is its power to see the Torah as Judaism, the category shift that changed everything else (or that ratified all other changes).

Judaism Enters the Category Religion

The category *religion* recognizes as distinct from "all of life" matters having to do with the church, the life of faith, the secular as against the sacred—distinctions lost on the received system of the dual Torah, which legislated for matters we should today regard as entirely secular or neutral—for example, the institutions of state (king, priest, army). I have already noted that, in the received system as it took shape in eastern and central Europe, Jews wore garments regarded as distinctively Jewish, and some important traits of these garments indeed derived from the Torah. They pursued sciences that only Jews studied—for instance, the Talmud and its commentaries. In these and other ways, the Torah encompassed all of the life of Israel, the holy people. The recognition that Jews are like others, that the Torah falls into a category into which other and comparable matters fall—that recognition was long in coming.

For Christians it had become commonplace in Germany and other Western countries to see religion as distinct from other components of the social and political system. While the Church in Russia identified with the tsarist state, or with the national aspirations of the Polish people, in the German states two churches, Catholic and Protestant, competed. The terrible wars of the Reformation in the sixteenth and seventeenth centuries, which ruined Germany, had led to the uneasy compromise that a prince might choose the religion of his principality; and, from that self-aware choice, people understood that "way of life and world view" in fact constituted a religion, and that any one religion might be compared with some other. By the nineteenth century, moreover, the separation of church and state ratified the important distinction between religion, where difference would be tolerated, and the secular, where citizens were pretty much the same.

That fact of political consciousness in the West reached the Judaic world only in the late eighteenth century for some intellectuals and in the nineteenth century for large numbers of others. It registered, then, as a fundamental shift in the understanding and interpretation of the Torah. The Jews who formed the Orthodox Judaic system had the creative power to shift the fundamental category in which they framed their system, and thus made Orthodoxy a Judaism on its own, not simply a restatement, essentially in established classifications, of the received system of the dual Torah.

If we ask how Orthodox Judaism, so profoundly rooted in the canonical writings and received convictions of the Judaism of the dual Torah, at the same time made provision for the prevailing issues of political and cultural change, we recognize the importance of this shift in category. Orthodox Judaism took the view that one can observe the rules of the Judaic system of the ages and at the same time keep the laws of the state. More important, Orthodox Judaism took full account of the duties of citizenship, so far as being a good citizen imposed the expectation of conformity in certain aspects of everyday life. So a category, *religion*, could contain the Torah, and a counter category, *secular*, could allow Jews a place in the accepted civic life of the country. The importance of the shift in category therefore lies in its power to accommodate the political change so important, also, to Reform Judaism. The Jews' differences from others would fit into categories in which difference was (in Jews' minds at any rate) acceptable, and would not violate those lines to which all citizens had to adhere.

For example, Jews no longer wished to wear distinctively Jewish clothing, or to speak a Jewish language, or to pursue only Jewish learning and study solely under Jewish aus-

126

pices. Yet the received system, giving expression to the rules of sanctification of the holy people, did entail wearing Jewish clothing, speaking a Jewish language, learning only, or mainly, Jewish sciences. Now clothing, language, and education fell into the category of the secular, while other equally important aspects of everyday life remained in the category of the sacred. Thus, Orthodox Judaism, as it came into existence in Germany and other Western countries, found it possible, by recognizing the category of the secular, to accept the language, clothing, and learning of those countries. And these matters served openly to denote a larger acceptance of gentile ways—not all, but enough to lessen the differences between the holy people and the nations. Political change of a profound order, which made Jews call into question some aspects of the received system—if not most or all of them, as in Reform Judaism—presented to Orthodox Jews the issues at hand: How separate? How integrated? And the answers required, as I have said, picking and choosing—different things, to be sure—just as much as, in principle, the Reform Jews picked and chose. Both Judaisms understood that some things were sacred, others not; and that understanding marked these Judaisms off from the system of the dual Torah.

Once the category shift had taken place, the difference was to be measured in degree, not in kind. For Orthodox Jews maintained those distinctive political beliefs in the future coming of the Messiah and in the reconstitution of the Jewish nation in its own land—beliefs that Reform Jews rejected. But, placing these convictions in the distant future, the Orthodox Jews nonetheless prepared for a protracted interim of life within the nation at hand, where like the Reform they differed in religion but not in nationality, for all were citizens. Thus, Orthodoxy, as much as Reform, signals remarkable changes in the Jews' political situation and—more important—in their aspirations. They did want to be different, but not so different as the received system would have made them.

Still, Orthodoxy in its nineteenth-century formulation claimed to carry forward, in continuous and unbroken relationship, the tradition. That claim assuredly demands a serious hearing, for the things that Orthodoxy taught, the way of life it required, the Israel to whom it spoke, the doctrines it deemed revealed by God to Moses at Sinai—all of these conformed more or less exactly to the system of the received Judaism of the dual Torah as people then knew it. So any consideration of the issue of a linear and incremental history of Judaism has to take at face value the character, and not merely the claim, of Orthodoxy. But we do not have to concede that claim without reflection. Each Judaism, after all, demands study in categories defined not by its own claims of continuity, but by its own distinctive and characteristic choices. For a system takes shape and then makes choices—in that order. But the issue here is whether Orthodoxy can be said to have made any choices at all. For is it not what it says it is: "just Judaism"? Indeed so, but the dual Torah of the received tradition hardly generated the base category *Judaism*. And any single Judaism, Orthodox or otherwise, is not Torah.

Here is where self-conscious choice enters discourse. For the Orthodoxy of the nineteenth century—that is, the Judaism that named itself "Orthodox"—exhibited certain traits of mind that marked its framers as distinctive, as separate from the received Judaism of the dual Torah as were the founders of Reform Judaism. To state the matter simply: the founders of Orthodoxy's act of choosing—that is, adopting for themselves the category *religion* and recognizing a distinction between religion and the secular, between the holy and other categories of existence—defines them as self-conscious: the received system was not for them self-evident.

The Torah was now transformed into an object, a thing out there, a matter of choice, deliberation, affirmation. In that sense, Orthodoxy both recognized a break in the line of the received tradition and proposed to repair that break: a self-conscious, a modern decision. The issues addressed by Orthodoxy, the questions its framers found ineluctable—these took second place. The primary consideration in my assessment of Orthodoxy's claim to carry forward, in a straight line, the incremental history of a single Judaism carries us to the fundamental categories within which Orthodoxy pursued its thought, but the Judaism of the dual Torah did not. How so? The Judaism of the dual Torah had no word for Judaism, and Orthodoxy did (and does).

Let me dwell on this matter of the category *Judaism*, a species of the genus *religion*. The fact is that those Jews for whom the received Judaism retained the standing of self-evident truth in no way recognized the distinctions implicit in the category *religion*. Those distinctions separated one dimension of existence from others—specifically, faith and religious action from all other matters, such as politics, economic life, incidental aspects of everyday life such as clothing, vocation and avocation, and the like. As I have stressed, the Judaism of the dual Torah, for its part, encompasses every dimension of human existence, both personal and public, both private and political. The Jews constitute a supernatural people; their politics form the public dimension of their holiness; and their personal lives match the most visible and blatant rules of public policy. The whole forms a single fabric, an indivisible and totally coherent entity, at once social and cultural, economic and political—and, above all, religious. The recognition, therefore, that one may distinguish the religious from the political, or concede as distinct any dimension of a person's life or of the life of the community of Judaism, forms powerful evidence that a fresh system has come into existence.

The Death of Judaism and the Birth of Judaisms

For nineteenth-century Reform and Orthodox theologians alike, the category *Judaism* defined what people said when they wished all together and all at once to describe what the Jews believe, or the Jewish religion, or similar matters covering religious ideas viewed as a system and as a whole. It constituted, therefore, a philosophical category, an -ism, instructing thinkers to seek the system and order and structure of ideas: the doctrine of this, the doctrine of that, in Juda*ism.* The nineteenth-century Judaic religious thinkers invoked the category *Judaism,* when they proposed to speak of the whole of Judaic religious existence. Available to the Judaism of the dual Torah are other categories, other words, to tell how to select and organize and order data: all together, all at once to speak of the whole.

To the Jews, therefore, who abided within the received Judaism of the dual Torah, Orthodoxy represented an innovation, a shift from the perceivedly self-evident truths of the Torah. For their word for Judaism was *Torah;* and when they spoke of the whole all at once, they used the word *Torah*—and for them also, the word *Judaism* encompassed different things than it did when used by nineteenth-century theologians. The received system not only used a different word but referred to different things. The two categories—*Judaism* and *Torah*—which were supposed to refer to the same data in the same social world, in fact denoted different data.

Judaism falls into a philosophical or ideological or theological classification: a *logos,* a "word"; while *Torah* falls into the classification of a symbol: that is, a symbol that in itself encompassed the whole of the system that the category at hand was meant to describe. The species *ism* falls into the classification of the genus *logos;* while the species *Torah,* while using words, transcends them and becomes a species of the genus *symbol.* How so? The *ism* category invokes not an encompassing symbol but a system of

130

thought. Judaism is an it, an object, a classification, an action. Torah, for its part, is an everything-in-one-thing, a symbol. I cannot imagine a more separate and unlike set of categories than *Judaism* and *Torah*, even though both encompass the same way of life and world view and address the same social group. So *Torah* as a category serves as a symbol, everywhere present in detail and holding all the details together.* *Judaism* as a category serves as a statement of the main points: the intellectual substrate of it all.

The conception of Judaism as an organized body of doctrine—as in the sentence "Judaism teaches" or "Judaism says"—derives from an age when people further had determined that Judaism belonged to the category of religion and—of still more definitive importance—that a religion was something that *teaches* or *says.* That is to say, Judaism is a religion; and a religion, to begin with, is (whatever else it is) a composition of beliefs. The age at hand was the nineteenth century; and the category of religion as a distinct entity emerged from Protestant theological thought. For in Protestant theological terms, one is saved by faith. But the very components of that sentence—"one" (individual, not the people or holy nation), "saved" (personally, not in history, and saved, not sanctified), "faith" (not *mitzvot*)—prove incomprehensible in the categories constructed by Torah.† Constructions of Judaic dogmas, the specification of a right doctrine—an orthodoxy—and the insistence that one can speak of religion apart from such adventitious matters as clothing and education (for the Orthodox of Germany who dressed like other Germans and studied in uni-

---

* That is why I called my prime textbook *The Way of Torah*, and its companion-reader, *The Life of Torah;*[6] but I see other ways to compose an introduction to Judaism and am now experimenting with one of them. My tentative title says it all: *From Testament to Torah.*

† My more sustained critique of the Protestant definition of religion and its effects upon the academic study of religion is in my forthcoming article "Theological Enemies of Religious Studies," *Religion* (1987).

versities, not only in yeshivas) or food (for the Reform), testify to the same fact: the end of self-evidence, the substitution of the distinction between religion and secularity, the creation of *Judaism* as the definitive category.

In fact, in the idiomatic language of Torah speech, one cannot make such a statement in that way about, or in the name of, Judaism—not an operative category at all. In accord with the modes of thought and speech of the received Judaism of the dual Torah, one has to speak of Israel, the community, to address not only individual life but all of historical time. The word *saved* by itself does not suffice. The category of sanctification, not only salvation, must find its place. Most important, one native to the speech of the Torah will use the word *mitzvot,* or religious duties, not speaking of salvation by faith alone. So the sentence serves for Protestant Christianity but not for the Torah. Of course, for its part, Judaism, Orthodox or Reform, will also teach things and lay down doctrines, even dogmas.

The counterpart, in the realm of self-evidence comprised by the received Judaism of the dual Torah, of the statement "Judaism teaches" can only be "The Torah requires"; and the predicate of such a sentence would be not ". . . that God is one," but ". . . that you say a blessing before eating bread." The category *Judaism* encompasses, classifies, and organizes doctrines: the faith, which, by the way, an individual adopts and professes. The category *Torah* teaches what "we," God's holy people, are and what "we" must do. The counterpart to the statement of Judaism "God is one," then, is ". . . who has sanctified us by his commandments and commanded us to. . . ." The one teaches—that is, speaks of intellectual matters and beliefs; the latter demands—social actions and deeds of us, matters of public consequence, including, by the way, affirming such doctrines as God's unity, the resurrection of the dead, the coming of the Messiah, the revelation of the Torah at Sinai, and

132

on and on: "we" can rival the Protestants in heroic deeds of faith. So it is true, the faith demands deeds, and deeds presuppose faith. But, categorically, the emphasis is what it is: Torah on God's revelation; the canon—to Israel and its social way of life, Judaism—on a system of belief. That is a significant difference between the two categories, which, as I said, serve a single purpose—namely, to state the thing as a whole.

Equally true, one would (speaking systemically) also "study Torah." But one studied not an intellectual system of theology or philosophy but rather a document of revealed Scripture and law. I do not mean to suggest that the theologians of Judaism, Orthodox or Reform, of the nineteenth century did not believe that God is one, or that the philosophers who taught that "Judaism teaches ethical monotheism" did not concur that, on that account, one has to say a blessing before eating bread. But the categories are different; and, in consequence, so too are the composites of knowledge. A book on Judaism explains the doctrines, theology or philosophy, of Judaism. A book of the holy Torah expounds God's will as revealed in "the one whole Torah of Moses, our rabbi," as sages teach and embody God's will. I cannot imagine two more different books, and the reason is that they represent totally different categories of intelligible discourse and of knowledge. Proof, of course, is that the latter books are literally unreadable. They form part of a genuinely oral exercise, to be cited sentence by sentence and expounded in the setting of other sentences, from other books, the whole made cogent by the speaker. That process of homogenization is how Torah works as a generative category. It obscures other lines of structure and order.

True, the two distinct categories come to bear upon the same body of data, the same holy books. But the consequent compositions—selections of facts, ordering of facts, analyses of facts, statements of conclusion and interpretation, and, above all, modes of public discourse, meaning who says what to whom—bear no relationship to one another, none whatsoever. Indeed, the compositions more likely than not do not even adduce the same facts or refer to them.

How is it that the category I see as imposed, extrinsic, and deductive—namely, *Judaism*—attained the status of self-evidence? Categories serve because they are self-evident to a large group of people. In Orthodoxy, therefore, the category *Judaism* serves because it enjoys self-evidence as part of a larger set of categories that are equally self-evident. The source of the categorical power of *Judaism* derives from the Protestant philosophical heritage that has defined scholarship, including category formation, since the time of Kant. *Juda* plus *ism* do not constitute self-evident, let alone definitive, categories. Judaism constitutes a category asymmetrical to the evidence adduced in its study; the category does not apply because the principle of formation is philosophical and does not emerge from an unmediated encounter with the Torah. Orthodoxy can have come into existence only in Germany—and, indeed, only in that part of Germany where the philosophical heritage of Kant and Hegel defined the categories of thought, also, for religion.

Creator of a New Judaism: Samson Raphael Hirsch

The importance of Samson Raphael Hirsch (1808–88), first great intellect of Orthodoxy, derives from his philosophy of joining Torah with secular education, producing a synthesis of Torah and modern culture. He represents the strikingly new Judaism, exhibiting both its strong tie to the received system but also its essentially innovative character. Sometimes called "neo-Orthodox,"[7] Hirsch's position, with its stress on the possibility of living in the secular world and sustaining a fully Orthodox life, rallied the Jews of the counterreformation. But he and his followers took over one principal position of Reform—the possibility of integrating Jews in modern society. What made Hirsch significant was that he took that position not only on utilitarian grounds, as Moshe Samet says, "but also through the acceptance of its [that society's] scale of values, aiming at creating a symbiosis between traditional Orthodoxy and modern German-European culture; both in theory and in practice this meant abandonment of Torah study for its own sake and adopting instead an increased concentration on practical halakhah [law]."[8] On that basis Orthodoxy is rightly identified as a Judaism distinct from the system of the dual Torah. Hirsch himself studied at the University of Bonn, specializing in classical languages, history, and philosophy.[9] So, as I noted, he did not think one had to spend all one's time studying Torah; and in going to a university, he implicitly affirmed that he could not define, within Torah study, all modes of learning. Gentile professors knew things worth knowing. But continuators of the Judaism of the dual Torah thought exactly the opposite: whatever is worth knowing is in the Torah.

In his rabbinical posts, Hirsch published works aimed at appealing to the younger generation. His ideal for the young was the formation of a personality that would be both enlightened and observant: that is, educated in Western knowledge and observant of the Judaic way of life. This ideal took shape through an educational program that included the Hebrew language and holy literature and also German, mathematics, sciences, and the like. In this way, he proposed to respond to the Reformers' view that Judaism in its received form constituted a barrier between Jews and German society, impeding the sort of integration they thought wholesome and good. Hirsch concurred in the ideal and differed on detail. Distinctive Jewish clothing, in Hirsch's view, was not important. He himself wore a Protestant ministerial gown at public worship, which did not win the approbation of the traditionalists; and when he preached, he referred not only to the law of the Torah but to other biblical matters, equally an innovation. He argued that Judaism and secular education could form a union, one that would require recognition of externals, which could be set aside, and emphasis on principles, which would not change. Thus, Hirsch espoused what, according to Jews wholly within the mentality of self-evidence, constituted selective piety and therefore, while details differed, fell within the classification of reform.

In his selectivity, Hirsch included changes in the conduct of the liturgy, involving a choir, congregational singing, sermons in the vernacular—a generation earlier, sure marks of Reform. He required prayers to be said only in Hebrew and Jewish subjects to be taught in that language. He opposed all changes in the Prayer Book. At the same time he sustained organizational relationships with the Reformers and tried to avoid schism. Halfway through his career, however, toward the middle of the century, Hirsch could not tolerate the Reformers' abrogation of the dietary laws and those affecting marital relationships, and made his break, accusing the Reformers of disrupting Israel's unity. In the following decades, he encouraged Orthodox Jews to leave the congregations dominated by Reform, even though, in a particular locale, the latter was the only synagogue. Separationist synagogues formed in the larger community.

In framing issues of doctrine, Hirsch constructed an affirmative system, not a negative one. His principal argument stressed that the teachings of the Torah constitute facts beyond all doubt, as much as the facts of nature do not allow for doubt. This view of the essential facticity—the absolute givenness—of the Torah led to the further conviction that human beings may not deny the Torah's teachings even when they do not grasp its meaning. Wisdom is contained within the Torah; God's will is to be found there. Just as the physical laws of nature are not conditioned by human search, so the rules of God's wisdom are unaffected by human search. The Torah constitutes an objective reality; and, in Simha Katz's words, its laws form "an objective disposition of an established order that is not dependent on the will of the individual or society, and hence not even on historical processes."[10] Humanity nonetheless may through time gain religious truth.

What makes Israel different is that the people gain access to the truth not through experience but through direct revelation. Gentile truth is truth, but derives from observation and experience. What Israel knows through the Torah comes through a different medium: the people stand outside history and do not have to learn religious truth through the passage of history and changes over time. Israel, then, forms a supernatural entity, a view certainly in accord with the Judaism of the dual Torah. But when it came to explaining the way of life, Hirsch went his own way, pursuing a theory of the practice of the religious life through concrete deeds—the commandments—in a highly speculative and philosophical way. He maintained that each of the deeds of the way of life represents something beyond itself, serves as a symbol, not as an end in itself. So when a Jew carries out a holy deed, the deed serves to make concrete a revealed truth. This mode of thought transforms the way of life into an exercise in applied theology and practical, practiced belief.

Specifically, in Katz's words, "the performance of a commandment is not determined by simple devotion but by attachment to the religious thought represented in symbolic form by the commandment. Symbolic meanings must be attributed . . . particularly to commandments which are described by the Torah itself as signs . . . and commandments which are established as pointing to historical events . . . and commandments whose entire content testifies to their symbolic character." The diverse commandments all together stand for three principles: justice, love, and "the education of ourselves and others."[11]

Hirsch's theory of who is Israel stood at the opposite pole from that of Geiger and the Reformers. To them, as we have seen, Israel fell into the classification of a religious community, that alone. To Hirsch, Israel constituted a people, not a religious congregation, and he spoke of "national Jewish consciousness": "The Jewish people, though it carries the Torah with it in all the lands of its dispersion, will never find its table and lamp except in the Holy Land." Israel performs a mission among the nations, to teach "that God is the source of blessing." Israel then falls between, forming its own category, because it has a state system, in the land, but also a life outside.[12] In outlining this position, Hirsch was reaffirming the theory of the supernatural Israel laid forth in the dual Torah. For him, the power of the national ideal lay in its polemical force against the assimilationists and Reformers, whom he treated as indistinguishable:

> The contempt with which the assimilationists treat David's [fallen] tabernacle and the prayer for the sacrificial service clearly reveals the extent of their rebellion against Torah and their complete disavowal of the entire realm of Judaism. They gather the ignorant about them to whom the Book of Books, the Divine national document of their Jewish past and future, is closed with seven seals. With a conceit engendered by stupidity and a perfidy born from hatred they point to God's Temple and the Divine Service in Zion as the unholy center of the "bloody cult of sacrifices." Consequently, they make certain to eliminate any reference to the restoration of the Temple service from

138

our prayers. . . . The "cultured, refined" sons and daughters of our time must turn away with utter disgust from their "prehistoric, crude" ancestors who worship their god with bloody sacrifices.

Hirsch reviewed the long line of exalted leaders who affirmed sacrifice and were not crude—for example, Moses, Isaiah, Jeremiah, and on—and concluded:

> The Jewish sacrifice expresses the highest ideal of man's and the nation's moral challenge. Blood and kidney, head and limbs symbolize our service of God with every drop of blood, every emotion, every particle of our being. By performing the act of sacrifice at the place chosen by God as the site of His Law, we proclaim our determination to fulfill our lofty moral and ethical tasks to enable God to bless the site of the national vow with the presence of this glory and with the fullness of this love and grace.[13]

Hirsch's spiritualization of the sacrifices—with an ample tradition of precedent, to be sure—derived from the challenge of Reform. Demanding an acceptance at face value of the Torah as the revelation of God's wisdom, Hirsch nonetheless made the effort to appeal to more than the givenness of the Torah and its commandments.

On the contrary, he entered into argument in the same terms—spiritualization, lofty moral and ethical tasks—as did the Reformers, thus marking his thought as new and responsive to a fresh set of issues. As to the Reformers, he met them on their ground, as he had to; and his principal points of insistence, to begin with, derived from the issues defined by others. Hence, he belongs in the larger discourse among the Judaisms of the nineteenth century, each one a product of the end of self-evidence and the beginning of a self-conscious explanation for what had formerly, and elsewhere in that age, the authority of the absolutely given.

The Death of Judaism and the Birth of Judaisms

The Issue of Revelation and the Dual Torah

The Judaism of the dual Torah by definition maintained that not only the Hebrew Scriptures (Old Testament) but also the entire canon of rabbinic writings constituted that one whole Torah that Moses received at Sinai. The three Judaisms of the nineteenth century met that issue head on. Each of the possibilities—only Scripture; everything; some things but not others—found proponents. Any consequent theory of revelation had to explain the origin and authority of each component of the received canon. And, further, that theory of revelation had to explain what, precisely, revelation meant. The position of Orthodoxy on this matter takes on significance only in the larger context of the debate with Reform. Reform through Geiger took the view that revelation was progressive: the Bible derived from "the religious genius of the Jewish people." Orthodoxy through Hirsch as the example saw the Torah as wholly and completely God's word. A middle position, represented by Conservative Judaism, espoused both views: God revealed the written Torah, which was supplemented by "the ongoing revelation manifesting itself throughout history in the spirit of the Jewish people."[14]

Orthodoxy could not concur. The issue involved the historical identification of those responsible for the rabbinic writings. The Conservatives, in the person of Zechariah Frankel (see chapter 4), a contemporary of Hirsch, maintained that the whole of the rabbinic corpus derived from scribes and their successors, who had adapted the system of Scripture by inventing the notion of the oral Torah—a break the Orthodox could not concede. The Positive Historical School, in Katzburg and Wurzburger's description, held that "the religious consciousness of the Jewish people

140

provided the supreme religious authority, [while] the Orthodox position rested upon the belief in the supernatural
origin of the Torah which was addressed to a 'Chosen
People.' "[15] So the theory of who is Israel joined the issue
of revelation: how, what, when. The Orthodox position, as
outlined by Hirsch, saw Israel as a supernatural people that
has in hand a supernatural revelation. The entirety of the
dual Torah and the writings flowing from it constitute that
revelation. Quite how this notion of a long sequence of revealed documents differs from the conception of a progressive revelation is not entirely clear, but in context it made
a considerable difference. For in his affirmation of the entirety of the Torah, written and oral, as the revealed will of
God, Hirsch marked the boundaries of Orthodoxy and
made them coincide with the precise ones of the received
dual Torah. It is doubtful, however, whether those Jews to
whom the supernatural character of Israel and the entirety
of Torah formed self-evident truths understood Hirsch's
careful explanations of matters outside the received modes
of apologetics. For the one thing the traditionalist
grasped—the absolute givenness of the whole—Hirsch
could not concede. How do we know? Because he explained
and explained and explained.

The Birth of a Judaism

Hirsch spent much energy defending the practice of the
religious duties called "commandments"—such as circum-
cision, the wearing of fringes on garments, the use, in
morning worship, of *tefillin* (commonly translated "phy-
lacteries"), and the sacrificial cult and Temple. These he
treated not as utter data—the givens of the holy life—but

rather as transformed into symbols of a meaning beyond. And that exercise, in his context, testifies to the utter self-consciousness of the Judaism at hand; hence, to the formation of a new Judaism out of received materials, no less than Reform Judaism constituted a new Judaism out of those same received materials. For the sole necessity for making up such symbolic explanations derived from decision: defend these, at all costs. The contemporaries of Hirsch living in the villages of the East did not feel the need to defend these—to them, self-evidently holy—beliefs and practices.

When, therefore, Hirsch invoked the parallel, to which I have already alluded, between the study of nature and the study of the Torah, he expressed the freshness, the inventiveness, of his own system and thereby testified to the self-consciousness at hand. A sizable abstract provides a good view of Hirsch's excellent mode of thought and argument:

One word here concerning the proper method of Torah investigation. Two revelations are open before us, that is, nature and the Torah. In nature all phenomena stand before us as indisputable facts, and we can only endeavor a posteriori to ascertain the law of each and the connection of all. Abstract demonstration of the truth, or rather, the probability of theoretical explanations of the acts of nature, is an unnatural proceeding. The right method is to verify our assumptions by the known facts, and the highest attainable degree of certainty is to be able to say: "The facts agree with our assumption"—that is, all the phenomena observed can be explained according to our theory. A single contradictory phenomenon will make our theory untenable. We must, therefore, acquire all the knowledge possible concerning the object of our investigation and know it, if possible, in its totality. If, however, all efforts should fail in disclosing the inner law and connection of phenomena revealed to us as facts in nature, the facts remain, nevertheless, undeniable and cannot be reasoned away.

The same principles must be applied to the investigation of the Torah. In the Torah, even as in nature, God is the ultimate cause. In the Torah, even as in nature, no fact may be denied, even though the reason and the connection may not be understood. What is true in nature is true also in the Torah: the traces of divine wisdom must ever be sought. Its ordinances must be accepted in their entirety as undeniable phenomena and must be studied in accordance with their connection to each other, and the subject to which they relate. Our conjectures must be tested by their precepts, and our highest certainty here also can only be that everything stands in harmony with our theory.

In nature the phenomena are recognized as facts, though their cause and relationship to each other may not be understood and are independent of our investigation. So too the ordinances of the Torah must be law for us, even if we do not comprehend the reason and the purpose of a single one. Our fulfillment of the commandments must not depend on our investigations.[16]

Here we have the counterpart, in his own argument, to Hirsch's theory of Torah and worldly learning. Just as he maintained the union of the two, so in the deepest structure of his thought he worked out that same union. Natural science dictated rules of inquiry—specifically, the requirement that one explain phenomena through a theory that one can test. The phenomenon is the given. Then, for the Torah, its requirements constitute the givens, which demand explanation but must be accepted as facts even when explanation fails. Clearly, Hirsch addressed an audience that had come to doubt the facticity of the facts of the Torah in a way in which none doubted the facticity of the facts of nature.

Once compared with nature, the Torah no longer defines the world view and the way of life at hand but takes its place as part of a larger world view and way of life, in which the Israelite–human being (in Hirsch's happy concept) has to accommodate both the received of the Torah and the given of nature. The insistence on the process of accommodation—"studied in accordance with their connection . . . and the subject to which they relate"—testifies to a world view essentially distinct from that of the received

143

system of the dual Torah. In this new world view, the Torah demands explanation; its rules are reduced to the lesser dimensions of an apologia of symbolism, so that they form not givens in an enduring and eternal way of life but objects of analysis, of defense, above all, of reasoned decision. True, Hirsch insisted, "Our fulfillment of the commandments must not depend on our investigations."[17] But the investigation must go forward; and that allegation of Hirsch's, in and of itself, tells us we deal with a new Judaism.

Let me now summarize the argument, because what I have maintained runs contrary to the prevailing view of Orthodoxy. Orthodoxy never claimed to mark the natural next step in the history of Judaism, but saw itself as nothing other than Judaism. In its near-total symmetry with the received system, Orthodoxy surely made a powerful case for that claim. But the fact that the case had to be made, the context and conditions of contention: these indicate that another Judaism was coming into being. The asymmetrical points, moreover, demand attention, though, on their own, they should not decisively refute the position of Orthodoxy. What does refute it is the very existence of an Orthodoxy. The single most interesting instance of a Judaism of self-consciousness, Orthodoxy defends propositions that, in the received system, scarcely reached a level of articulate discourse: for instance, the absolute necessity to conform to the holy way of life of the Torah. The necessity for making such an argument testifies to the fact that people, within Orthodoxy, thought they confronted the need to choose and did choose. True, the choices, from the viewpoint of Orthodoxy, fell in the right direction. But Orthodoxy formed an act of restoration and renewal; therefore, an act of innovation. The modes of argument of Hirsch, representative as they are of the mentality of the Orthodoxy he defined, call into question the linear descent of Orthodoxy from what people called "tradition." An incremental progress, perhaps; but a lineal and unbroken journey, no. But even the incremental theory of the history of Judaism, which, in the case of Orthodoxy, identifies Hirsch's Orthodoxy with the system of the dual Torah, fails to take note of facts; and, as Hirsch himself argued, that failure sufficed. The facts were that people, Hirsch included, made clearcut choices, identifying some things as essential, others not (clothing, for one important instance). If the piety of Reform proved selective, the selections that Hirsch made place him into the classification also of one who sorted out change and made changes. Just as the Reformers of the nineteenth century laid emphasis on the points of continuity they located between themselves and the past, so, of course, did the Orthodox (and, from their perspective, with better reason). Just as the Orthodox of the nineteenth century specify what mattered more than something else, so, of course, did the Reform (and, from their perspective, with greater relevance to the situation at hand).

The political changes that in the aggregate created an abyss between the Judaism of the dual Torah and the new, theological Judaisms of the nineteenth century affected both the Reform and the Orthodox of the age. They stood in a single line—one that broke off en route to (so to speak) Sinai—that is, to the Judaism of the dual Torah. So in Orthodoxy we find a system that is clearly incremental with the received system, but still more striking symptoms of a system formed afresh and anew.

Continuity or new creation? Both—but, therefore, by definition, new creation. Piety selected is by definition piety invented, and Hirsch emerges as one of the intellectually powerful creators of a Judaism. "Torah and secular learning" defined a new world view, dictated a new way of life, and addressed a different Israel. To those who received the Judaism of the dual Torah as self-evident, what the Torah did not accommodate was secular learning; nor did the Torah as they received it approve changes in the familiar way of life or know an Israel other than the one at hand. So the perfect faith of Orthodoxy sustained a wonderfully selective piety. The human greatness of Hirsch, and of the many Jews who found self-evident the possibility of living the dual life of Jew and German or Jew and American, lay in the power of the imagination to locate in a new circumstance a rationale for inventing tradition.

The human achievement of Orthodoxy demands more than routine notice. Living in a world that only grudgingly accommodated difference and did not like Jews' difference in particular, the Orthodox followed the rhythm of the week to the climax of the Sabbath, of the seasons to the climactic moments of the festivals. They adhered to their own pattern of daily life, with prayers morning, noon, and night. They married only within the holy people. They ate only food that had been prepared in accord with the rules of sanctification. They honored philosophy and culture, true, but these they measured by their own revealed truth as well. It was not easy for them to keep the faith when many within Jewry, and many more outside, wanted Jews to be pretty much the same as everyone else. The human costs cannot have proved trivial. To affirm when the world denies, to keep the faith against all evidence—that represents a faith that in other settings people honored. It was not easy for either the Orthodox of Germany or the immigrant Jews of America, whom an ocean voyage carried from the world of self-evident faith to one of insistent denial of that faith.

My grandmother was one of those Jews for whom the way of Torah defined the path of life. Raised as a Reform Jew, I know through her the pride, the dignity, the courage of the Judaisms of both the dual Torah and Orthodoxy. Challenged by the rabbi of our temple, advocate of Reform in its most vigorous formulation, that keeping the dietary laws involved violating the American Constitution, she did not answer; she did not think the argument important. At my bar mitvzah, held on Simhat Torah in 1945, when the Torah was carried about the sanctuary, the congregation remained seated, as was their custom, but she stood up all by herself—silently, without comment—as was hers. So we cannot miss the costs, but we recognize also the consequences, for humanity, of those who continued the received system and those who, come what may, sustained it and found in it sustenance for their lives. Each Judaism, Reform and Orthodox, demanded its price, but both richly rewarded those who paid that price. We the living inherit them all.

CHAPTER 4

CONSERVATIVE JUDAISM: ORTHOPRAXY AND ANACHRONISM

The order of the formation of the several Judaisms of the nineteenth century is first Reform, then Orthodoxy, finally Conservatism—the two extremes, then the middle. Reform defined the tasks of the next two Judaisms to come into being. Orthodoxy framed the clearer of the two positions in reaction to Reform; but, in intellectual terms, the Historical School in Germany met the issues of Reform in a more direct way. The Historical School comprised a group of nineteenth-century German scholars, who provided the principal ideas that were realized by Conservative Judaism, a twentieth-century Judaism in America. Each in its own setting took the middle position. We treat them as a single Judaism, because they share a single viewpoint.

The Historical School in Europe and Conservative Judaism in America stressed two matters: first, scholarship, with historical research assigned the task of discovering those facts of which the faith would be composed; and, second, observance of the rules of the received Judaism. A professedly free approach to what was called "critical scholarship" therefore would yield an accurate account of the essentials of the faith. But the scholars and lay people alike would keep nearly the whole of the tradition, just as the Orthodox did. The ambivalence of Conservative Judaism, speaking in part for intellectuals deeply loyal to the received way of life, but profoundly dubious of the inherited world view, came to full expression in the odd slogan "Eat kosher and think *traif*," meaning that people should keep the rules of the holy way of life but ignore the convictions that made sense of them. *Orthopraxy* is the word that denotes correct action and unfettered belief, as against orthodoxy, or right doctrine. Conservative Judaism in America could thus be classified as an orthoprax Judaism defined through works or practices, not through doctrine.

The middle position, then, derived equally from the two extremes. The way of life was congruent in most aspects with that of the Orthodox; the world view, with that of the Reform. Conservative Judaism saw the Jews as a people, not merely a religious community, and celebrated the ethnic as much as the more narrowly religious side of the Jews' common life. Orthodoxy took a separatist and segregationist position, leaving the organized Jewish community in Germany as that community fell into the hands of Reform Jews. Reform Judaism, for its part, rejected the position that the Jews constitute a people, not merely a religious community. Conservative Judaism emphasized the importance of the unity of the community as a whole and took a stand in favor of Zionism as soon as that movement got under way at the end of the nineteenth century.* What separated Conservative Judaism from Reform was the matter of observance. Fundamental loyalty to the received way of life distinguished the Historical School in Germany and Conservative Judaism in America from Reform Judaism in both countries. When considering the continued validity of a traditional religious practice, the Reform asked *Why?* and the Conservatives, *Why not?* The Orthodox, of course, asked no questions. Conservative Judaism for a long time enjoyed the loyalty of fully half of the Jews in the United States and today retains the center and the influential position of Judaism in this country.

The viewpoint of the center today predominates even in the more traditional circles of Reform and the more modernist sectors of Orthodoxy—even though the institutions of organized Conservative Judaism, the Jewish Theological Seminary of America, the Rabbinical Assembly, and the United Synagogue have faced various difficulties in the past decade and a half. The reason we distinguish institutions from systems is that a Judaism is not identical with the organizations and institutions that at one time or another serve that Judaism. Conservative Judaism as the Judaism of

---

* Since the Second World War, Reform Judaism has affirmed the ethnic aspect of the Jews' common life and become highly pro-Israel; and Orthodoxy, in its modern or Western mode, has entered into collaboration with Reform and Conservative Judaisms. The description at hand pertains to the situation characteristic of the first century of the three Judaisms, down to the Second World War, in Germany and America alike.

the center has never enjoyed a more paramount position than it does today throughout the world, even though the way of life and world view here identified as Conservative Judaism do not enjoy recognition as such elsewhere. In the State of Israel are many more who call themselves "traditional" than "religious," meaning Orthodox. That title, "traditional," in effect marks the Israeli who uses it as the equivalent of Conservative in America. In the Judaic life of many European Jewish communities, as well as those in Australia and South Africa and Canada, the basic situation of Conservative Judaism—observance of many basic rules by rabbis and of some by lay people, a moderate and rational reading of the received holy books, emphasis upon the ethnic as much as upon the narrowly religious side to things— characterizes the practiced Judaism. The rabbis are mainly Orthodox; the congregations mostly non-observant—just as in Conservative Judaism in America. So while calling themselves Orthodox and their Judaism, Orthodoxy, the religious sector of the Diaspora over all exhibits the distinctive indicators of Conservative Judaism, in its paradigmatic power the single most important Judaism of modern times.

The strength of the "Historical School,"[1] and therefore of Conservative Judaism, lay in that compromise defining the centrist position. The Historical School in Germany and Conservative Judaism in America affirmed a far broader part of the received way of life than Reform did, while rejecting a much larger part than did Orthodoxy of the world view of the system of the dual Torah. The Judaism at hand concurred with the Reformers that change was permissible, and claimed that historical scholarship would show what change was acceptable and what was not. But the proponents of the Historical School differed in matters of detail. The emphasis on historical research as a means of settling theological debates explains the name of the group. Arguing that its positions sprang from historical fact rather

151

than theological conviction, Conservative Judaism maintained that "positive historical scholarship," joined to far stricter observance of the law than the Reformers required, would prove capable of purifying and clarifying the faith.

The history of Conservative Judaism in the nineteenth and twentieth centuries began in 1886, when rabbis of the centrist persuasion organized the Jewish Theological Seminary of America; and from that rabbinical school developed the Conservative Movement. For its part, as we have seen, the Historical School in Germany did not constitute a Judaism but a handful of scholars writing books, and a book is not a Judaism. In the United States and Canada, by contrast, the Conservative Movement in Judaism (as it sometimes called itself) or Conservative Judaism reached full realization in a way of life characteristic of large numbers of Jews; in a world view that, for those Jews, explained who they were and what they must do; and in a clearly articulated account of who is Israel—a Judaism. From the end of the First World War, Conservative Judaism became the dominant movement among American Jews. In *Conservative Judaism*, Marshall Sklare argued that that Judaism served to express the viewpoint of the children of the immigrants to America from eastern Europe who came at the end of the nineteenth century.[2] Those children laid emphasis on the folk aspect—the way of life—while rejecting the world view—the supernaturalism—of the received system of the dual Torah. That forms the counterpart in the life of ordinary people of the slogan, "Eat kosher and think *traif.*" Sklare further identified Conservative Judaism with the area of second settlement, that is to say, the neighborhoods to which the Jewish immigrants or their children moved once they had settled down in this country. The enormous success of Conservative Judaism in the third generation beyond the initial migration—that is, among the grandchildren of the immigrants, from the Second World War to the

1970s—and the power of Conservative Judaism to establish itself in distant suburbs calls into question the thesis at hand. But in its own terms, Sklare's reading of the second generation assuredly illuminates matters.

The still greater attraction of Conservative Judaism for the third and fourth generations lay in two factors: first, its capacity to attract to a life of observance Jews who had grown up outside the religious world of Judaism; and, second, its power to mediate between the received tradition and the intellectual and social facts of the contemporary world. The center's fundamental definition of the urgent issues and how they were to be worked out, in both nineteenth-century Germany and twentieth-century America, therefore proved remarkably uniform and successful, from the beginning to the present.

The World View of Historical Scholarship: Zechariah Frankel and Heinrich Graetz

If history, the chosen discipline for Judaic theological argument in the nineteenth century, gave its name to the Judaism at hand, the particular area of history that defined discourse was by no means accidental. People made a deliberate choice in the matter. They did not study Scripture in the critical way, but they did study the documents of the oral Torah in accordance with the canons of contemporary academic scholarship. Why the difference? While no one argued about whether Moses gave the Ten Commandments, people did have to work out their relationship to the Judaism of the dual Torah—and, by definition, to the documents of the oral Torah. At issue was its origin and standing. The Orthodox answers, as we recall, left no ambiguity: The entirety of the Torah comes from God, not from mortal humanity; the entire Torah retains authority, such as it had from the very beginning; and, of course, the Talmud and the other rabbinic writings form part of the revelation of Sinai. The Reform answers took an opposite position: The oral Torah is an accident of history; it comes from human authors; it is not part of the Torah of Sinai. Now in addressing these issues, scholars thought that they could produce "positive" historical knowledge, which would secure reliable facts in answer to questions of faith.

The historians Zechariah Frankel (1801–75) and Heinrich Graetz (1817–91) founded the study of rabbinic literature, of the Talmud, as a historical source in Germany, in the 1850s, when Reform was well defined and Orthodoxy was coming to an articulate view of itself. Thus, the modern debate about the Talmud as history took shape in the single decade from 1851 to 1859. In less than ten years, four books were published that defined the way the work would be done for the next century: Leopold Zunz's posthumous publication of Nahman Krochmal's *Moreh nebukhe hazzeman* ("Guide to the Perplexed of Our Times" [1851], a title meant to call to mind Maimonides's *Guide to the Perplexed*); Heinrich Graetz's fourth volume of his *History of the Jews from the Earliest Times to the Present* (1853), which is devoted to the talmudic period; Abraham Geiger's *Urschrift und Uebersetzungen der Bibel* (1857); and Zechariah Frankel's *Darkhé hammishnah* ("Ways of the Mishnah" [1859]). These four volumes—Zunz and Geiger marking the Reform contribution; Graetz and Frankel, the Historical School's contribution (and Krochmal posthumously)—placed the Talmud into the very center of the debates on the reform of Judaism and addressed the critical issues of the debate: the divine mandate of rabbinic Judaism.[3] For three generations, there would be no historical

154

work on the Talmud deriving from Orthodoxy; and what came later bore no constructive program at all.

In the struggle over reform, both Reform and Conservative theologians proposed that, by exposing the historical origins of the Talmud and of the rabbinic form of Judaism, they might "undermine the divine mandate of rabbinic Judaism."[4] As Ismar Schorsch points out, Geiger's work is the highwater mark of the attack on rabbinic Judaism through historical study. He treated it in a wholly secular way. Krochmal, Graetz, and Frankel presented a sympathetic and favorable assessment of rabbinic Judaism and, then, took their leave of Reform Judaism to lay the foundations for the Historical School of Conservative Judaism. In so doing, however, they adopted the fundamental supposition of the Reformers: the Talmud can and should be studied historically. They conceded that there is a history for the period in which the Talmud came forth. The Talmud itself was a work of men in history.

Both Graetz's and Frankel's method was essentially biographical. The two provided spiritual heroes, a kind of academic hagiography, imparting color and life to the names of the talmudic canon. One-third of Frankel's book is devoted to biographies of personalities mentioned in the Talmud. He collected the laws given in the name of a particular man and stated that he appears in such and such a tractate, and the like. Frankel's "card file," though neatly divided, yields no more than what is filed in it. Joel Gereboff comments on Frankel as follows:

> For Frankel Rabbi was the organizer and the law-giver. He compiled the Mishnah in its final form, employing a systematic approach. The Mishnah was a work of art; everything was "necessary" and in its place. All these claims are merely asserted. Frankel gives citations from Mishnaic and Amoraic sources, never demonstrating how the citations prove his contentions. Frankel applied his theory of positive-historical Judaism, which depicted Jewish life as a process combining the lasting values

155

from the past with human intelligence in order to face the present and the future, to the formation of the Mishnah. The Mishnah was the product of human intelligence and divine inspiration. Using their intelligence, later generations took what they had received from the past and added to it. Nothing was ever removed. Frankel's work has little lasting value. He was, however, the first to analyze the Mishnah critically and historically; and this was his importance.[5]

What is important is not what Frankel proves but, as I said, what he implicitly concedes, which is that the Mishnah and the rest of the rabbinic literature are the work of men. Graetz likewise stresses the matter of great men. Schorsch characterizes his work:

> Graetz tried valiantly to portray the disembodied rabbis of the Mishnah and Talmud as vibrant men, each with his own style and philosophy and personal frailties, who collectively resisted the disintegrating forces of their age. . . . In the wake of national disaster, creative leadership forged new religious institutions to preserve and invigorate the bonds of unity. . . . He defended talmudic literature as a great national achievement of untold importance to the subsequent survival of the Jews.[6]

Now historians of the day in general wrote biographies. History was collective biography. Their conception of what makes things happen was tied to the theory of the great man in history, the great man as the maker of history. The associated theory was of history as the story of politics, of what great men have done. Whether the Jewish historians of the talmudic period were good, average, or poor historians in general terms I cannot say. The important point is that the beginnings of the approach to the Talmud as history centered on biography. But while most contemporary historians neither laid the foundations for religious movements nor engaged in vigorous debate on theological questions,

156

Graetz and Frankel strongly opposed Reform and criticized not only the results of Reform scholarship but the policies of Reform Judaism. The program of these two historians fitted more comfortably into a theological than a critical-historical classification, however much they invoked critical-historical and positive-historical knowledge to support their results. Thus, the Historical School, measured by the standards of its day, proved far less critical, far less historical, and far more credulous and believing than its adherents admitted—and, indeed, was methodologically obsolete.

For a broad range of critical questions concerning the reliability of sources escaped the attention of the Historical School. Specifically, in both classical and biblical studies, long before the middle of the nineteenth century, a thoroughgoing skepticism had arisen, formed in the Enlightenment of the previous century and not to be eradicated later. This critical spirit did not accept the historical allegations of ancient texts as necessarily true. So for biblical studies in particular, the history of ancient Israel no longer followed the paths of biblical narrative, from Abraham on. In the writing of the life of Jesus, for example—the contradictions among the several gospels, the duplication of materials, the changes from one gospel to the next between one saying and story and another version of the same saying and story, the difficulty in establishing a biographical framework for the life of Jesus—all of these and similar, devastating problems had arisen. The result was a close analysis of the character of the sources: for example, the recognition, before the nineteenth century, that the Pentateuch consists of at least three main strands—JE, D, and P. It was well known that behind the synoptic Gospels was a source (called "Q," for the German *Quelle*, "source") containing materials assigned to Jesus, upon which the three evangelists drew but which they reshaped for their respective purposes. The notion that ancient storytellers cannot be relied on as sources was thus well established. For the founders of talmudic history—Graetz, Frankel, and Krochmal—however, either did not know or did not find useful the discoveries of biblical and other ancient historical studies—and did not use them. The issues that concerned these scholars derived from a religious and not an academic or narrow scholarly debate, as is apparent when we examine the scholarly methods of the Historical School.

No German biographer of Jesus, for example, could, by the 1850s, have represented his life and thought by a mere paraphrase and harmony of the Gospels, in the way in which Graetz and Frankel and their successors down to the mid-twentieth century would paraphrase and string together talmudic tales about rabbis and call the result history and biography. Few were the scholars who, by the end of the nineteenth century, completely ignored the redactional and literary traits of documents, let alone their historical and social provenance. Yet the historians of positive-historical Judaism believed that whatever was given to a rabbi, in any document, of any place or time, provided evidence of what that rabbi really said and did in the time in which he lived. Thus, while the theologians of the Historical School claimed to present "mere" facts, as well substantiated as those of contemporary historians, the bulk of such facts derived from a reading of sources in as believing, not to say credulous, a spirit as the Orthodox brought to Scripture.

The middle position emerged in a simple way. On the one side, the historian-theologians of the Historical School chose to face the Orthodox with the claim that the Talmud was historical. On the other, they chose to turn their backs on the critical scholarship of their own day with that very same claim that the Talmud *was* historical. That formed a powerful weapon against Reform, and it was the weapon of

158

the Reformers' own choice. Thus, as with the Reformers and the Orthodox, so for the Conservatives the place and authority of the oral Torah, embodied in the Talmud, formed the arena for debate. Facing the one side, the Historical School treated the Talmud as a document of history, therefore as a precedent for attending to context and circumstance, so as to admit to the possibility of change. But facing the other side, the Historical School treated the Talmud as a uniformly reliable and unerring source of historical information. The Talmud was the target of opportunity. The traditionalists trivialized the weapon, maintaining that history was essentially beside the point of the Talmud. But the real debate was not with Orthodoxy but with Reform.

Graetz set the style for such history as was attempted; Frankel, for biography of talmudic sages. Finally, let me quote Schorsch's judgment of Graetz, which constitutes an epitaph to the whole enterprise of talmudic history:

> Above all, Graetz remained committed to the rejuvenation of his people. His faith in God's guiding presence throughout Jewish history . . . assured him of the future. His own work, he hoped, would contribute to the revival of Jewish consciousness. He succeeded beyond measure. As a young man, Graetz had once failed to acquire a rabbinic pulpit because he was unable to complete the delivery of his sermon. There is more than a touch of irony in the remarkable fact that the reception accorded to Graetz's history by Jews around the world made him the greatest Jewish preacher of the nineteenth century.[7]

That none of this indicates a historical task scarcely requires proof. The reliance on precedent, of course, did not surprise proponents of the dual Torah, but they were surprised and deeply offended by the entire program, with its treating as this-worldly and matters of history what the received system of Judaism understood to form an entirely supernatural realm.

The Way of Life of Orthopraxy: Alexander Marx and Louis Ginzberg

We thus come to the question of who joined the Judaism of the Historical School in Europe and Conservative Judaism in America. It was in the way of life formed here that the world view was realized in a Judaism. Of particular interest are the system builders, the intellectuals: historians, talmudists, and other scholars. They are the ones, after all, who defined the ideas in concrete terms and expressed the values and the attitudes that made whole and complete all of the Judaisms I am considering, each with its world view, way of life, theory of an Israel—and each with its powerful appeal to an Israel as well. Since nearly all of the first generations of Conservative Jews in America and of the Historical School in Europe had made their way out of the received system of the dual Torah, the motivation for the deeply conservative approach to that system, the orthopraxy, requires explanation. For that motivation assuredly did not emerge from matters of doctrine. Indeed, once scholar-theologians maintained that the oral part of the Torah derived from mortals, not from God, disagreements with Reformers on matters of change can have made little difference. For by admitting to the human origin and authority of the documents of the oral Torah, the historian-theologians had accomplished the break with Orthodoxy, as well as with the received system. Then differences with Reform were of degree, not of kind. But these differences sustained a Judaism for a very long time, a Judaism that would compose its world view, its way of life, its audience of Israel, in terms that marked off that system from the other two successor Judaisms I have already considered.

Two Europeans-turned-American typify the first mature

160

generation of Conservative Judaism and show how the differences emerged: Louis Ginzberg and Alexander Marx, counterparts to Abraham Geiger and Samson Raphael Hirsch. Ginzberg and Marx, who were professors at the Jewish Theological Seminary of America for the first half of the twentieth century and important authorities in their fields of learning—Talmud and history, respectively—will serve as our interlocutors in pursuing the questions of this study. For what we want to find out—to remind ourselves of—is not the sociology, or even the theology, of the successor Judaisms of the nineteenth century, but where and how people made the passage from self-evidence to self-awareness, and how we may identify what changed, and specify what continued, within the received way of life and world view. The answers to these questions tell us how people identified and answered urgent questions and so constructed a social world in which to live out their lives.

In the case of the Historical School of Germany in the nineteenth century and of Conservative Judaism in the United States, the answers are clear. Keeping the way of life of the received tradition, to which the Conservatives felt deep personal loyalty because of upbringing and association, would define the way of life of Conservative Judaism. Ignoring the intellectual substance of the received system and striking out in new directions would define the method of thought, the world view. Conservative Judaism began— and for many years persisted—as a blatant orthopraxy— think what you like but conform to the law, as in the cynical apothegm I quoted earlier (page 149). The inherited way of life exercised profound power over the heart of the Conservative Jew of the early generation. The received viewpoint persuaded no one. So they decided to keep what could not be let go, and relinquish what no longer possessed value. To justify both sides, historical scholarship would find reassuring precedents, teaching that change is not Re-

The Death of Judaism and the Birth of Judaisms

form after all. But no precedent could provide verification for orthopraxy, the most novel, the most interesting reform among the Judaisms of continuation.

Of the two substantial figures who show us how Conservative Judaism actually worked in the lives of first-rate intellects, I turn first to Alexander Marx (1878–1953) who, in his *Essays in Jewish Biography* (1948), introduces scholars he knew and loved. His book presents a classic statement of the philosophy of the founders of Conservative Judaism. Marx teaches us where that Judaism came from—which, in his person, was out of the Westernized Orthodoxy of nineteenth-century Germany. He carried forward the legacy of his father-in-law, David Hoffmann, and of Hoffmann's father-in-law, Rabbi Azriel Hildesheim—two intellectual giants, after Hirsch, of Orthodoxy in Germany. Marx explains the choices of those whose biography he undertook: "The works of Rashi [a medieval Bible commentator] have attracted me since my early youth"; and, "My interest in Saadia [a philosopher] was aroused by the greatness and originality of his work and the unusual story of his life." As to the eight modern scholars whose work he describes, he says, "I had a personal reason for selecting these men. In one way or another each of them either affected my own scholarly career or was bound to me by ties of close friendship."[8] Hoffmann, for example, was his father-in-law; and Solomon Schechter, the founding president of the Jewish Theological Seminary of America just after the turn of the twentieth century, his friend. We see, therefore, how Marx's personal life affected his choice of heroic figures for biography.

But there is more to it than that. The notion that orthopraxy without a world view characterized Conservative Judaism is wrong. Marx expressed a system, and that system emphasized the same critical approach that characterized the Historical School. As I have already noted, the mode

162

of scholarship in the study of the talmudic corpus, while different from that of both Orthodoxy and the system of the dual Torah called "traditional," in fact remained entirely within the programmatic and topical interests of Orthodox and traditionalists alike. In the case of Marx, this fact emerges clearly. His book, in its values and choice of heroes, is a party document—a work of theology masquerading as descriptive history. Orthopraxy contained its own world view, remarkably like that of Orthodoxy—except where it differed. There are deep convictions in his book, beliefs about right and wrong, not only about matters of fact. Hence, Marx proves more interesting than people who knew him in his day as a dry-as-dust factmonger might have predicted. He wrote an intellectual autobiography, expressed through the biographies of others—a powerful and subtle medium. In his pages, a reticent but solid scholar reflects on himself through what he says about others, reveals his ideals through what he praises in others. Here is an authentic judgment on the nineteenth and twentieth centuries and its principal intellectual framers: Marx's masters, friends, and heroes.

Marx himself was born in Eberfeld, in what is now East Germany. In his youth he served as a horseman in a Prussian artillery regiment—hardly a routine vocation for a rabbinical student, any more than was Hirsch's attendance at a university. Only later did Marx go to the Rabbinical Seminary in Berlin. There, in that center of Orthodoxy, he married the daughter of David Hoffmann, the son-in-law of the founder of that same seminary. So there was a continuity within the intellectual leadership of Western Orthodoxy: Hildesheim; Hoffmann; then, via the Jewish Theological Seminary of America, Marx. But then there was a break: while Hoffmann was an intellectual founder of Germany's westernized Orthodoxy, Marx in 1903 accepted Schechter's call to America. For Marx was one of the major European scholars Schechter brought to the Jewish Theological Seminary of America.

Perhaps Marx hoped that the Jewish Theological Seminary would reproduce the intellectual world of German Orthodoxy: intellectually vital and religiously loyal to tradition. In any case he became professor of history and librarian at the Jewish Theological Seminary. To be Conservative in Judaism then meant to make minor changes in the law but to make much of them, and at the same time to make major innovations in the intellectual life of Judaism and minimize them. Marx fit that pattern—as did many of those about whom he wrote. As a result, Marx's scholarship was erudite but not terribly original or productive. He embodied a Judaism that made much of facts—observances—but did little with them in a kind of intellectual counterpart to orthopraxy.

He carried on the intellectually somewhat arid tradition of Frankel and Graetz, collecting information and making up sermons about it, but engaging in slight analysis or sustained and sophisticated inquiry. He published in the areas of history and bibliography. His most popular work was his *History of the Jewish People* (written with Max L. Margolis), published in 1927.[9] The work, a one-volume history, must rank as among the most boring of its uninspired genre, but it does provide an accurate catalogue of important facts. So Marx's intellectual strength lay in his massive erudition, not in his powers of imagination and interpretation. To him history was a sequence of facts of self-evident importance and obvious significance—a theological, not merely an academic, conviction. For the theological data of the Historical School derived from historical facts, whose consequence was then self-evident.

But that view did not derive from Marx; it was commonplace then and is so even today that the facts of history bear self-evident theological meaning. That view would main-

164

tain, for instance, that if we know how a given belief or practice originated, we are guided as to the meaning of that belief, the legitimacy of that practice. If we can prove that the taboo against mixing milk with meat began in a Canaanite custom, or that the taboo against pork began because that meat spoiled so rapidly in the hot desert (as has been alleged), then we can dismiss those taboos as no longer valid, there being today no Canaanites but ample refrigeration. Called the "genetic fallacy," that position on the authority of history characterized the generation in which Marx did his work. Thus, Conservative and Reform theologians alike believed that people today should not feel compelled to do or not to do, to believe or to disbelieve—just because things once happened that way. To this view of theology Marx, with his entire generation of German and American scholars of Judaism, subscribed.

The important point, then, was the fact, and facts were to be defined one by one. Consequently, the episodic point, expressed in a brief article, formed the natural vehicle for scholarly expression. The alternative was a lengthy book, systematically working out and sustaining a proposition or problem with many implications. Marx wrote no such book, nor did many scholars in his day. Scholarship for Marx and his fellows was comprised of brief, topical, *ad hoc*, and unconnected papers—and, of such ideas, too. Graetz's history, made up of tales, and Frankel's biographies, thumbnail sketches based on paraphrases of talmudic stories, fall into the same classification. Given the stress on the self-evident meaning of facts, we can understand why the simple establishment of a fact allowed Marx and his generation to see in it a message and derive from it a meaning. But even as short essays, Marx's papers and those of his contemporaries contain important statements of broad significance. The modern figures of interest to Marx were at the center of the movement for the intellectual modernization of Judaism. All of them stood within the Western camp, but also took a traditionalist position in that camp. When we reflect on those Marx did not choose to write about—for example, Zunz and Geiger, founders of Reform Judaism; Zechariah Frankel, founder of the Positive Historical School that yielded Conservative Judaism—we see his points of sympathy and concern.

And that brings me to Louis Ginzberg (1873–1953), a still more typical and influential figure.[10] He typifies the entire group of theologian-historians, in that he grew up within the heartland of the Jewish world of eastern Europe, but left for the West. In that important respect, he stands for the experience of departure and of alienation from roots that characterized most of the early Reformers, the earliest generations of Conservative theologians, and the Orthodox of the age as well. Later some of these thinkers would lay down the rule that, to be a scholar in Judaism, one had to grow up in a yeshiva—and leave—a counsel that raised alienation to a norm. Conservative Judaism's world view bore no relationship whatsoever to the received system of the dual Torah. None of the representative men in the early generations found urgent the replication of the way of life and world view in which Ginzberg grew up.* The policy of orthopraxy, then, formed a mode of mediating between upbringing and adult commitment—that is, of coping with change.

Born and brought up in Lithuania, heartland of the intellectual giants of the received system, Ginzberg left it for Berlin and Strasbourg, where he studied with Semitists, historians, and philosophers—practitioners of disciplines unknown in the sciences of the dual Torah. Ginzberg's next move, from the central European universities, brought him to the United States, where, in 1899, he found employ-

* There were no women of note: A century would have to pass before women found their rightful place in the life of Judaisms.

166

ment at Hebrew Union College. But his appointment was canceled when it became known that he affirmed as valid the critical approach to the Hebrew Scriptures—a point of view, central to Reform and Conservative positive-historical scholarship, that made it impossible for him to be accepted by any Reform seminary.

In 1900, he found employment with the *Jewish Encyclopedia* and, in 1903, accepted an appointment in the Talmud at the Jewish Theological Seminary of America, yet another of the founding faculty collected by Solomon Schechter. Why Schechter found Ginzberg's views on biblical scholarship acceptable I do not know; but, of course, Ginzberg taught Talmud, not Scriptures. He taught at the Jewish Theological Seminary for fifty years, and has been called by Hertzberg simply "a principal architect of the Conservative movement."[11]

Ginzberg's scholarly work covered the classical documents of the oral Torah, with special interest in subjects not commonly emphasized in the centers of learning he had left. He studied the Talmud, just as he had done as a youth in Lithuania—but concentrated on the Talmud of the Land of Israel, which was not usual there, rather than on the Talmud of Babylonia, which was. And in the Talmud, he took a special interest not in legal problems but in folklore, and so compiled *The Legends of the Jews.*[12] Further, he offered a fresh and novel angle, hitherto unexplored entirely—namely, the issue of economic interest—claiming that sages had taken certain legal positions owing to particular class interests. In these striking ways, Ginzberg did something new with texts that were very, very old. The canon persisted, but the subject changed, and changed radically. Yet, despite the fresh questions and perspectives, the mode of learning remained constant. Ginzberg's work emphasized massive erudition, with a great deal of collecting and arranging, and was primarily textual and exegetical. When he entered into historical questions, the received mode of talmudic discourse—deductive reasoning, *ad hoc* arguments—predominated. For example, in the 1929 essay where he propounded the theory—famous in its day—that differences on issues of the law represented class differences, repeated enunciation of the thesis followed by examples of how that thesis might explain differences of opinion took the place of rigorous analysis and cool weighing of its implications.[13] Maintaining that liberals expressed the class interests of the lower classes, and conservatives of the upper classes, he then found in details of the law, as two parties debated it, ample exemplifications of this same theory. Just as in the yeshiva world Ginzberg had left, enthusiastic argument took the place of sustained analysis and critical testing, so in the world he chose to build, the same mode of thought persisted, changed in context, unchanged in character. For talmudists such as Ginzberg who acquired a university training, including an interest in history, and also continued to study talmudic materials, never fully overcame the intellectual habits ingrained from their beginnings in *yeshivot*.

Characteristic of talmudic scholarship is the search, first, for underlying principles to make sense of discrete, apparently unrelated cases; second, for distinctions to overcome contradictions between apparently contradictory texts; and third, for *hiddushim*, or new interpretations of a particular text. The exegetical approach to historical problems that stresses deductive thought, while perhaps appropriate for legal studies, produces egregious results for history, too often overlooking the problem of evidence: How do we know what we assert? What are the bases in actual data to justify *hiddushim* in small matters or, in large ones, the postulation of comprehensive principles (*shitot*) of historical importance? Ginzberg did not support, with archeological or even extratalmudic literary evidence, his theory that dis-

168

putes reflect economic and social conflict. Instead, having postulated that economic issues are everywhere present, he proceeded to use this postulate to "explain" a whole series of cases. The "explanations," intended to demonstrate the validity of the postulate, in fact merely repeat and illustrate it. None of these theses in their exposition and demonstration bears much in common with then-contemporary humanistic learning: humanistic history, even then, was deriving its propositions from inductive, not deductive, proof. Ginzberg, for each of his hypotheses, failed to demonstrate that the data could not be equally well explained by some other postulate or postulates. At best he leaves us with "this could have been the reason" but provides no concrete evidence that this *was* the reason.

Ginzberg was more than a great scholar. He also provided for Conservative Judaism a full and systematic statement of its world view, clarifying its issues and methods and defining its attitudes. He explicitly stressed the orthopractic view that Judaism "teaches a way of life and not a theology." At the same time, he conceded that theological systems do "expound the value and meaning of religion in propositional form," but that doctrines follow practices: "Theological doctrines are like the bones of the body, the outcome of the life-process itself and also the means by which it gives firmness, stability, and definiteness of outline to the animal organism." So Ginzberg rejected "the dogma of a dogma-less Judaism." Religious experience—that is, observance of the way of life—comes first and generates all theological reflection. As for the role of history: "Fact, says a great thinker, is the ground of all that is divine in religion and religion can only be presented in history—in truth it must become a continuous and living history." This extreme statement of the Positive Historical School, which would not have surprised Frankel and Graetz, provides a guide to the character of Conservative Judaism in the context of the political changes of the nineteenth and twentieth centuries. The appeal to fact in place of faith, the stress on practice to the subordination of belief—these form responses to the difficult situation of sensitive intellectuals brought up in one world but living in another. To understand the reason orthopraxy proved appealing, we have to recall a simple fact. Growing up within the received way of life, the now-alienated Jews retained warm memories of home and family, joined to Sabbath, festival, the holy pattern of the life of the community. Facing the conflict between a way of life found affecting and appealing and a world view in conflict with "the facts," whether of history or science, the first generation beyond the tradition preserved what it valued and dropped what it did not. So it kept alive the way of life, while adopting positions contradicting the familiar premises of that way of life.* In line with the human problem solved by the appeal to orthopraxy, Ginzberg's judgment placed experience prior to thought: "Religious phenomena are essentially reactions of the mind upon the experienced world, and their specific character is not due to the material environment but to the human consciousness."[14] Ginzberg's capacity for a lucid statement of his own theological views belied his insistence that theology followed upon, and modestly responded to, what he called "religious experience" but was, in fact, simply the pattern of religious actions that he had learned in his childhood to revere.

So orthopraxy eased the transition from one world to another. The next generation found no need to make such a move; it took as normal, not to say normative, the stress on deed to the near exclusion of intellect that, for Ginzberg and the Historical School, as much as for Orthodoxy, ex-

---

* Modern Orthodoxy did no less, but it did so in a way that, in its view, would not at all violate the convictions of the received Judaism's world view.

plained why and how to keep in balance a world view now utterly beyond belief and a way of life very much in evidence. His address in 1917 to the United Synagogue of America, of which he served as president, provides a stunning statement of his system of Judaism:

> Looking at Judaism from an historical point of view, we become convinced that there is no one aspect deep enough to exhaust the content of such a complex phenomenon as Judaism, no one term or proposition which will serve to define it. Judaism is national and universal, individual and social, legal and mystic, dogmatic and practical at once, yet it has a unity and individuality just as a mathematical curve has its own laws and expression. By insisting upon historical Judaism we express further our conviction that for us Judaism is no theory of the study or school, no matter of private opinion or deduction, but a fact. . . . If we look upon Jewish History in its integrity as a simple and uniform power, though marked in portions by temporary casual parenthetical interruptions, we find that it was the Torah which stood forth throughout the history of Israel as the guiding star of [the Jews'] civilization.[15]

While some readers may find this statement gibberish, affirming as it does everything and its opposite, it is nonetheless a serious effort to state deeply held convictions. The key to much else lies in the capital *H* assigned to the word *History*, the view that history possesses "integrity as a simple and uniform power." What we have is none other than the familiar notion that history—fact—proves theological propositions.

That position cannot surprise us when we remember that the facts of the way of life impressed Ginzberg far more than did the faith that, in the context of the dual Torah, made sense of those facts and formed of the whole a Judaism. In fact Ginzberg did not possess the intellectual tools for the expression of what he had in mind, which is why he found adequate resort to a rather inchoate rhetoric. Assuming that he intended no merely political platform, broad enough to accommodate everyone whom he hoped would stand on it, we reach a single conclusion: Conservative Judaism, in its formative century from Frankel to Ginzberg, stood for the received way of life, modified in only minor detail, along with complete indifference to the received world view. To take the place of the missing explanation—of theology—"Jewish History" would have to make do. That history, of course, supplied a set of theological propositions; but these demanded not faith but merely assent to what were deemed ineluctable truths of history: mere facts.

The Birth of a Judaism

In its formative century, Conservative Judaism carried forward the received way of life—hence it was a Judaism professedly continuous with its past. But in its forthright insistence that no world view one could delimit and define accompanied that way of life, Conservative Judaism imposed on itself a still more radical break with the received tradition than did Reform Judaism. Above all, Conservative Judaism denied the central fact of its system—its novelty. The change effected by Frankel, Graetz, and Ginzberg involved not a scarcely articulated change of attitude, as with Hirsch, but a fully spelled out change of doctrine. For the one thing that Hirsch—all the more so his critics in the traditionalist world—could not concede proves central to Ginzberg's case: "Judaism" is everything and its opposite, so long as Jewish History defines the matter. So if we ask, incremental development or new beginning? the answer is self-evident. Conservative Judaism formed a deeply original response to a difficult human circumstance.

In its formative century, Conservative Judaism solved, not only for scholars and rabbis, the urgent problem of alienation. To people who had grown up in one place, under one set of circumstances, and now lived somewhere else, in a different world, the question of change proved urgent. They had to find ways of retaining ties to a past that, they knew, they had lost. They cherished that past, but they themselves had initiated the changes they now confronted. Some did so simply by emigrating from the old village in eastern Europe to a city in Germany, Britain, or America. That new circumstance imposed strains on the capacity to live in the familiar patterns. It certainly called into question the givenness of received attitudes, the established world view, as well. In the doctrine of orthopraxy, a generation in transit held on to the part of the past its memoirs found profoundly affecting and made space for the part of its present circumstance it did not, and could not, reject. A Judaism that joined strict observance to free thinking kept opposed weights in equilibrium—to be sure, in an unsteady balance. By definition such a delicate juxtaposition could not hold. Bridged with a fragile chain of words, the abyss between the way of life, resting on supernatural premises of the facticity of the Torah (as Hirsch rightly understood), and the world view, calling into question at every point the intellectual foundations of that way of life, remained. But the experience of change through migration affected only the founders. They produced a Judaism that served beyond their time and distinctive circumstance. We turn to a second-generation Conservative theologian to show us the more lasting statement of the system. He will indicate how the successor generation proposed to bridge the gap, to compose a structure resting on secure foundations.

The claim of Reform Judaism to constitute an increment of Judaism, we recall, rested on the position that the only constant in Judaism is change. The counterpart for Conser-

The Death of Judaism and the Birth of Judaisms

vative Judaism was provided by the writings of Robert Gordis (1903–) which, for their day, set the standard and defined the position of the center of the religion. Specifically, we ask how Gordis viewed the Judaism of the dual Torah and how he proposed to relate Conservative Judaism to it. Here is his forthright account of the "basic characteristics of Jewish tradition":

> The principle of development in all areas of culture and society is a fundamental element of the modern outlook. It is all the more noteworthy that the Talmud . . . clearly recognized the vast extent to which rabbinic Judaism had grown beyond the Bible, as well as the organic character of this process of growth. . . . For the Talmud, tradition is not static—nor does this dynamic quality contravene either its divine origin or its organic continuity [all italics his]. . . . Our concern here is with the historical fact, intuitively grasped by the Talmud, that *tradition grows.*

Gordis's appeal is to historical precedent—a precedent that derives from a talmudic story, which by itself is scarcely historical at all. The story, as Gordis reads it, recognizes that tradition is not static. Let us read the story in Gordis's words and ask whether that is, in fact, its point:

> Moses found God adding decorative crowns to the letters of the Torah. When he asked the reason for this, the lawgiver was told: "In a future generation, a man named Akiba son of Joseph is destined to arise, who will derive multitudes of laws from each of these marks." Deeply interested, Moses asked to be permitted to see him in action, and he was admitted to the reason of the schoolhouse where Akiba was lecturing. To Moses' deep distress, however, he found that he could not understand what the scholars were saying and his spirit grew faint within him. As the session drew to a close, Akiba concluded: "This ordinance which we are discussing is a law derived from Moses on Sinai." When Moses heard this, his spirit revived![16]

While Gordis's view—that the story "clearly recognized

the vast extent to which rabbinic Judaism had grown beyond the Bible, as well as the organic character of this process of growth"—certainly enjoys ample basis in the sense of the tale itself, his interpretation of the story hardly impressed the Orthodox and traditionalists who read the same story. More important, if we did not know in advance that "the principle of development . . . is . . . fundamental," we should not have necessarily read the story in that context at all. For the emphasis of the story when it is not adduced as a proof-text for the Conservative position lies on the origin at Sinai of everything that came later. And that point sustains the principal issue at hand: the divine origin of the oral Torah, inclusive even of the most minor details adduced by the living sage. We know, of course, the issue urgent to the storytellers both of the Talmud of the Land of Israel and of Babylonia: namely, the place of the sages' teachings in the Torah. And that position, fully exposed here, was that everything the sages said derived from Sinai—precisely the opposite of the meaning imputed to the story by Gordis. It is not that Gordis has "misinterpreted" the story, but he has interpreted it in a framework of his own, not in the system that, to begin with, created the tale. This is evidence of creativity and innovation, of an imaginative and powerful mind proposing to make use of a received tradition for fresh purpose: not incremental but a new birth.

This small excursus on talmudic exegesis serves only to underline the fresh and creative character of Conservative Judaism. For without the slightest concern for anachronism, the Conservative theologians found in the tradition ample proof for precisely what they proposed to do, which was, in Gordis's accurate picture, to preserve in a single system the beliefs in both the divine origin and the "organic continuity" of the Torah: that middle ground, between Orthodoxy and Reform, that Conservative Judaism so massively occupied. For Gordis's generation, the argument directed itself against both Orthodoxy and Reform. In the confrontation with Orthodoxy, Gordis pointed to new values, institutions, and laws "created as a result of new experiences and new felt needs." But to Reform, he pointed out "instances of accretion and of reinterpretation, which . . . constitute the major modes of development in Jewish tradition."[17] That is to say, change comes about historically, gradually, over time, and does not take place by the decree of rabbinical convocations. The emphasis of the Positive Historical School upon the probative value of historical events serves the polemic against Reform as much as against Orthodoxy. To the latter, history proves change; to the former, history dictates modes of appropriate change.

Gordis thus argues that change deserves ratification after the fact, not deliberation beforehand: "Advancing religious and ethical ideals were inner processes, often imperceptible except after the passage of centuries." To his credit, he explicitly claims that Conservative Judaism is part of an incremental and continuous, linear history of Judaism:

> If tradition means development and change . . . how can we speak of the continuity or the spirit of Jewish tradition? An analogy may help supply the answer. Biologists have discovered that in any living organism, cells are constantly dying and being replaced by new ones. . . . If that be true, why is a person the same individual after the passage of . . . years? The answer is twofold. In the first instance, the process of change is gradual. . . . In the second instance, the growth follows the laws of his being. At no point do the changes violate the basic personality pattern. The organic character and unit of the personality reside in this continuity of the individual and in the development of the physical and spiritual traits inherent in him, which persist in spite of the modifications introduced by time. This recognition of the organic character of growth highlights the importance of maintaining the method by which Jewish tradition . . .

continued to develop. This the researches of Jewish scholars from the days of Zacharias Frankel ... to those of ... Louis Ginzberg have revealed.[18]

The incremental theory follows the modes of thought of Reform, with their stress on the continuity of process, that alone. Here, too, just as Marcus saw the permanence of change as the sole continuity, so Gordis sees the ongoing process of change as permanent. The substance of the issues, however, accords with the stress of Orthodoxy on the persistence of a fundamental character to Judaism. The method of Reform, then, produces the result of Orthodoxy, at least so far as practice of the way of life would go forward.

While, like Orthodoxy, Conservative Judaism defined itself as Judaism pure and simple, it did claim to mark the natural next step in the slow evolution of the tradition, an evolution within the lines and rules set forth by that tradition itself. Appeals to facts proved by scholars underlines the self-evidence claimed in behalf of the system in its fully articulated form. Scholars could not see the anachronism in their reading the past in line with contemporary concerns. Everything was alleged to be self-evident. But, of course, it was not. What truths Conservative theologians held to be self-evident they uncovered through a process of articulated inquiry. The answers may strike them as self-evident; but they themselves invented the questions.

The appeal to an incremental and linear history, a history bonded by a sustained method and enduring principles that govern change, comes long after the fact of change. Assuredly, Conservative Judaism forms a fresh system, a new creation, quite properly seeking continuity with a past that has, to begin with, been abandoned. For processes of change discerned after the fact, and in the light of change already made or contemplated, are processes not discovered but de-

177

fined, then imputed by a process of deduction to historical sources that, read in other ways, scarcely sustain the claim at hand. The powerful scholarship of Conservative Judaism appealed to a reconstructed past, an invented history: a perfect faith in a new and innovative system, a Judaism discovered by its own inventors.

Conservative Judaism solved a profound human problem, rather than answering an urgent question. The problem was how to make a graceful and dignified exit from a world view and a way of life that people had come to find alien. As between the two, the Conservatives abandoned the world view—ideas are cheap, words do not have to mean much—but sustained the way of life, imparting to it all sorts of fresh meanings, as best they could. The insistence on continuity yielded a certain cynicism, a going through motions. But the human anguish for a generation deeply loyal to a world it rejected cannot escape our notice. For Conservative Judaism in its formulation as orthopraxy was transient. Ginzberg kept the cultic laws of the Torah. The next generation did not. The future of Conservative Judaism lay in its serving as a road not out, but into, the Judaic system of the dual Torah—as by the mid-1950s, it had begun to do.

NEW AND OLD IN THE JUDAISMS OF CONTINUITY

The notion that the Judaisms of the nineteenth century look, from a later perspective, remarkably alike would have surprised their founders and framers, who fought bitterly among themselves. But, as we have already noticed, the three Judaisms of continuity exhibit striking traits in common. All looked backward, at the received system of the dual Torah. All sought justification in precedent out of a holy and paradigmatic past. All viewed the documents of that system as canonical, differing, of course, on the relative merit of the several components. They concurred that texts to prove propositions deemed true should derive from those canonical writings (or from some of them). All took for granted the enduring, God-given authority of those writings. None doubted that God had revealed the (written) Torah at Sinai. All looked for validating precedent in the received canon. Differing on issues important to both world view and way of life, all three Judaisms concurred on the importance of literacy in the received writings, on the lasting relevance of the symbolic system at hand, on the pertinence of the way of life (in some, if not in every detail), on the power of the received Judaism of the dual Torah to stand in judgment on whatever, later, would serve to continue that Judaism.

True, the differences among the three Judaisms impressed their framers and with good reason. The Reformers rejected important components of the Judaism of the dual Torah, and said so: written Torah, yes; oral Torah, no. The Orthodox explicitly denied the validity of changing anything, insisting on the facticity, the givenness, of the whole. The Conservatives, in appealing to historical precedent, shifted the premise of justification entirely: written Torah, yes; oral Torah, maybe. They sought what the Orthodox thought pointless and the Reform, inconsequential: namely, justification for making some few changes in the present in continuation of the processes that had effected development in the past. None of these points of important difference proved trivial. But all of them, all together, should not obscure the powerful points of similarity that mark all three Judaisms as continuators of the Judaism of the dual Torah—continuators, but not linear developments, not the natural next step, not the ineluctable increment of history, such as all claimed to be—each with good reason, and, of course, all wrong.

Not only were the differences in the grounds of separation from the received system formidable, but still more striking and fresh were the several arguments adduced once more to establish a firm connection to the Judaism of the dual Torah or, more acurately, to the "tradition" or to "Judaism." In my view, all three established a firm position within the continuation of that Judaism. While the allegation made by each of priority as the next step in the linear and incremental history of Judaism scarcely demands serious analysis, the theory, for each one respectively, enjoys ample, if diverse, justification. For the Judaisms of continuation differed in the several ways in which each on its own proposed to establish its continuity with a past perceived as discontinuous—as Jewish History dictates, a considerable difference.

The Reform position proved least ambiguous: things change all the time, and we change things too. So Reform carries forward the method of the received Judaism. Stated differently, Reform simply pursues the precedent of all former Judaisms.

Taking account of that same principle but expressing it in its distinctive way, the Conservative theologians concurred that change is perennial and traditional. But they maintained, as Gordis amply spelled out, two qualifications— one trivial, the other not. The minor qualification was that change must take place slowly and deliberately, on which point the Reform can readily have concurred. The major contribution laid emphasis on the possibility of identifying patterns of change, modes by which the tradition changed over time, the principles of change implicit in the history— the facts—of the tradition. So, the Conservatives argued, change by itself falls outside all available modes of verification. We cannot know whether change out of the context of the tradition is right or wrong. But we can know that change within the lines already dictated by the history of the tradition is legitimate and right. Change within the norms by which change has taken place marks the way forward, because that kind of change—which, the Conservatives held, historical research tells the Conservatives how to define and effect—is legitimate. Indeed, change following from the natural pattern of the tradition represents nothing more than the natural next step of the tradition itself, and that claim constituted Conservative Judaism's most powerful apologetic. Conservative Judaism accepted change in principle, only with the proviso that the tradition dictate its own next step; and, as Gordis expresses matters in an authoritative way, Conservative Judaism constitutes that natural next step. That theory of continuity with the tradition in no way compares to the one worked out by Reform Judaism.

The Orthodox theory scarcely requires articulation: there is no change. Everything Orthodoxy teaches simply states the doctrine, the way of life, the world view, received from Sinai: all from God, through us. And yet the pattern of apologetics perceived in Conservative thought recurs: Orthodoxy, too, forms the natural next step. The sole point of difference between that position and the one of Conservative theologians is that Orthodoxy perceived no difference between itself and the tradition, while Conservative Judaism recognized the difference and constructed the required apologetic for it. So in the aspect of establishing continuity, Reform stood apart from the other groups, while Orthodox and Conservative invoked pretty much the same principle, though in different ways. The incremental theory of the linear history of Judaism, established within Orthodox and recapitulated by Conservative Judaism, would serve the Reformers as well, if playing a less central part in their theory of themselves.

If I had to specify the three Judaisms' single most striking trait in common, it would be their power to endure. Orthodoxy, Reform, Conservative Judaism, as well as their variations and extensions, today continue to flourish. Nearly two hundred years have seen the birth and death of movements in the arts and philosophy, literature and music, and also religion. But the Judaisms of continuation retained, even to the beginning of the third century of Reform Judaism, the power to set the issues within Jewry and to sustain their institutions as well. We may readily lose sight of that fact and miss its surprising quality, until we realize that the more vigorous and popular movements of the twentieth century exhibited in common the opposite quality: transience. True, one came to an end because of its success, and another perished with the European Jews who were murdered in the Second World War, and in the cultural genocide practiced in Stalin's Soviet Union and into our own day. But aside from the adventitious effects of real history—as distinct from Jewish History—the Judaisms of continuation did endure. And, with their success, they preserved (and, I would say, enhanced) that Judaism of the dual Torah that, in diverse ways, these continuator systems made their own.

That fact will appear most vividly when I turn to three systems of the twentieth century, which took shape more than a century beyond the initial separation from the received system of the dual Torah. The farther a Judaism is from the point of departure, the more attenuated its links to that system. The three systems that would reach prominence in the twentieth century laid no claim to continue the Judaism of the dual Torah, in no way placed themselves in relationship to it, implicitly denied all relevance, all right of judgment, to that Judaism. So in fact they formed essentially new Judaisms, none exhibiting the claim, or the mark, of continuity. True, as a matter of form or convention, each claimed antecedents, even precedents; all adduced proof-texts. Yet in the mythic ideologies of the twentieth century, we find a new set of questions; a new body of proof-texts; above all, a new definition of imperatives confronting the Jews as a group.

The Judaisms of the nineteenth century differ from those

183

of twentieth over the issue of continuity. The nineteenth-century Judaisms outlined the grounds for establishing a single and continuous relationship with the "past," as the Conservatives put it; with the revealed, written Torah, as the Reformers emphasized; or with Sinai and God's will, as the Orthodox said. That mattered. So, too, did one other thing: all of the Judaisms of continuity paradoxically recognized their separation from the received tradition and proposed to account for it and to treat it as important, to be explained. So each composed a statement of a self-conscious explanation of who it was in relationship to the received system.

The systems of the future, discontinuous with the received system, found no urgency in such a self-conscious accounting but treated their several compositions—world views, ways of life, addressed to an identified Israel—as essentially self-evident. So the Judaisms of continuation responded to the knowledge of change with an account of the meaning of change, with the self-aware explanation of how change gave way before continuity, whether of doctrine, or method, or historical force. The Judaisms that made the total break from the received system lost the perspective gained from the external point of viewing themselves. Appealing to a fully formed system of their own, they went in search not of proof-texts, whether in literature or in history, so critical to the Reform, Orthodox, and Conservative theologians, but of mere pretexts: rhetoric to conform to an available rhetoric. So if the prophets said what the Socialists or Zionists wished to hear, the prophets would provide the requisite texts, to be affixed, so to speak, to the doorposts of the houses and to the gates, but not to be bound on mind and heart. Of such self-evidence is made: of a myth become the medium for making meaning out of the messages of the twentieth century.

One last point: my real purpose—realized only in the final chapter—requires a comparison of systems, of one set of systems to another.

As an initial generalization toward the larger work of interpreting the whole all together, seen all at once, let me cite this simple fact. The Judaisms of the nineteenth century have in common a single point of origin. All of them took shape in the world of intellectuals. All focus upon issues of doctrine and regard as important the specification of why people should do what they do, how Israel within their several definitions should see the world and live life. The Judaisms of the twentieth century address questions not of intellect but of public policy. They regard as important not ideology (which they identify with propaganda), let alone theology (which lies beyond their imagination altogether), but collective action. That action works itself out through large-scale institutions of government, politics, economics. In the categories of charisma and routine—individual initiative through intellectual charisma and collective action through bureaucracy—the nineteenth century was the age of Judaisms of intellect; the twentieth, of bureaucracy.

For the Judaisms of the twentieth century, as we shall now see, all take shape in a world that requires the gifts not of intellectuals (though the founders all were persons of substantial intellect and vision) but of organizers, people who could create vast institutions and organizations: unions, bureaucracies, even (in Zionism) entire governments. What mattered to nineteenth-century Judaisms demanded the genius of individual minds: writers, scholars, theologians. What made a difference later on would require a different order of abilities altogether: not personal charisma or intellect but the capacity to organize and administer—bureaucrats, lawyers, politicians, businessmen. To such as these, ideas formed not a world view to make sense of life, but an ideology to make possible persuasion through

185

propaganda. From men and women of individual vocation, we shall move on to those who can transform the gifts of charisma into the structures of routine and order.

And the reason for the shift stands near at hand: the urgent issues of the nineteenth century called attention to doctrine and individual deed: What should I think? What should I do? The critical concerns of the next century focused upon public policy: How shall we survive? Where should we go? So the Judaisms of an age testify to the character and quality of that age. Jews could evade the intellectual issues of the nineteenth century. The world forced on their attention the political crises of the twentieth. And that accounts for the difference between the one system and the other.

So we conclude our brief encounter with the Judaisms of a century in which mind still mattered, and, in the end, we shall find reason to admire the work of the nineteenth-century intellectuals, continuators of the grand tradition represented by the Judaism of the dual Torah. We shall wonder quite how, in the end, the Judaisms of the twentieth century measured up to their task. In intellect, none did. In practice, alas, none could. No Judaic system ever quite matched the human circumstance of the twentieth century. In that incongruence, Israel, the entirety of the Jewish people, would find its ultimate vindication. Never, with such an age, could it have found its fit.

PART III
Perfect Faith
Redivivus

THE TWENTIETH CENTURY'S MYTHIC IDEOLOGIES

Three Judaisms were born in the twentieth century—two in 1897, one in 1967. The first was Jewish socialism and yiddishism; the second, Zionism; and the third, three generations later, the American Judaic system of Holocaust and Redemption. Jewish socialism took shape in the Bund, a Jewish union organized in Poland in 1897. Zionism was founded in the World Zionist Organization, created in Basel in the same year. American Judaism as I am considering it came to powerful expression in the aftermath of the 1967

189

War in the Middle East. All three Judaic systems answered profoundly political questions. Their agenda attended to the status of the Jews as a group (Zionism, American Judaism), to the definition of the Jews in the context of larger political and social change (Jewish socialism, Zionism). In the twentieth century, powerful forces for social and economic change took political form, in movements meant to shape government to the interests of particular classes or groups—the working classes or racial or ethnic entities, for instance.

Jewish socialism presented a Judaic system congruent to the political task of economic reform through state action. The Jews would form unions and engage in mass activity of an economic—and ultimately, therefore, political—character.

In that same century, the definition of citizenship, encompassing ethnic and genealogical traits, presented the Jews with the problem of how they were to find a place in a nation-state that understood itself in an exclusionary and exclusive racist way—whether Nazi Germany or nationalist Poland or Hungary or Rumania or revanchist and irredentist France. Zionism declared the Jews "a people, one people" and proposed as its purpose the creation of the Jewish State.

Later on, shifting currents in American politics, a renewed ethnicism and emphasis on intrinsic traits of birth, rather than on extrinsic ones of ability, called into question Jews' identification with the democratic system of America as that system defined permissible difference. A Jewish ethnicism, counterpart to the search for roots among diverse ethnic groups, responded with a tale of Jewish "uniqueness"—unique suffering—and unique Jewish ethnic salvation, redemption in the Jewish State—far away, to be sure.

So three powerful and attractive movements—Jewish socialism and Zionism and American Judaism—presented answers to critical issues confronting groups of Jews. As I said, all of these movements addressed political questions and responded with essentially political programs. Zionism wanted to create a Jewish state, American Judaism wanted the Jews to form an active political community on their own, and Jewish socialism in its day framed the Jews into political, as much as economic, organizations, seeing the two as one, a single and inseparable mode of defining economic activity and public policy.

In arguing that the several systems constitute Judaisms, of course, I do not propose that these Judaisms are like the ones that came to formation in the nineteenth century. First of all, on the surface the three Judaic systems of the twentieth century took up political, social, and economic but not theological questions. That is self-evident. Second, while the nineteenth-century Judaisms addressed issues particular to Jews, the matters of public policy of the twentieth-century Judaic systems concerned everyone, not only Jews. So none of the Judaisms of the twentieth century proves congruent in each detail of structure to the continuator Judaisms of the nineteenth. All of the new Judaisms intersected with comparable systems—like in character, unlike in content—among other Europeans and Americans. Socialism then is the genus, Jewish socialism the species; American ethnic assertion the genus, American Judaism the species.

Accordingly, we move from a set of Judaisms that form species of a single genus—the Judaism of the dual Torah—to a set of Judaisms that bear less in common among themselves than they do between themselves and systems wholly autonomous of Judaic world views and ways of life. The reason is clear. The issues addressed by the Judaisms of the twentieth century, the crises that made those issues urgent, did not affect Jews alone or mainly. The crises in common derived from economic dislocation, which generated socialism, and also Jewish socialism; the reorganization of political entities, which formed the foundation of nationalism, and also of Zionism; and the reconsideration of the theory of American society, which produced, alongside the total homogenization of American life, renewed interest in ethnic origins, and also American Judaism. So as is clear, the point of origin of the nineteenth-century Judaisms was the dual Torah; Jews in the twentieth century had other things on their minds.

For the twentieth-century systems were born within another matrix altogether: the larger world of socialism and linguistic nationalism, for Jewish socialism and yiddishism; the realm of the nationalisms of the smaller peoples of Europe, rejecting the government of the international empires of central and eastern Europe, for Zionism; the reframing, in American culture, of the policy governing social and ethnic difference, for American Judaism. None of these Judaic systems of believing and behaving drew extensively on the received Judaic system of the dual Torah, and all of them for a time vastly overshadowed, in acceptance among the Jewish group, the Judaisms that did. So the passage of time, from the eighteenth to the twentieth century, produced a radical attenuation of the bonds that joined the Jews to the Judaism of the dual Torah.

The contrast between the nineteenth- and the twentieth-century systems should be drawn. The Judaisms of the nineteenth century retained close and nurturing ties to the Judaism of the dual Torah. All three confronted its issues, drew heavily on its symbolic system, cited its texts as proof-texts, eagerly referred to its sources in justification for the new formations. All of them looked backward and assumed responsibility toward that long past of the Judaism of the dual Torah, acknowledging its authority, accepting its program of thought, acceding to its way of life—if only by way of explicit rejection. While the nineteenth-century Judaisms made constant reference to the received system of the dual Torah, its writings, its values, its requirements, its viewpoints, its way of life, the twentieth-century Judaisms did not. True, each Judaism born in the nineteenth century faced the task of validating change; but all of the new Judaisms of the nineteenth century articulated a principle of change guiding relationships within the received system, which continued to define the agenda of law and theology alike. All the Judaisms of that age recognized themselves as answerable to something they deemed the tradition. We cannot point to a similar relationship between the new Judaisms of the twentieth century and the received Judaism of the dual Torah. For none of them made much use of the intellectual resources of that system, found important issues deemed urgent within that system, or even regarded itself as answerable to the Judaism of the dual Torah.

Just as, in the second century, the important thinkers of Christianity found only mildly interesting the issues urgent for Peter and Paul in the first, but rather pursued a quite fresh program of thought on issues generated by Christian experience utterly alien to the Judaic world, of either the first or the second century, so the Judaisms of the twentieth century had absolutely no interest in the received Judaism of the dual Torah. They looked forward, and they drew heavily upon contemporary systems of belief and behavior. But they turned to the received system of the dual Torah only adventitiously, merely opportunistically, and—if truth be told—cynically. For that received Judaism provided not reasons but excuses. Appealing to its proof-texts provided not authority for what people wanted to do anyhow, but mere entry to the mind and imagination of Jews themselves not far separated from the world that took for granted the truth of Scripture and the wisdom of the oral Torah. So the shift from the Judaisms that responded to the received system to those that essentially ignored it except (at most) after the fact marked the true beginning of the modern age: that is, the point at which the old system held to be a set of self-evident truths gave way to a new set of systems, all of them equally self-evident to their adherents. What intervened was a span of self-consciousness, in which people saw choices and made decisions about what had formerly appeared obvious and beyond argument. At what cost did the shift come from a reading of the received texts to an ignoring of them? And what price did people pay when what had served as a source of proof-texts for the nineteenth century turned into a treasury of pretexts for twentieth-century ideologists?

The Judaisms of the nineteenth century attained a high measure of self-consciousness because they had before their eyes the image of the innocent faith of their predecessors—and of many in their own time as well. The Judaisms of the twentieth century, abandoning all pretense at a connection to the received Judaism, lost also the awareness that change had taken place, that people had made choices. So they entered a new phase of self-evidence, appealing now for vindication not to received texts but to the obvious facts of the everyday world. History, meaning events, now proved propositions for the new Judaisms, and the text of these Judaisms was the world out there. Proof-texts derived from headlines in newspapers.

The continuators of the Judaism of the dual Torah developed systems of belief and behavior that invariably fell into the category of religion—in our setting, Judaisms. Whether the twentieth-century successor systems constitute religions, Judaisms, is a question of only slight consequence. Clearly, Jewish socialism and Zionism provided the deep meaning for the lives of millions of Jews, so that, defining ways of life and world views and the Israel subject to realize both, they functioned entirely as did the religions, the Judaisms, of the nineteenth century and of the twentieth as well.

194

But socialism-yiddishism and Zionism differ from the continuator Judaisms, because neither of the former invoke a supernatural God, revelation of God's will in the Torah, belief in Providence, or any other indicator of the presence of the family of closely related religions, the Judaisms; and, moreover, their framers and founders did not claim otherwise. Had the framers alleged that theirs was a continuator Judaism, I should have to introduce that fact into this analysis and interpretation, but none did. The Socialists took a position actively hostile to religion in all forms, and the Zionists compromised with the religious Judaisms of the day but in no way conceded that theirs was a competing Judaism. American Judaism forms a separate set of problems; but in its contemporary form, in its appeal to the salvific myth of Holocaust and Redemption, it crosses the border between a genuinely religious and an entirely secular system addressed to Jews, and falls on both sides of the not-unmarked boundary between the one and the other.

Since we are not dealing with systems that claim to continue the dual Torah, we may now facilely dispose of the question that occupied us in part II, and define a more interesting one for part III. We asked Reform, Orthodoxy, and Conservative Judaism to tell us whether they were old or new, and found that, in all three cases, they were both—therefore new. We further wanted to know how each of the religious systems of the nineteenth century explained the continuity between itself and the system of the dual Torah which each one of them insisted rendered its Judaism legitimate. And we could find the mode of establishing that connection: change is the sole constant and therefore legitimate; there is no change; change is acceptable within limits, which historical scholarship discovers. Now when we turn to Socialism, Zionism, and American Judaism as Judaic systems, we need not ask whether they are old or new. All of them are new, without clear precedent and with slight pretense to the contrary. It follows that none of them proposed to legitimate its system by invoking precedents, proof-texts, or points of continuity in doctrine or deed.

A further set of questions arises from the fact that, so far as I can observe, to the adherents of the Judaisms before us, the truths embodied in the way of life and the world view of socialism, Zionism, and American Judaism enjoyed that same status of self-evidence as had characterized the beliefs and behavior of the system of the dual Torah. So I want to show how, within the acknowledged limits of an inquiry into systems and their structures, the systems at hand attained that self-evidence, that authority beyond all argument, that, for the participants, each one possessed. And that issue requires me to specify the urgent questions taken up by the several systems in succession. Knowledge of the points of stress and emphasis of the system may also lead to a theory on why the system worked so well where and when it did—a theory to be tested not here, but by social research, to be sure—and why, more to the point, the received system did not serve at all. For what enjoyed the standing of self-evident truth for fifteen hundred years lost that standing and fell to the wayside in scarcely a hundred years—a fact that, while familiar as the ground of Judaic existence in the twentieth and twenty-first centuries, remains astonishing. For none of the successor Judaisms gives promise of so long a spell of success as one hundred, let alone fifteen hundred, years; and two of the three born at the eve of the twentieth century had died before the end of the century, socialism-yiddishism and Zionism in its original formulation.

For in the end the difference between the twentieth-century and the nineteenth-century Judaisms is much more than a century. It is the difference between the civilization of the West in its Christian form and that same civilization as it took new forms altogether. What pertinence had the

Judaism formed in response to Christianity, with its interest in Scripture, Messiah, the long trends of history and salvation? The new world imposed its own categories: class and class struggle, the nation-state composed of homogeneous cultural and ethnic units—the lowest common denominator of bonding for a society; the search, among diverse and rootless people, for ethnic identity. These issues characterized a world that had cast loose the moorings that had long held things firm and whole.

Between the twentieth-century and the nineteenth-century Judaisms lay a century, but the passage of time explains little. The real explanation for the character of the Judaisms of the twentieth century derives from what was going on in that worst of all centuries in the history of humanity: the age of total death. Confronting the urgent and inescapable questions of the twentieth century, the system makers of Judaisms in the end came up with no self-evident answers. There were none. There could have been none. What is there to say in the face of "extermination"—that is, of the murder of human beings because they were Jews? And what system could have answered the urgent question of life?

CHAPTER 5

SOCIALISM AND YIDDISHISM AS A JUDAIC SYSTEM

In 1897, Jews of Poland formed the General Jewish Workers Union, known as the "Bund," which embodied Jewish socialism and gave the movement its institutional expression. The working-class Jews of Poland and Russia, as well as of America, in huge numbers affiliated with the Jewish unions and Socialist political parties (and later with the Democratic party of Franklin Roosevelt's New Deal). These facts contribute to the study of Judaic systems because Jews derived from Jewish socialism not merely economic benefits or political identity but—of greater interest to us—a life's ideal, a view of the future, a reason for action

198

in the present: a Judaism. Jewish socialism was a movement that joined the social and economic ideals of socialism to a deep commitment to the formation of a way of life and a world view for an Israel—specifically, the impoverished and working-class Jews of Eastern Europe. It presented a complete picture of how one should live life (namely, as an active worker for political change and social improvement), of how one should see the world (namely, as something to be perfected within the ideals of the biblical prophets and the program of Socialist theorists), and of how to so form a new Israel, among the united working people of the world. This new Israel would take its place within the international working classes, but as a distinct component, just as the Russian or the Polish Socialists recognized their ethnic origins as well.

But can we call it a Judaism? Not for the many Communists and Socialists who happened to be Jews—that is, to have come from Jewish families. For them, socialism had no bearing on their Jewish origins, and they had no special relationships to other Jews. But for Jews who opted for a socialist ideal, who organized labor unions and other institutions in particular for the betterment of the life of the Jewish masses, socialism bonded with certain aspects of the received holy literature to form a distinctively Jewish version of socialism—indeed, one that in the lives of the participants formed their way of "being Jewish."

One considerable component of that "way," moreover, involved the Yiddish language, the vehicle that brought socialism to the Jewish masses. Hence Jewish socialism joined to yiddishism—an ideology of turning a language into the foundation for a way of life—constituted a powerful and important Judaism. Before taking up the ideology of yiddishism, I shall consider the world view, the life ideal, of the Jewish Socialists. For a statement of the world view of the radicals—a statement in Hebrew, but an example of Socialist poetry—I turn to the poem "We Believe," published in 1872. Here we find that set of truths held to be self-evident that express the way of explaining the world and the purpose of life that made Jewish socialism a statement of meaning:

> We believe
> —that misdeeds, injustice, falsehood, and murder will not reign forever, and a bright day will come when the sun will appear.
> —there is hope for mankind; the peoples of the world will not destroy each other for a piece of land, and blood will not be shed for silly prestige.
> —Men will not die of hunger, and wealth not created by its own labor will disappear like smoke.
> —People will be enlightened and will not differentiate between man and man; will no longer say, "Christian, Moslem, Jew," but will call each other "Brother, friend, comrade."
> —The secrets of nature will be revealed and people will dominate nature instead of nature dominating them.
> —Man will no longer work with the sweat of his brow; the forces of nature will serve him as hands.[1]

The passage in the original may be more evocative than it is in English, but our interest in its banalities is only to discern the ideals of Jewish socialism, and they emerge with clarity. The world view of the Jewish Socialists laid emphasis on the building of a better world through science and technology. It elicited commitment and generated hope because of this powerful promise of a better tomorrow. Jewish socialism promised a bright future, a better tomorrow; spoke of an eschatology; addressed issues of economic justice; took up the Jews' concern for anti-Semitism as part of a larger ideal of universal tolerance; expressed a commitment to science and technology. That, sum and substance, frames the world view: an amalgam of the Jews' social aspirations and contemporary complaints, a solution to the Jewish problem as part of a solution to the problem of class conflict.

This brings us to the other, the Yiddish component of this popular Judaism. Yiddishism was the Judaic movement that identified in the language, Yiddish, a set of cultural values and ideals of personal conduct that, all together, comprise a way of life and a world view. The union of Jewish socialism and yiddishism formed the single most popular Judaism of the first half of the twentieth century, appealing to the mass of Jews in both Poland and Russia as well as in America. In her classic essay, Ruth R. Wisse defines yiddishism as a system: "*Yiddishkeyt* [that is, the ideology of Yiddish] has come to signify both the culture that is embodied in the Yiddish language and a standard of ethical conduct that preserves the essence of Judaism without the requirements of ritual and law." Since the language is treated as the bearer of ideals and values, the speaking of that language constitutes the principal component of a way of life; and those values, the world view. The Israel at hand, of course, comprises Yiddish-speaking Jews. The connection to socialism, moreover, proves critical. Jewish Socialists pointed to the Yiddish language, and its supposedly distinctive values of compassion and social idealism, as the cultural vehicle for their movement. They espoused Yiddish as the language of Jewish socialism. So yiddishism and Jewish socialism joined together, even though each Judaism preserved its particular points of stress and concern. As to the special ideology of yiddishism, again in Wisse's words we find "an ideal of behavior in which the whole religious discipline of Jewish life is transmuted into the practice of kindness and decency." We are dealing here then with yearning not for a language but for a social and political ideal. That ideal, moreover, for its holders serves, in Wisse's words, as "a model for the present and the future."[2]

The poem I have just cited provides a model for present and future, and we see the congruity—if also the distinction—between Jewish socialism and yiddishism.

The appeal to language as an ideology, Wisse points out, has its roots in the end of the nineteenth and beginning of the twentieth century in eastern Europe. Compensating for the loss of religious belief and for the absence of territorial unity and autonomous politics, advocates of Yiddish resorted to language to "express . . . cultural autonomy, so that same language would now cement a culturally autonomous community." Wisse observes, in this connection, that the recognition of language as a separate category for Jews runs parallel to the recognition of religion as something subject to discrete definition.[3] This, too, seems to me a positive indication that the language nationalism represented by Yiddish forms an encompassing system, not merely a matter of adventitious choice.

The linking of yiddishism to socialism requires explanation. Wisse explains the appeal of yiddishism to the socialist:

> A Jew who lived in accordance with the religious tradition could presumably maintain his Jewishness in Spanish as well as English, in German as well as Yiddish, or even in modern Hebrew. A secular Zionist could abandon religious practice and many of the "trappings" of Jewish culture, secure in the belief that statehood would generate a new national identity. The Jewish Left, however, had only its culture to set it apart from the Polish Left and the Russian Left, and that culture, stripped of its religious content, added up to Yiddish—the language, the folklore, the literature.

Hence, the formation of yiddishism, now no longer an ideology of language but an ideology of the people. The Jewish socialist-yiddishist Chaim Zhitlowsky held, Wisse points out, that "Yiddish had absorbed the Jewish ethics to such a degree that anyone who spoke it was permeated by the Jewish spirit." The difficulty with the ideology at hand, both on its own and when joined to socialism, hardly escapes notice. Wisse states it simply: "Yiddish had developed out of the religious way of life of the Jews, both to express and to protect Jewish separateness. Yiddishists now hoped that a secular way of life, with no other ideological justification for separateness, could be sustained by language alone." Joined to socialism and class struggle, treated as the language of oppressed classes, Yiddish found itself bearing a still heavier burden: "The transfer of a system of values from religion, where it was appropriately lodged, to language, where it was assuredly not, placed upon Yiddish a new burden of exceptionalism, and one for which there was no national consensus."[4]

The issue of yiddishism for us frames a different question from the one so ably answered by Wisse. While she explains "the failed politics of Yiddish," for our purpose the ideology built on language forms an excellent example of the move from the Judaism of the dual Torah to other Judaisms. And we cannot deny to yiddishism, by itself and in union with socialism, the status of a sociopolitical ideology. The prophetic tradition contributed proof-texts, but yiddishism did not emerge from prophetic writings. The values of the Judaism of the dual Torah made their contribution, but yiddishism joined to socialism did not take shape to restate these values in a language or a structure continuous with the one that had gone before. Concern for the poor and oppressed of all nations sustained an established value of the received system, but that concern, in Wisse's words, was "really socialism with a Jewish face."[5] So, in her judgment, the bonds uniting socialism and yiddishism to the received form of Judaism proved tenuous and weak, ready to snap under the slightest pressure.

The Judaic System of Jewish Socialism

Clearly, Jewish socialism formed a Jewish component of international socialism, as the General Jewish Workers Union, the Bund, claimed. But what was Jewish about it? It was a version of a general movement, bearing no particular message to Jews and addressing no problem unique to them. Socialism and Jewish socialism form a case in point. Jewish socialism exercised enormous appeal to large numbers of Jews (the "masses," in the parlance of the day), constituting the largest single movement, the most successful Judaic system in its time. And yet, joining the noun *socialism* with the adjective *Jewish* will surprise those who quite properly regard socialism as an international movement of the working class, transcending all boundaries and erasing all ethnic and national distinctions. The appeal of socialism to Jews, indeed, derived in part from its promise of doing away with ethnic and religious difference. The world view of Jewish socialism laid emphasis on overcoming ethnic difference, not on reaffirming it as Zionism and American Judaism did. But that phenomenon—that is, a political and social movement affecting large numbers of Jews—while interesting for the history and sociology of Jews in modern Europe and the United States, does not constitute a Judaism: a way of life, a world view, addressed in particular to (an) Israel. One might as well invoke the Democratic party of the New Deal as a Judaism, if the sole criterion is Jews' adherence to a movement "as Jews" (in the quaint term of that time). Quite to the contrary, socialism, while a movement attractive to Jews, has no bearing on the study of the birth of Judaisms in modern and contemporary times any more than does, for example, psychoanalysis or political neoconservatism, each with its sizable component of Jewish participants.

Jewish socialism and yiddishism, however, formed—out of (1) aspects of the received system of the dual Torah as defined in eastern Europe, (2) the Yiddish language, and (3) the social ideals of the prophets and rabbis of old—a distinctive ideology. Jewish socialism demands attention in the study of the birth of Judaisms beyond the death, for many, of the Judaism given literary substance in the fourth and early fifth centuries, because, as I argued in the opening section to this chapter, the movement at hand when reshaped to the special interests of Jews—hence, Jewish socialism—offered to Jews in particular an ideology, a mode of social organization, a way of life and a world view, explaining who is Israel and why the Jews must do as they do: a Judaism. I do not mean to suggest that all Jews who joined socialist parties or movements formed a single movement, Jewish socialism; the opposite is the case.

Many Socialists who derived from Jewish families explicitly rejected that Jewish heritage. In Germany, Poland, and Russia, important Socialist and Communist figures of Jewish origin in no way sought in socialism or communism a mode of "being Jewish," or a Judaic system. Quite to the contrary, Rosa Luxemberg, a leading German Socialist, Leon Trotsky, a major Bolshevik leader in the early stages of the Russian Revolution, and the Jews in the leadership of the Polish Communist party, though afflicted by anti-Semitism, treated as trivial or distasteful particularly Jewish concerns, and said so. Nor should we imagine that because, in some circumstances, socialism was particularly attractive to Jews, that movement demands attention in the study of the Judaisms of modern and contemporary provenance. Not everything Jews adopt as a way of life and a world view constitutes a Judaism; and most such things, in the nature of modern life, do not.

205

True, Jews were attracted to socialism in western Europe, partly by the appeal of "building a 'just society' based on the teachings of the prophets, partly by the hope that socialism would overcome anti-Semitism." Still others turned to socialism as an instrument for their own exodus from the Jewish group, as Schneier Zalman Levenberg wrote: "There were also Jews who saw in it a way of getting rid of their Jewish heritage and serving the cause of the 'Brotherhood of Man.' Socialism was particularly attractive for Jews anxious to leave the ghetto behind them and who, disappointed with the slow progress of 19th century liberalism, were keen to embrace a new universal faith."[6] None of this has any bearing on our subject, though these themes have a considerable place in the study of the ideas and politics of Jews in modern Europe and the United States as well, of course, as in the State of Israel.

Ezra Mendelsohn, the master of the subject of Jewish socialism, describes the matter: "[Jewish socialism] refers to specifically Jewish movements and parties which envisaged the creation of a socialist society as an essential aspect of the solution to the Jewish question. This definition, while far from perfect, has the virtue of excluding Jews who happened to be socialist as well as socialist movements in which many Jews were active but which had no specifically Jewish content or aims."[7] Mendelsohn's definition amply justifies asking whether and how a Jewish socialism took shape as a Judaic system. By every criterion, Jewish socialism serves. Informing its adherents how to conduct their lives, supplying them with a purpose and a meaning to existence, providing them with an explanation for history and a world view encompassing the entirety of existence, defining for them the meaning of Israel and the place of Israel, the people, in the world—in all these, Jewish socialism qualifies as a Judaism. In ways in which, despite its appeal to Jewish practitioners, psychoanalysis did not form a Judaism, the Jewish Socialist system did. Not every Judaism falls into the classification of a religion. Whether Jewish socialism fell into the classification of a religion, it assuredly fitted nicely into the category of a Judaism. As Mendelsohn stresses, Jewish socialism, in addressing "the Jewish question," developed a system that would not only function like a Judaism but would exhibit those traits that, all together, indicate a Judaism.

When through the nineteenth and into the twentieth century, Jews in eastern Europe ceased to find self-evident the system of the dual Torah, they did not become Reform, Conservative, or Orthodox. Reform answered questions of political definition that those Jews did not face, since they were never offered the promise of political emancipation. Conservative Judaism relied upon Reform for its motive energy. Reacting against what it deemed excess, Conservative Judaism drew its power from the tensions of the center position. But in eastern Europe (as in the State of Israel today) it was difficult to locate that center among contending groups of a religious order. Orthodoxy had no message not delivered more eloquently by the life of the villages and the streets imbued with the received system. To explain to Jews within that system that the facts of nature and of supernature were equally facts was to answer a question of faith in a context of doubt that few within the received system perceived.

And those who did come to doubt sought, in the main, some system other than the one retained and intellectually enriched by Orthodoxy in its philosophical mode. Those who found the Judaism of the dual Torah self-evidently irrelevant did not then seek a revision of that Torah. The reason is that the problems that occupied their lives scarcely intersected with the issues of that Torah, in any of its versions. What defined those problems was a long-term depression, severely aggravated by political stress in the very regions of Jewish settlement; by the decline of agriculture and the economy that served it; by the growth of population and consequent unemployment, for Jews in particular; by the growing and violent anti-Semitism of the state, of one ethnic identification, the Russian, and the population, of several others—Polish, Ukrainian, Hungarian, and Rumanian, for instance. These, as I have observed, constituted a crisis of a different order from the one addressed by the dual Torah.

One of the several interesting systemic alternatives derived from socialism, and it was the Jewish kind that mattered. It mattered because it constituted a kind of "anti-Judaism," a systemic response, of a negative order, to the received system among those choosing to reject that system. Again, Mendelsohn:

> Jewish socialism, so understood, could originate only in Eastern Europe, [where there were] . . . thousands of workers, the Yiddish-speaking "masses" so evident in the cities of western and southern Russia. Moreover, by the late nineteenth century a secular Jewish intelligentsia had developed in the Pale, consisting of students and professionals, many of whom were influenced by radical Russian ideologies. That they should be so was quite predictable, given the all-pervasive anti-Semitism which awakened their demands for social justice and made public activity, outside of radical circles, impossible. These Jewish intellectuals . . . were in revolt against the values and traditions of the ghetto. In many cases socialism, the acceptance of which in itself was a sign of assimilation, led them to discover the Jewish proletariat; this discovery, in turn, led them back to the Jewish people, to whom they preached the new doctrine.[8]

So much for the audience. What can we say of the doctrine, and can we describe the system in terms also of a way of life and an address to (an) Israel?

208

The first stages in the formation of a doctrine of Jewish socialism had to take up the issue with which I began: How can an internationalist movement recognize a particular ethnic group? The special needs of the Jewish working class, Jewish Socialists maintained, made Jewish socialism not a kind of nationalism but a legitimate outgrowth of international socialism. What was needed, however, was no more—in the earliest phase of the movement—than Jewish unions. The movement's original aim was to establish a school for socialism among Jews.[9] By the early 1890s, however, a distinct Jewish socialist movement began to take shape. In 1897, the year of the formation of the Zionist organization, the Jewish socialist movement founded the General Jewish Workers Union, or Bund, in Russia and Poland. Russian Marxists in the Russian Social Democratic Workers' party declined to recognize the Jewish Union, a position consistently taken by Lenin and the Bolsheviks.

The ideology of the Bund took the shape of a Jewish national program, as Mendelsohn explains: "The Jewish proletariat, bearer of the Marxist mission, was also seen as the bearer of the Jewish national tradition as against the assimilated, Russified, or Polonized Jewish middle class."[10] The mode of expression of this program was to be celebration of the Yiddish language and literature. The Jewish Socialists adopted the Yiddish language as the language of the working class, maintained that reading Yiddish literature formed an expression of the movement, and argued that the Jews formed a group deserving national self-determination, like the other ethnic nations of eastern Europe in both the Russian and the Austro-Hungarian empires. The Bund moved into system building as it began to speak of the Jews' national rights; so forming a doctrine of Israel, aiming at the right to foster Yiddish cultural activities; so beginning to define a distinctive, public way of life for the Jewish entity ("people"? "nation"?) of the Russian and Austrian empires.

209

So, in all, the marriage of socialism and nationalism yielded that Jewish socialism that formed an absorbing and encompassing system: a way of life, a world view, addressed to Israel. If we ask about the way of life distinctive to the system, we discover a panoply of institutions—unions, youth groups, and the like—that the Jewish Socialist movement formed for the organization of the working class. These institutions, with their meetings, rehearsals of the faith, enactment of recurrent rites, defined a kind of Jewish "civil religion"; and, as we shall see in the next section, that civil religion appealed to the ideals and emotions of the faithful in much the same spirit as had the received system of the dual Torah. In other words, Jewish socialism absorbed the devotee, explaining what one should do with one's life (with women enjoying a more substantial role than in the Judaism of the dual Torah), and how one should understand and interpret national and personal existence—so, again, a way of life and a world view. These claims of the Judaic-systemic classification of Jewish socialism await the evidence of how, in a given system of life and thought, they worked themselves out: the concrete system as an interesting intellect gave it substance.

The Judaic System of Yiddishism

Just as Jewish socialism developed out of recalcitrant materials a distinctively Judaic world view and a way of life, so nothing can have proved less likely to yield an ideology than a language. But in the age in which (merely) speaking Yiddish became a statement of meaning, rather than a vehicle for the expression of meaning, there was a long list of languages that, in their respective settings, served the same purpose: Polish, Armenian, Afrikaans, Flemish, French in Canada, to name but a few. Indeed, one of the recurrent traits of group life in the twentieth century would come to exemplary expression in yiddishism: namely, the position that a language bears the meaning—the world view, the way of life—of the group. Whether the celebration of Afrikaans, marking the inauguration of a renaissance of Afrikaans national politics in the Republic of South Africa, or the strong affirmation of Flemish in Belgium, or of French in Canada, among numerous candidates worldwide, the picture proves uniform. What marks yiddishism as especially interesting is the joining of linguistic assertion to the values of the class struggle espoused in Jewish socialism. In the study of Judaic systems, that is the aspect of yiddishism that attracts our interest.

The use of the Yiddish language as a vehicle for reaching the Jewish working class and organizing the labor movement became a matter of ideology. Yiddish found itself transformed from an instrument of communication into a "cultural asset of national and intrinsic value." Clearly, if speaking Yiddish constituted a statement, then speaking some other language had also to matter; and, among the Jews of eastern Europe, the choice was Yiddish or Hebrew or the vernacular (Polish or Russian, for example). Yiddish, the language of the working class, took on the status of a symbol of a broader position—that outlined in our rapid look at Jewish socialism; and speaking Yiddish rather than some other language became an instrument of self-identification. So in observing that the systems of the twentieth century took on the character of self-evidence, we must not miss the entirely self-aware choices made by people in adopting one or another of the modes of living out life. Because speaking Hebrew stood for the Zionist position, speaking Yiddish constituted a mode of identification with the Jewish socialist movement. The writers of Yiddish then enunciated an ideology of struggle against the exploitation of the worker, summoning the Jew "to struggle against his exploiters within and without and to sacrifice himself for social, political, and national liberation."[11]

As to who participated in that system we identify as yiddishism, there were, first of all, writers and poets and, then, those to whom they spoke: those who spoke the language and throughout asserted the values of the system at hand, of class struggle within Jewry, aiming at a liberation of all workers everywhere—so an international movement's Jewish section. Any Judaism has to identify its distinctive type of hero: for Jewish socialism, it was the labor union leader; for yiddishism, the poet, the writer. That the writers and poets served as counterparts to the rabbis and saints of the received system was proved in the former's treatment by the enemies of yiddishism and Jewish socialism. On 12 August 1952, the most important Yiddish authors living in the Soviet Union were put to death by its Communist government, which thereby liquidated proponents of a world view and a way of life to which that country took exception.

Accordingly, we scarcely exaggerate if, looking back, we classify the speaking and the writing of a language as definitive components of a world view and a way of life. And that conception, so difficult of access for the speakers of American English, a homogenizing force in the lives of diverse groups, finds its best proof in the fact that Yiddish was recognized as a competing force. In declaring his implacable opposition to Jewish socialism even before 1917, Lenin gave evidence of discerning precisely that same trait: namely, that that set of organizations and views constituted a competing system with its distinctive world view and way of life. Nonetheless, these external testimonies to the character of Jewish socialism, with yiddishism as a mode of organizing life and making sense of it, leave open the question of how the system at hand actually worked. To answer that question, I turn to the testimony of individuals, who expressed in their own words that larger world view and way of life by which they formed their identity.

Socialism and Yiddishism: Vladimir Medem and Chaim Zhitlowsky

The definition of the joined system of Jewish socialism and yiddishism gains concreteness when we consider the lives of its important heroes, which vividly demonstrate how this Judaic system functioned. What we see in Vladimir Medem and Chaim Zhitlowsky is a trait characteristic of the Judaisms of the twentieth century: the creative power of once-alienated Jews in the forming of Judaic systems. Both of these exemplary heroes of the Judaic system before us began their lives and careers as outsiders and came back to a Judaism but not to the Judaism of the dual Torah or to its continuators. What they came back to and what they brought with them would define the Judaic system at hand: they came back to the group and brought with them things they had learned elsewhere, much as Moses came back to Israel but was identified, by the Israelites, as an Egyptian.

Vladimir Medem (1879–1923), after an upbringing in the Orthodox Church and as a Russian, identified himself as a Jew only through Jewish socialism. He rejoined the Jews in his early twenties and identified, as Jew and Marxist, with the Bund. The way of life of the Bund finds exemplification in Medem. He spent his life in the service of the Jewish Union, as writer and organizer and public speaker. That way of life encompassed his existence, as much as spending his days in the study of the Talmud would otherwise have

213

absorbed his life's energies. He represented the Bund at the second convention, in 1903, of the Russian Social Democratic Party in London,[12] served on the Committee Abroad of the Bund, contributed to Bund newspapers, served on the Bund's Central Committee, and on and on. So the way of life of Jewish socialism, for the élite at least, involved public activity in organizations. Medem took the view that the Bund should take an interest in Jewish community organization and encourage the teaching of Yiddish, in Yiddish; he strongly opposed Zionism while favoring Jewish national-cultural autonomy in the countries of eastern Europe, and opposed communism in the Bund.

How, then, to invoke the categories of our analysis? Let us make up a questionnaire to administer to each of our heroic figures, to a devotee of the system.

Way of life? Politics.

That is to say, the principal activities of the Jewish Socialist leaders encompassed political organization and activity. They wrote to persuade, lectured to organize, spent their lives forming of the Jews a political entity to accomplish economic and social goals.

World view? The issues of international socialism.

The Jewish Socialist heroes viewed the world through the perspective of socialism, seeing the oppression of the working classes and their exploitation by capitalism as the force of evil against which to struggle, and identifying activities in support of the working classes as the power of good in the world. History, moreover, found structure and explanation and purpose in this same class struggle.

Judaism? In every fiber of the heroes' being. For in their language, their social concern, their every breath, the heroes devoted themselves to the welfare of the Israel they identified, to the Jewish working classes, the speakers of Yiddish, in the sweatshops of Poland, England, and America.

214

The form of life derived from a pattern common among diverse Socialist groups, each in its own country and language. The substance of this socialism came to expression among Jews, in the Yiddish language, wholly within the idiom of the life of the Israel identified by the Judaism at hand.

Medem, raised as a gentile by converted parents, regained his identification with Jews through Jewish socialism; and the movement of his life—from one system to the other—strongly points to the comparability, in terms of his existence, between the one and the other. I do not mean to argue that Jewish socialism for Medem formed a religion comparable to the (Russian, Christian) Orthodoxy of his youth. The two could not have differed more radically. One was a religion in the narrow and accepted sense, a system of sacred duties in the service of God; the other was a secular identity, also in a conventional sense. But Medem moved from the one to the other and, to the second, gave precisely those energies and commitments that he had devoted to the first. So for him one world view and way of life gave way to another, each addressing the enduring issues of human life and society that he found required sorting out. And in his movement from outside to inside via Jewish socialism and yiddishism, he typified the passage of Jews of the twentieth century—indeed, prefigured what would be the norm: traveling the road back. For characteristic of the movement in the nineteenth century was the way out; and in the twentieth (for those who sought the path), the way back. For many already outside, yiddishism and Jewish socialism showed the way.

How did Medem express this "Jewishness" that he discovered in Jewish socialism? For one thing, he learned Yiddish. Speaking that language formed his entry into the Israel he would serve. For another, he identified with the Jews, describing the worship of a synagogue in these terms:

215

It was as though I had fallen among torrential waves. Hundreds upon hundreds of worshippers—each one taking his own case to God, each in a loud voice with passionate eagerness. Hundreds of voices ascended to the heavens, each for himself, without concord, without harmony, yet all joining together in one tremendous clamorous sound. No matter how strange to the Western ear, it makes a deep impression and has a great beauty derived from the passion of mass feeling.

The power that brought him to the Jews derived from "constant association with Jews and Jewish life": "I cannot exactly determine how this 'nationalizing' influence of the Jewish labor circles expressed itself. It was the quiet effect of day to day living. This life became dear and important to me. It was Jewish and it drew me into its environs."[13]

Now, as I have said, translating statements such as these into a clear construction, a system composed of a way of life and a world view, faces obstacles. We see no clear ideology, comparable to the theology that identifies with God's will the way of life so cherished by Medem; no well-defined way of life emerges from (merely) associating with other Jews. Yet for Medem, exemplary of a great many Jews, that is what Jewish socialism provided—association, together with an articulated appreciation of that association; an ideal of life, in the service of the laboring masses; a teleology of class struggle to which were imputed strong affinities with the prophetic texts found pertinent; a definition of Israel, as apart from the international working classes; an ideal of how to use one's life on earth, and with whom: a Judaism, as self-evidently valid to Medem as was Orthodoxy to Hirsch.

The joining of yiddishism to socialism finds its best representative in Chaim Zhitlowsky (1865–1943). Lucy S. Dawidowicz describes him as "the example par excellence of the modern radical Jew drawn to non-Jewish intellectual and revolutionary society, yet reluctant, despite his ambivalence toward the Jewish group, to divorce himself from it." Hostile to Judaism as a supernatural religion, Zhitlowsky provided for Yiddish the ideological position as the foundation for the renewal of Jewish culture, parallel to a renewal of the Jewish people along economic lines: "Jews were to become 'productive' and 'nonparisitic' elements in a socialist economy."[14] So Yiddish would serve as the vehicle of national cultural identity, along with socialism as the definition of the entity's organization of its productive life. Yiddish was meant to serve as a weapon in the class war, Dawidowicz points out. Since, in later times, ideologists identified the Jews' participation in socialism—or, in the United States, in liberal politics—as part of their prophetic heritage, it is important to note that that identification, for Zhitlowsky, came much after the fact:

> Did I assimilate this concept of internationalism from our Jewish prophets? True, the best of them first promulgated the pure internationalist ideal of a fraternizing society. . . . But I knew almost nothing of the prophets. We had learned about them in heder, but only incidentally and according to the interpretation of a later Jewry uninterested in such "trivialities." . . . Did my internationalism originate in a Jewish religious world view which reigned in our world of Jewish ideas? . . . First, Jewish religion was of no interest to me . . . the idea of chosenness was conspicuous for its glaring chauvinism. Second, national diversity in the Jewish world view was distorted to mean that Jews differed from Gentiles, but all Gentiles were alike. Third, even nationalism, a basic element of internationalism, was not quite a pure element because it was pervaded with religion.[15]

Any claim, therefore, that the received system took its natural next steps toward socialism finds little proof in Zhitlowsky's memoirs; he is explicit to the contrary. Zhitlowsky found in socialism a road out of the Jewish condition of being victim of anti-Semitism: "For me personally, the idea of cosmopolitanism was for a time like healing balm for the pain I had felt ever since it had been explained to me that we Jews lived a parasitic existence." What struck Zhitlowsky was the need for a language and a literature that would explain to Jews their lives, ideas, hopes, and aspirations, and he sought a socialist theory "that harmoniously united socialist ideals with the problems of Jewish life." Describing a sequence of conversion experiences, he explains that, to carry out his moral responsibility to remain faithful to the Jewish people, he would devote his life to a work of "enlightenment and struggle for those universal foundations of human progress which could be advocated even under Russian censorship":

> The decision to issue the journal [that he founded] in Yiddish did not originate from any conscious Yiddishism. The theoretical works on nationality . . . gave no particular importance to language. . . . My reasoning then went something like this: One must talk to a people in its own language. But our people use two languages, Hebrew and Yiddish. In the world in which I grew up, both languages had the same prestige. . . . The question facing me was to decide in which language to appeal to Jews, not just the ignorant masses, but the whole people, to train an avant-garde to fight for the ideals of universal progress and for their realization in Jewish life. I decided on Yiddish. This was my calculation: We, the carriers of ideas of universal human progress, had to appeal to the people with our message about quite a new world, the world of modern, progressive, West European culture. Vis à vis this world, the whole Jewish people were like the ignorant masses. . . . One had to use the language that everyone understood. That was Yiddish, the vernacular of every Jew.[16]

Zhitlowsky's contribution, therefore, was the advocacy of Yiddish as the instrument of socialism and reform. Critics of his position held that the use of Yiddish would form an obstacle to the assimilation of the Jews. Zhitlowsky, for his part, demanded equal rights for the Jews, as a distinct national group in the Russian empire.[17] These rights would be effected through their sustaining their own national language. Socialism would transform the Jews into part of the working class. The Yiddish language would express their ideals of productive labor and solidarity with humanity. Socialism did not require cosmopolitanism but allowed nations to develop in a multinational community. So Melech Epstein states: "Yiddish literature . . . did not originate in a drawing room. . . . Yiddish literature was a people's art, a conscious medium for uplifting. It carried an impelling social and moral message to the ordinary man and woman."[18]

The Yiddishists found themselves drawn by humanitarian impulses; the Socialists, by a more rigorous theoretical vision. Together they formed a powerful phalanx within Jewry. But did they add up to a Judaism? The Jewish Socialists, in the definition of Mendelsohn, assuredly thought so: They clearly formed a consciousness of "uniquely Jewish needs and dilemmas." They did make the effort to draw on inherited writings, "a past culture which could not be totally denied or repressed," and recognized the need of Jewish workers "to find a Jewish, as well as socialist, identity."[19] Language of this kind points to the formation of a Judaism: a way of life, joined to a world view, addressed to an Israel. The way of life involved union activity and political agitation in causes in no way distinctively Jewish; the world view was taken over from socialism in its eastern European redaction; the Israel was the working class of Jewish origin. Yet Medem and Zhitlowsky found in these components common to all Socialist lives, all socialist systems of thought, the wherewithal for what they regarded as a distinctive doctrine, which accounted for a life particular to Jews: encompassing, ample, adequate to the purpose.

219

Socialism and Yiddishism as a Judaism
of Self-Evidence

The claim that in Jews' particular expression of socialism
we have a Judaism, and that in Jews' framing of the linguistic nationalism of the age we have another, must puzzle
people who take for granted that a Judaism must be a religion. In such a definition of a Judaism, we invoke the classification of religion, then treat Judaism as a subdivision of
that classification, and, within Judaism, diverse Judaisms.
But as we have seen, that conception of matters imposes on
Jews categories alien to their diverse historical and cultural
expressions. Singling out as a distinct and distinctive aspect
of culture something we define as religion violates the classification system of the Judaism of the inherited sort, the
system of the dual Torah, and indicates—by itself—a pecu-
liarly nineteenth-century and Protestant view of matters.
So I have argued in reference to Orthodoxy. That same
stress on a Judaism as a type of a religion, moreover, lays
enormous emphasis on systems of ideas, theology or ideology, since, when we define a religion, we ordinarily focus
upon things people believe, rather than on things they do,
and we treat belief as an aspect of the definition of an individual's world view rather than as the principal component
of a whole society's conceptual basis.

But if we come to matters from the angle of the society—
the particular Israel at hand—we have no difficulty in treating as a Judaism something that in no way constitutes a religion. A Judaism addresses an Israel, and an Israel finds its
self-understanding in the world view of a Judaism, its way
of living as a society in the way of life posited by a Judaism.
Among the three components of a social and cultural system—way of life, world view, and social definition—there-

220

fore, we select the third, not the first two; and when we do, we have no difficulty in understanding why a massive movement made up only of Jews—and that by definition (so to speak!)—should constitute a Judaism. Yiddishism therefore is critical to our understanding of why Jewish socialism and yiddishism constitute a Judaism, just as the Zionist ideal of resurrecting the Hebrew language and the Jewish State makes Zionism—a Jewish movement of national emancipation—into a Judaism. And that view also encompasses the Judaic system of Holocaust and Redemption that today flourishes among American Jews.

Claiming a continuity in values with the received Judaism of the dual Torah, yiddishism, both with and without socialism, to its founders and framers solved important problems. These problems, for those who confronted them, proved urgent and pressing. The way of life—the use of language, the devotion to organizations or to writing or to reading—and the world view, bound up with a particular evaluation of the Jews and their values (one Wisse calls moral hubris[20]), do coalesce and present a cogent and coherent answer to a large and encompassing question. Self-evident? To those who found the question urgent, the answer scarcely demanded argument and apology. It was beyond all doubt a Judaism. But the urgent questions in no way corresponded to those answered by the received system, and the answers originated in other places than the Torah. So in yiddishism and socialism we discern a Judaism out of all relationship with the Judaism of the past, articulately and explicitly alienated from the Judaism of the dual Torah.

Let me cursorily revert to the generative issue, the linear and incremental theory of the history of Judaism. In no way do yiddishism and socialism, severally or jointly, develop in an incremental relationship to the Judaism regnant for fifteen hundred years, and in no way do they mark the natural next step out of that earlier and established system. The difference between this Judaism and the nineteenth-century ones is blatant. First, no one carried out the pretense of claiming continuities that people in any case did not want. And no one found in the received literature more than a set of evocative and useful texts for the persuasion of people who, unlike those who made the selections, responded to the authority and to the values of those words. In contrast, the new Judaisms of the nineteenth century carefully spelled out the continuity between themselves and the inherited system—whether the appeal was to exact replication, as with Orthodoxy; to replication of the ongoing processes by which change may take place, as with Conservative Judaism; or to replication only of the paramount trait of the whole, change itself, as with Reform. Socialism and yiddishism did not trouble to explain how they related to the received Judaism, because, to begin with, their framers proposed to break the ties utterly and completely. Thus, they undertook the labor of shaping and defining a system of their own. And that is precisely what they accomplished. And yet none can deny that they set forth a Judaic system, precisely as they claimed to do. They specified their Israel, the Yiddish-speaking working classes; they worked out their world view, the amalgam of socialist theory and shards and remnants of appropriate sayings; and, above all, they knew just who Israel was. Some would question characterizing socialism and yiddishism as a Judaism, but the framers of the system maintained that we can and should so characterize it. Wisse's excellent critique of the system confirms that, in its founders' view, the union yielded a new entity, but—unlike the Judaisms of the nineteenth century—a born, not a reborn Judaism.[21] It did posit a way of life. It told the founders the meaning of history and linked the individual to the large movement of time.

Here an important qualification requires attention. Jewish socialism and yiddishism lacked staying power. Their way of life served only the first generation of Jewish Socialists and yiddishists, which therefore proved to be a transitional generation. The Judaic system of social action and linguistic preference did not produce a second generation for itself; again, Wisse: "It is not simply that the children of the Yiddishists no longer speak to their children in Yiddish. . . . Yiddishism, which was meant to serve Jewish cohesion, had no . . . self-regenerating powers, and Yiddishkeyt was but a transitional phase in which a secular generation enjoyed the fruits of a religious civilization."[22] But for that first generation, the system did answer the same questions as did other systems. And that is what marks as a Judaism the set of ideas, the doctrine of how life is to be lived, the definition of the Israel at hand. How long a system lasts, where it comes from, where it heads—these form the epiphenomena of description, not the center and heart of analysis. A system serves for as long as it serves, whom it serves, when and where it proves serviceable: a butterfly or a boulder, it hardly matters.

Had the vast populations to whom these mated Judaisms proved self-evidently true survived the Second World War and endured in societies prepared to accommodate them on terms of their own, who knows the terms those populations might have defined for themselves? I, for one, cannot say what might have been had there been no Holocaust, other than to offer one certain judgment: Jewish socialism and yiddishism, in their nature, would have formed the single most powerful force within whatever Judaisms the reconstituted Jews of Poland, Rumania, Hungary—not to mention the lands of the Soviet empire—might have made for themselves. But they are all dead and gone. As to the truth or even the functionality of Jewish socialism and yiddishism, history therefore proves nothing. So we encounter for the first time the leitmotif of the Judaisms of the twentieth

223

and twenty-first centuries: the as yet uncalculated costs, to the living Judaisms, of the death of most of the Jews of Europe. Only as we contemplate the twenty-first century in the retrospective glance at the Judaisms of the twentieth do we grasp something of the terrible cost to Judaic *systemopoeia* (the power to create systems for the formation of a social entity, a term I shall more fully explain in chapter 9) of the murder of the Jews. The charge against the future exacted a toll beyond mere numbers. The living: they die too, today, every day.

CHAPTER 6

ZIONISM: REVERSION TO AN INVENTED PAST

Zionism constituted the Jews' movement of self-emancipation, in response to the failure, by the end of the nineteenth century, of promises of political improvement in their status and condition. Zionism called to the Jews to emancipate themselves by acknowledging that gentiles in general hated Jews, and founding a Jewish state where Jews could free themselves of anti-Semitism and build their own destiny.

Zionism came into existence at the end of the nineteenth century, with the founding of the Zionist Organization in

1897, and reached its fulfillment, and dissolution in its original form, with the founding of the State of Israel in May 1948. Zionism defined, first of all, its theory of Israel: a people, one people, in a secular sense. So Jews all over the world now formed a single entity, not alone (or at all) in God's view, but in humanity's. Then came the world view, which composed of the diverse histories of Jews a single, singular history of the Jewish people (nation), leading from the Land of Israel through exile back to the Land of Israel. Again, this recapitulation of the biblical narrative derived not from a religious but from a nationalist perspective. The way of life of the elitist or activist required participation in meetings, organizing within the local community, attendance at national and international conferences—a focus of life's energy on the movement. Later, as settlement in the Land itself became possible, Zionism defined as the most noble way of living life migration to the Land and, for the Socialist wing of Zionism, building a collective community (kibbutz). So Zionism presented a complete and fully articulated Judaism and, in its day, one of the most powerful and effective of them all.

Since Zionism carried out a political program, its relevance to the study of Judaisms born in modern times requires explanation. For not everything Jews did constituted a Judaism, as I remarked in regard to the Jewish system of socialism. But Zionism did constitute a Judaism. In fact, among the Judaic systems of the twentieth century, Zionism took second place only to Jewish socialism and yiddishism in its appeal to large numbers of Jews. And after the Second World War, Zionism offered the sole explanation for what had happened and what people then should do: a way of life and a world view meeting the ineluctable crisis assigned to it by history. Like Jewish socialism joined with yiddishism, therefore, Zionism supplied a sizable part of the Jews of Europe and America with a comprehensive account of themselves and what they should do with their lives. And that account involved deeply mythic Judaic truths, as we shall see.

True, Zionism forms part of a larger idiom of international and modern life, just as much as does socialism. Zionism takes shape against the "general background of European and Jewish history since the French Revolution ... and the spread of modern anti-Semitism."[1] Not only so, but Zionism also arose "within the milieu of European nationalism." But Zionism bears traits all its own, as Hertzberg points out in his classic account: "All of the other nineteenth-century nationalisms based their struggle for political sovereignty on an already existing national land or language. ... Zionism alone proposed to acquire both of these usual preconditions of national identity by the élan of its nationalist will."[2] Our interest in Zionism, of course, requires a different focus altogether: that is, the analysis of Judaic systems and comparison of one system to another (see chapter 9).

The modern word *Zionism* came into use in the 1890s, connoting a political movement of "Jewish self-emancipation." Since the word *emancipation* had earlier referred to the Jews' receiving the political rights of citizens in various nations, "self-emancipation" turned on its head the entire political program of nineteenth-century Jewry. That shift alerts us to the relationship between Zionism and the political changes of which, at the start of the century, Reform Judaism had made so much. Clearly, the history of the Jews then as earlier would contribute the main themes for emerging Judaisms. But the particular themes of the Zionist system derived from specific events.

Two factors shifted the discourse in the nineteenth century from emancipation to self-emancipation: first, the disappointing persistence of anti-Semitism in the West; second, the disheartening failure to attain political rights in eastern Europe. As a result, Jews began to conclude that they would have to attain emancipation on their own terms and through their own efforts. The stress on Zionism as a political movement, however, came specifically from Theodor Herzl (1860–1904), a Viennese journalist who, in response to the recrudescence of anti-Semitism he witnessed in covering the Dreyfus trial in Paris in 1896, discovered the Jewish problem and proposed its solution. To be sure, Herzl had earlier given thought to the problem of anti-Semitism, and the public anti-Semitism that accompanied the degradation of Alfred Dreyfus marked merely another stage in the development of Herzl's ideas. What he contributed, in the beginning, was the notion that the Jews all lived in a single situation, wherever they were located. They should, then, live in a single country, in their own state (wherever it might be located). Anti-Semitism formed the antithesis of Zionism; and anti-Semites, growing in strength in European politics, would assist the Jews in building a state and thereby also solve their own "Jewish problem."

The solution entailed the founding of a Jewish state—a wholly new conception, with its particular world view and, in the nature of things, its concrete and detailed program for the conduct of the life of the Jews. For the Jews were now to become something they had not been for that "two thousand years" of which Zionism persistently spoke: a political entity. The Judaism of the dual Torah made no provision for a this-worldly politics, and no political tradition had sustained itself during the long period in which that Judaism had absorbed within itself and transformed all other views and modes of life. In founding the Zionist Organization in Basel in 1897, Herzl said that he had founded the Jewish state, and that, in half a century, the world would know it—as, indeed, the world did.

Three main streams of theory flowed abundantly and side

by side in the formative decades. One, represented by cultural Zionists, laid stress on Zion as a spiritual center, to unite all parts of the Jewish people. This "spiritual Zionism" emphasized psychological preparation, ideological and cultural activities, and the long-term intellectual issues of persuading the Jews of the Zionist premises.[3] Another stream, the political one, from the beginning maintained that the Jews should provide for the emigration of the masses of their nation from eastern Europe (then entering a protracted state of political disintegration and already long suffering from economic dislocation) to the land of Israel— or somewhere, anywhere. Herzl in particular placed the requirement for legal recognition of a Jewish state over its location and, in doing so, set forth the policy that the practical salvation of the Jews through political means would form the definition of Zionism. He stressed that the Jewish state would come into existence in the forum of international politics.[4] The instruments of state—a political forum, a bank, a mode of national allegiance, a press, a central body and leader—came into being in the aftermath of the first Zionist congress in Basel. Herzl spent the rest of his life—less than a decade—seeking an international charter and recognition of the Jews' state.

A third stream derived from socialism and expressed a Zionist vision of socialism or a socialist vision of Zionism. The Jewish state was to be socialist—as, indeed, for its first three decades, it was. Socialist Zionism in its earlier theoretical formulation (before its near-total bureaucratization) emphasized that a proletarian Zionism would define the arena for the class struggle within the Jewish people to be realized. Ber Borochov (1881–1917), an ideologist for this Zionism, explained:

> Jewish immigration is slowly tending to divert itself to a country where petty Jewish capital and labor may be utilized in

such forms of production as will serve as a transition from an urban to an agricultural economy and from the production of consumers' goods to more basic forms of industry. . . . This land will be the only one available to the Jews. . . . It will be a country of low cultural and political development. Big capital will hardly find use for itself there, while Jewish petty and middle capital will find a market for its products. . . . The land of spontaneously concentrated Jewish immigration will be Palestine. . . . Political territorial autonomy in Palestine is the ultimate aim of Zionism. For proletarian Zionists, this is also a step toward socialism.[5]

The Socialist Zionists predominated in the settlement of the Land of Israel and controlled the political institutions for three-quarters of a century. They founded the labor unions, the large industries, the health institutions. They controlled the national institutions that were taking shape. They created the press, the nascent army—the nation. No wonder that for the first quarter-century after independence, the Socialist Zionists made all the decisions and controlled everything.

They formed a way of life of a distinctive order, finding their ideal in collective settlements in farming, and expressed a world view entirely their own: the building of an ideal society by Israel, the Jewish nation, on its own land, in agriculture. The Socialist Zionists accepted the Socialist critique of the Jews as a people made up of parasites, not productive workers, and held that the Jews should create a productive society of their own, so that they could enter the arena of the class struggle, which would result in due course in the creation of a classless society. It is a somewhat complicated notion. Socialist Zionism maintained that the Jews had first to constitute an appropriately divided society of classes. This they would accomplish only when they formed their own nation. They had further to enter productive economies and build an economy of their own. Then the Jews would work out the class struggle in terms appropriate to their nation and produce the classless society. The creation of a Jewish national economy then took on importance as the mode of establishing a healthy class struggle; and, above all, physical labor and the development of rootedness in the soil would accomplish that goal. This thesis, then, carried within itself the prescription of the way of life that would lead to the founding of collective farms and the building of a Jewish agricultural life in the Land of Israel.

Zionism as a political movement enjoys its own audience. For our purpose, it is the Zionism that functioned as a Judaism that draws our attention. In this regard, Ahad HaAm made the explicit claim that Zionism would succeed Judaism; so Hertzberg:

> The function that revealed religion had performed in talmudic and medieval Judaism, that of guaranteeing the survival of the Jews as a separate entity because of their belief in the divinely ordained importance of the Jewish religion and people, it was no longer performing and could not be expected to perform. The crucial task facing Jews in the modern era was to devise new structures to contain the separate individual of the Jews and to keep them loyal to their own tradition. This analysis of the situation implied . . . a view of Jewish history which Ahad HaAm produced as undoubted . . . , that the Jews in all ages were essentially a nation and that all other factors profoundly important to the life of this people, even religion, were mainly instrumental values.

Hertzberg contrasts that statement with one made a thousand years earlier, in the tenth century, by the philosopher Saadiah: "The Jewish people is a people only for the sake of its Torah."[6] That statement of the position of the Judaism of the dual Torah contrasts with Hertzberg's on Zionism and allows us to set the one against the other, both belonging to the single classification, a Judaism. For, as is clear, each proposed to answer the same type of question, and the answers provided by each enjoyed that same status of not

231

mere truth but fact, of not merely fact but just and right and appropriate fact.

Herzl's thesis, by contrast to that of cultural Zionism, stressed the power of anti-Semitism to keep the Jews together, and that was the problem the founder of the Zionist Organization proposed to solve. So Ahad HaAm's conception serves more adequately than Herzl's to express a world view within Zionism comparable to the world view of a Judaism. Hertzberg points out that Ahad HaAm described the Jews' "national spirit as an authoritative guide and standard to which he attributed a majesty comparable to that which the religious had once ascribed to the God of revelation." That conception competed with another, which laid stress on the re-creation of the Jews in a natural and this-worldly setting; again, Hertzberg: "a bold and earthy people, whose hands would not be tied by the rules of the rabbis or even the self-doubts of the prophets."[7]

Debates within Zionism focused on the differences between narrowly political Zionists, who wished to stress work in the Diaspora, and cultural Zionists. By the First World War, Zionism had made considerable progress among European Jewry. Then, with the British conquest of Palestine, a statement issued on 2 November 1917—the Balfour Declaration—supplied the charter that Herzl had sought in his lifetime: the British government declared itself to favor a Jewish national home in Palestine, provided that the civil and religious rights of non-Jews in the country were protected. This declaration won the endorsement of other countries, and Zionism began to move from the realm of system formation to the work of nation building. Its three principal theoretical statements had come to expression.

Zionism as Way of Life and World View

Let me return to the analysis of Zionism as a Judaic system. For one thing, Zionism enunciated a powerful doctrine of Israel: the Jews form a people, one people. Given the Jews' diversity, people could more easily concede the supernatural reading of Judaic existence than the national construction given to it. For, scattered across the European countries as well as in the Moslem world, Jews did not speak a single language, follow a single way of life, or adhere in common to a single code of belief and behavior. What made them a people, one people, and further validated their claim and right to a state, a nation, of their own, constituted the central theme of the Zionist world view. No facts of perceived society validated that view. In no way, except for a common fate, did the Jews form a people, one people. True, in Judaic systems they commonly did. But the Judaic system of the dual Torah and its continuators imputed to Israel, the Jewish people, a supernatural status, a mission, a calling, a purpose. Zionism did not: a people, one people—that is all.

Zionism is especially interesting in the context of an inquiry into the theory that imputes to Judaism a single, linear, and incremental history in that Zionist theory, more than yiddishist and socialist, sought roots for its principal ideas in the documents of the received Judaism of the dual Torah. Zionist theory had the task of explaining how the Jews formed a people, one people; and in the study of Jewish history, read as a single and unitary story, Zionist theory solved that problem. The Jews all came from some one place, traveled together, and were going back to that same one place: one people. Zionist theory therefore derived strength from the study of history, much as had Reform Judaism, and in time generated a great renaissance of Judaic

233

studies as the scholarly community of the nascent Jewish state took up the task. The history that emerged took the form of factual and descriptive narrative. But its selection of facts, its recognition of problems requiring explanation, its choice of what mattered and what did not—all of these definitive questions found answers in the larger program of nationalist ideology. So the form was secular and descriptive, but the substance was ideological in the extreme.

At the same time, Zionist theory explicitly rejected the precedent formed by that Torah, selecting as its history not the history of the faith, of the Torah, but that of the nation, Israel construed as a secular entity. Zionism defined episodes as history, linear history, Jewish History, and appealed to those strung-together events—all of a given classification, to be sure—as vindication for its program of action. Thus, a distinctive world view explains a particular way of life and defines for itself that Israel to which it wishes to speak. True, like Reform Judaism, Zionism found the written component of the Torah more interesting than the oral. And in its search for a usable past, it turned to documents formerly neglected or treated as not authoritative—for instance, the book of Maccabees. As we shall see, Zionism went in search of heroes unlike those of the present—warriors, political leaders, and others who might provide a model for the movement's future and for the projected state beyond. Instead of rabbis or sages, Zionism chose figures such as David or Judah Maccabee or Samson. David, the warrior king; Judah Maccabee, who had led the revolt against the Syrian Hellenists; Samson, the powerful fighter—these provided the appropriate heroes for a Zionism that proposed to redefine Jewish consciousness, to turn storekeepers into soldiers, lawyers into farmers, corner grocers into builders and administrators of great institutions of state and government. The Judaism of the dual Torah treated David as a rabbi. The Zionist system of Judaism saw David as a hero in a more worldly sense: a courageous nation builder.

In its eagerness to appropriate a usable past, Zionism—and Israeli nationalism, its heir and successor—dug for roots in the sands of history, finding in archaeology links to the past, even proofs for the biblical record to which, in claiming the Land of Israel, Zionism (in my view, quite rightly and persuasively) pointed. So both before and after the creation of the State of Israel in 1948, Zionist scholars and institutions devoted great effort to digging up the ancient monuments of the Land of Israel, finding in archaeological work the link to the past that the people, one people, so desperately sought. Archaeology uncovered the Jews' roots in the Land of Israel and became a principal instrument of national expression—much as, for contemporary believers in Scripture, archaeology would prove the truths of the biblical narrative. It was not surprising, therefore, that in the Israeli War of Independence (1948–49) and in later times as well, Israeli generals explained to the world that by following the biblical record of the nation in times past, they had found hidden roads, appropriate strategies—in all, the key to victory.

So Zionism framed its world view by inventing—or selecting—a past for itself. Its appeal for legitimation invoked the precedent of history—or, rather, Jewish History—much as had Reform. But Orthodoxy, in its (quite natural) appeal to the past as the record of its valid conduct in the present, produced an argument of the same sort. None of the exemplary figures Zionism chose for itself, of course, served as did their counterpart components in Reform, Orthodox, and Conservative Judaisms, to link the new movement to the received Torah. As I said, Zionism sought a new kind of hero as a model for the new kind of Jew it proposed to call into being. Like socialism and yiddishism, Zionism in its appeal to history was a deliberate act of rejection of the received Torah and construction of a new system altogether. But Zionism found far richer and more serviceable than had socialism and yiddishism the inherited writings, and made more ample use of them. Its particular stress, as time went on, was on the biblical portrait of Israel's possession of the Land of Israel. And the Torah (only in its written form; hence, "the Bible") represented for Zionism, as much as for the Judaism of the two Torahs, the validation of Israel's claim to the Land. But the Torah also contributed a usable past, in place of the one now found wanting; that is, the past made up of the dual Torah's sages and their teachings, on the one side, as well as of their iron control of the politics of the traditional sector of Israel, the people, on the other.

So we should not find surprising the power of Zionism to appropriate those components of the received writings that it found pertinent, and to reshape them into a powerful claim upon continuity—indeed, in behalf of the self-evidence of the Zionist position: the Jews form a people, one people, and should have the Land back and build a state on it. Above all, Zionism found in the writings of the biblical prophets about the return to Zion ample precedent for its program, linking today's politics to something very like God's will for Israel, the Jewish people, in ancient times. Thus, calling the new Jewish city Tel Aviv invoked the memory of Ezekiel's reference to a Tel Aviv, symbolizing much else. No wonder, then, that professors at the Hebrew University of Jerusalem in later times would confuse their own scholarly authority with Isaiah's promise that from Zion, Torah would go forth and from Jerusalem, the word of God. It was a perfectly natural identification of past and present, not an appeal for authority alone to a historical precedent, but, rather, a re-entry into a perfect world of mythic being, an eternal present. Zionism would reconstitute the age of the return to Zion in the time of Ezra and

Nehemiah, so carrying out the prophetic promises. The mode of thought, again, is entirely reminiscent of that of Reform Judaism, which, to be sure, selected a different perfect world of mythic being, a golden age other than the one that to Zionism gleamed so bright.

Yet the continuity should not be overstated. For alongside the search of Scripture, Zionism articulated a clear perception of what it wished to find there. And what it did not find, it deposited on its own: celebration of the nation as a secular, not a supernatural, category; imposition of the nation and its heroism in place of the heroic works of the supernatural God. A classic shift took the verse of Psalms, "Who will retell the great deeds of God" (20:44), and produced, "Who will retell the great deeds of Israel," in a typical example of the profound revisioning of Israel's history accomplished by Zionism. For Israel in its dual Torah (and not, by any means, only in that Judaism) formed a supernatural entity, a social unit unlike any other on the face of the earth. All humanity divided into two parts, Israel and the (undifferentiated) nations. The doctrine of Israel in the Judaism given literary expression in Constantine's day, moreover, maintained that the one thing Israel should not do is arrogant deeds. That meant waiting on God to save Israel, assigning to Israel the task of patience, loyalty, humility, obedience, all in preparation for God's intervention. The earliest pronouncements of a Zionist movement, received in the Jewish heartland of eastern Europe like the tocsin of the coming Messiah, for that same reason impressed the sages of the dual Torah as blasphemy. God will do it—or it will not be done. Considerable time would elapse before the avatars of the dual Torah could make their peace with Zionism, and some of them never did.

The doctrine of Israel joined with well-considered doctrines, competing with those of socialism, on how to solve what was then called the "Jewish problem." That same doctrine told Jews what they should do, which, as in the Socialist case, entailed a great deal of organizing and politicking. The world view, centered on Israel's (potential) nationhood, absorbed much of the idealism of liberal nationalism in the nineteenth century and imparted to it a distinctively Judaic character. So the claim that, in its formative decades, Zionism constituted a Judaism—way of life, world view, addressed to a social group and lived out by that group—certainly accords with the facts of the matter.

The world view of Zionism defined the Jews as a people with a single, linear, continuous history. But Zionism made its choices, within that history, of a past it found congenial and useful. Leaping over the long history of the Exile, which Zionism by definition rejected, the Zionist theorists selected Bar Kokhba, with his heroic war against Rome in the second century of the Common Era, as the final precedent prior to their own time. The Zionist world view then appealed to a unitary history, Jewish History, no less than did Conservative theologians or Reform scholars.

What about its way of life? My personal memories intervene, but before I explain them, let me state the matter in general terms. Upon reaching fulfillment, Zionism described in a simple way the way of life it prescribed: living in the Land of Israel and still, later, building the State of Israel. The world view of Zionism in contemporary times came to coincide with the policies and programs of the government of the State of Israel. But in the beginning, when Zionism fairly laid claim to compete with socialism and yiddishism, on the one side, and the continuator Judaisms of Reform and Orthodoxy, on the other, matters were different. Then Zionism formed a distinctive way of life, to be lived out in the everyday by adherents of the movement, and further taught a particular world view, very much its own, as I have already noted.

Zionism was a movement led by intellectuals—not

scholars, but also not workers. Its earliest members thought about action, debated with pleasure, and grounded their hopes in ideas. Speaking of the Zionist labor movement in what was then Palestine, Anita Shapira characterizes a large sector of the movement: "The labor movement was response to the written word, to education, to dialog. . . . Its faith in the power of words was an integral part of its belief that society could be changed by educating mankind and raising their social consciousness."[8] If I had to select a single activity characteristic of the several Judaisms of the twentieth century, it is the capacity to sit long and talk intensely at meetings.

This brings me to my humble encounter with—to use the idiot language of the age—the bureaucratization of systemic formations. I mean to say that Zionism found its way of life in organizational activity, much as did the other political and mass movements put forth by Judaisms of the twentieth century. In terms of concrete activity, nothing differentiated the Jewish Socialist from the Zionist in Warsaw or New York—except *which* meeting he or she went to. What Zionists did because they were Zionists, that is, was what Socialists did because they were Socialists, what labor unionists did to serve their union, Communists to serve their cause, and on and on. The diversity of world views yielded, in this century, a single way of life—idiomatically expressed, to be sure. Since my father was among the founders of the Zionist District of Connecticut, my earliest memories involve sitting in the car while he attended meetings that never seemed to end. In this regard, we cannot distinguish Zionism from the other twentieth-century Judaisms—and, self-evidently, not only from them!—in the emphasis on people gathering together for wordy debate. We should not miss the power of such activity, its ritual quality, its capacity to express in mundane and undistinguished gesture a deep commitment.

239

Accordingly, Zionism is to be compared with Jewish socialism and yiddishism. As to the former, its way of life encompassed a socialism of its own, as I have already noted, and the Zionist Socialists built a most attractive and distinctive way of life in the kibbutz communities, collective farms, which captured the imagination of world socialism and of Jewry as well. Zionism in its socialist version, furthermore, concurred with socialism that conflict derived from class struggle. National conflicts derived from social tensions, and fraternity between the workers of the peoples will resolve them.[9] The brotherhood of peoples will resolve the Zionist-Arab national conflict, so the Zionist Socialist maintained.

In its competition with yiddishism, Zionism adopted the renewed Hebrew language and made a principal indicator of Zionist loyalty the study of that language, which later became the national language of the Jews of the State of Israel. So, in these two ways, Zionism offered its counterpart to the ways of life posited by the competing movements: the one with its picture of class struggle and regeneration; the other with its doctrine of the language as bearer of values. But Zionism bore within itself traits to which the other movements lacked all counterpart; hence, its enduring power to capture the imagination of the Jewish people.

The Zionist world view explicitly competed with the religious. The formidable statement of Jacob Klatzkin (1882–1948) provides the solid basis for comparison:

> In the past there have been two criteria of Judaism: the criterion of religion, according to which Judaism is a system of positive and negative commandments, and the criterion of the spirit, which saw Judaism as a complex of ideas, like monotheism, messianism, absolute justice, etc. According to both these criteria, therefore, Judaism rests on a subjective basis, on the acceptance of a creed . . . a religious denomination . . . or a com-

munity of individuals who share in a Weltanschauung. . . . In opposition to these two criteria, which make of Judaism a matter of creed, a third has now arisen, the criterion of a consistent nationalism. According to it, Judaism rests on an objective basis: to be a Jew means the acceptance of neither a religious nor an ethical creed. We are neither a denomination or a school of thought, but members of one family, bearers of a common history. . . . The national definition too requires an act of will. It defines our nationalism by two criteria: partnership in the past and the conscious desire to continue such partnership in the future. There are, therefore, two bases for Jewish nationalism—the compulsion of history and a will expressed in that history.

Klatzkin's stress on a "will expressed in history" carries us back to the appeals of Reform and Conservative theologians to facts of history as precedents for faith. Zionism's historicism falls into the same classification of thought. But for the theologians the facts proved episodic and *ad hoc*—mere precedents. Zionists would find it necessary to reread the whole of the histories of Jews and compose of them Jewish History, a single and linear system leading inexorably to the point that, to the Zionist historians, seemed inexorable: the formation of the Jewish State at the other end of time. Klatzkin defined being a Jew not as something subjective but as something objective: "on land and language. These are the basic categories of national being." That definition would lead directly to calling the Jewish state "the State of Israel," and so making a clear statement of the doctrine formed by Zionism of who is Israel. In contributing, as Klatzkin said, "the territorial-political definition of Jewish nationalism," Zionism offered a genuinely fresh world view: "Either the Jewish people shall redeem the land and thereby continue to live, even if the spiritual content of Judaism changes radically, or we shall remain in exile and rot away, even if the spiritual tradition continues to exist."[10]

241

It goes without saying that, like Christianity in its original encounter with the task of making sense of history, so Zionism posited that a new era began with its own formation: "not only for the purpose of making an end to the Diaspora but also in order to establish a new definition of Jewish identity—a secular definition." In this way Zionism clearly stated the intention of providing a world view instead of that of the received Judaism of the dual Torah and in competition with all efforts of the continuators of that Judaism; so Klatzkin: "Zionism stands opposed to all this. Its real beginning is *The Jewish State*, and its basic intention, whether consciously or unconsciously, is to deny any conception of Jewish identity based on spiritual criteria."[11] Klatzkin's was not the only voice. But in his appeal to history, in his initiative in positing a linear course of events of a single kind leading to one goal, the Jewish State, he did express that theory of history that would supply Zionism with a principal plank in its platform. What the several appeals to the facts of history meant is that scholarship dealing with what ("really") happened would define the boundaries for debate on matters of faith. Consequently the heightened and intensified discourse of scholars would produce judgments not on secular facts but on deeply held truths of faith, identifying not correct or erroneous versions of things that happened but truth and heresy, saints and sinners.

Zionism and Israel's Salvation

Zionism offered not merely a political program, solving secular problems of anti-Semitism and political disabilities. It gave to its adherents a vision of a new heaven and a new earth, a salvific way of life and world view, that drew the system closer in overall structure to the more conventionally religious Judaic systems of the nineteenth century. The vision of the new Jerusalem, promised in Isaiah 65:17–19 and 66:22, can help us understand people who have yearned for, and then beheld, the new Jerusalem:

> For behold, I create
> new heavens and a new earth.
> Former things shall no more be remembered
> nor shall they be called to mind.
> Rejoice and be filled with delight,
> you boundless realms which I create;
> for I create Jerusalem to be a delight
> and her people a joy.
> I will take delight in Jerusalem and rejoice in my people;
> weeping and cries for help shall never again be heard in her.
>
> (Isaiah 65:17–19)

> For as the new heavens and the new earth
> which I am making shall endure in my sight,
> says the Lord,
> so shall your race and your name endure.
>
> (Isaiah 66:22)[12]

Any account of Zionism in the context of the new Judaisms of modern times will require a grasp of the mental world of the Zionists who lived out the experience of salvation. For Zionism was a crucial factor in the transition from self-evidence to self-consciousness to a new age of self-evidence.

The creators of the State of Israel, brilliantly described by the great Israeli writer Amos Elon,[13] formed a cadre of romantic messianists who realized their dream and attained their eschaton. Elon's account of the founders is pertinent to American Jewry (as we shall see in chapter 7), for the same Jews who created the State of Israel also created the American Jewish community as we now know it. They were the emigrants from the heartland of world Jewry, the east-European *shtetls* in Poland, Lithuania, the old Austro-Hungarian empire, White Russia, Rumania, and the Ukraine.* Those emigrants, whether to Palestine or to America, endowed their movement with more than this-worldly, rational meaning. They fled not starvation but hell, and their goal was not a better life but the Promised Land. Elon has given us a portrait of two generations of exceptional interest. From the perspective of modern Jewish messianism, it is the first—the founders'—that matters.

We deal with generations of individuals who fall into the classification of heroes and saints, not ordinary men and women. For the founders lived for a cause. They had little in the way of private lives. Theirs was a public task, a public arena. "Few had hobbies; hardly anyone pursued a sport. . . . They pursued and served the idea of Zion Revived. Socialists and Zionist, they were secular rabbis of a new faith of redemption"—so Elon. One cannot improve on his description of these seekers for the new earth and the new heaven: "Resolute and resourceful abroad, at home they often fought one another with a ferocity that seems to characterize the infighting of most revolutions. In their lifetime historical processes normally much longer had shortened sensationally. They had lived their Utopias in their own lives."[15]

And this Utopia was the Jewish State no less. What reasonable man in nineteenth-century Poland could take seriously such a notion, such an aspiration? The condition of the country was pitiful. Why bother?

---

* In this connection, I recommend Raphael Mahler's extraordinarily rich account of the various communities of European Jewry, especially in eastern Europe, in the modern formative period.[14]

The answer was: Because it is time to bother. Again Elon: "Zionism profoundly affected the lives of men. It gave people, thus far powerless and disenfranchised, a measure of power to decide their own fate."[16] And it gave them something to do—a sense that their private lives might be spent in a great, public, and meaningful cause. It further lent to the otherwise inconsequential affairs of small people a grand, even transcendental significance. Zionism means more than messianism; it transformed the worldly and natural to whatever modern, secular man may perceive as the other-other-worldly and supernatural. That is what makes Zionism one of the more interesting movements in the history of religions in the post-archaic epoch.

What has characterized the post-archaic epoch if not faith in the twin myths of secularity and democracy? The latter would open society to all people; the former would make the open society worthwhile. But as Elon writes:

> The crucial experience which lies at the origin of Israel as a modern state was the persecution generated by the failure of emancipation and democracy in Europe. Its myth of mission was the creation of a new and just society. This new society was to be another Eden, a Utopia never before seen on sea or land. The pioneers looked forward to the creation of a "new man." A national renaissance, they felt, was meaningless without a structural renewal of society.[17]

Zionism therefore represents the rejection of modernity, of the confidence of modern man in democracy and—because of Zionism's espousal of a "myth of mission" as a renaissance of society—in secularity. For there is nothing wholly secular about Zionism, and there never was. It is not modern but is, as some say, the first of the postmodern religious movements.

The Zionists, so devoted to that dream, did not take seriously their dependence, in the realization of that dream, on others who spent their lives in the "real" world. Seeing only visions, the Zionists did not perceive that their time to dream was paid for by more practical people, who also wanted a dream—one to be lived by others, to be sure—and who were willing to pay for the right to a fantasy. Elon portrays Baron Edmond de Rothschild (1848–1934), one of the rich patrons of Palestinian Jewry. "He resented his colonists' European clothes and wanted them to wear the local Arab dress; he insisted they observe meticulously the Jewish Sabbath, dietary, and other laws of orthodox Jewish religion, which he himself . . . ignored." Rothschild was the model for American Jewry later: "We shall pay a ransom for the absent soul. In exchange, give us pride, purpose, a trace of color and excitement for unheroic lives. We shall pay you to be the new and courageous Jew—to keep the Sabbath on a dangerous hill, to wear *tefillin* in a tank." Rothschild, too, was one of the founders; he, too, lives on. Elon calls the founders "beggars with dreams."[18] But they were honest brokers of dreams. And what they promised they delivered. In time they invested world Jewry with new purpose, gave meaning to its endurance, promised hope in its darkest hour.

Throughout Elon's account one discovers the evidences of a new rite, a new cult, along with the new myth. The Zionists commonly discarded Jewish names and took Hebrew ones. Elon stresses, however, that the changing of names was not mere routine:

> The Zionist mania for renaming was too widespread to be dismissed as a mere bagatelle. The new names they chose were too suggestive to be ignored as elements in the complicated jigsaw that represents the transient sensibility of an epoch. Names are elementary symbols of identity. They are seldom the heart of the matter, but they often shed a sharp light on where the heart can be found. . . . A Zionist settler, in changing his name

246

from Rachmilewitz to Onn ("Vigor"), was not only Hebraicizing a foreign sound. He was in fact re-enacting a piece of primitive magic, reminiscent of the initiation rites of certain Australian tribes, in which boys receive new names at puberty and are then considered reborn as men and the reincarnation of ancestors.

Likewise, the communities they founded were represented in the minds of some as religious communes:

> David Horowitz [a Zionist pioneer] . . . compared Bittania [a kibbutz] to a "monastic order without God." It was no simple matter to be accepted as a member; candidates passed a trial period, a kind of novitiate. Horowitz likened Bittania to a "religious sect . . . with its own charismatic leader and set of symbols, and a ritual of confessions in public reminiscent of efforts by religious mystics to exorcise God and Satan at one and the same time."[19]

No wonder, then, that the impact of Zionism is to be measured not merely in this-worldly matters.

Zionism did more than create a state, a country, a government: it regenerated a whole people. That the day of Zionism, in the form of which I speak, is past does not mean that the movement is dead. But for the second and third and later generations, the myth, evocative symbols, cult and rites of Zionism had to be revised and reworked. For the initial power of the movement to present a set of self-evident truths leading to necessary and legitimate actions worked itself out in its complete success. That very success explains why we have to speak of Zionism, as a Judaism, in the past tense. It yielded Israeli nationalism, a different composition altogether and, I shall argue in the appendix, not a Judaism at all. But in its day, from 1897 to 1948, Zionism emerged as a powerful movement of salvation and affected women's and men's lives in a more profound way than—if truth be told—Reform, Orthodoxy, and Conservative Judaisms all together.

Zionism as a Judaism of Self-Evidence

The extraordinary success of this Judaism requires explanation. For, as we have seen, the three continuators of the received system of the dual Torah worked out, mainly for intellectuals, certain conflicts between doctrine and contemporary academic dogma. But Zionism changed lives and accomplished its salvific goals. No wonder, then, that it enjoyed the status of self-evident truth to the true believers of the movement—which came, in time, to encompass nearly the whole of the contemporary Jewish world and to affect all the Judaisms of the day. It was, in other words, the single most successful Judaism since the formation, fifteen hundred years earlier, of the Judaism of the dual Torah. The reason for the success of Zionism derives from that very source to which, to begin with, Zionism appealed: history, Jewish History. In a way no one would have wanted to imagine, what happened to Jews—Jewish History—validated the ideology of Zionism, its world view and, furthermore, vindicated its way of life. When the surviving Jews of Europe straggled out of the death camps in 1945, Zionism came forth with an explanation of what had happened and a program to effect salvation for the remnant. Critical to the self-evident truth accorded to Zionism is the historical moment at which Zionism came to realization in the creation of the Jewish state, the State of Israel.

Until the massacre of the Jews of Europe, between 1933 and 1945, and the founding of the State of Israel, three years later, in 1948, Zionism remained very much a minority movement in Jewry. Jewish socialism and yiddishism, in the new nations of eastern Europe, and in the New Deal in American Democratic politics, attracted a far larger part of Jewry; and the former, though not the latter, formed a competing Judaic system in particular. Before 1948, the Jewish

248

population of the Land of Israel/Palestine had scarcely reached half a million, a small portion of the Jews of the world. In the United States and in western Europe, Zionist sentiment did not predominate, even though a certain romantic appeal attached to the pioneers in the Land. Until, indeed, 1967, Zionism constituted one choice among many for Jews throughout the world. Since, at the present time, Jewry nearly unanimously attaches to the State of Israel the status of the Jewish state, affirms that the Jews form a people, one people, concedes all of the principal propositions of Zionism, and places the achievement of the Zionist program as the highest priority for Jewry throughout the world, we may say that today, but not a great many days before, Zionism forms a system bearing self-evident truth for vast numbers of Jews, myself included.

And the truth has endured. Since I have already outlined the reasons for classifying Zionism as a Judaism, it must follow, on the surface at least, that Zionism constitutes a Judaism of self-evidence. Its truths are received as facts; its system—its way of life, involving emphasis on building the land or at least raising money for it through an absorbing round of meetings and activities, and its world view, placing the State at the center of Judaic existence—strikes vast numbers of Jews as self-evidently true, an obvious and ineluctable next step in their history. In that sense at least, it forms an inevitable increment in the history of Judaism as well. Zionism therefore inaugurated a long history for itself, as its competing systems did not. There was a second and a third generation. In America, as Wisse points out, yiddishism served a single generation only.[20] The children understood Yiddish; they spoke English. Yiddish served as a language not of systemic consequence ("ideology") but of nostalgia.

Why did Zionism persuade a second and a third and a fourth generation of Jews, while socialism and yiddishism

249

constituted movements of an essentially transient character? And why did Zionism gain the support—as a set of self-evident truths—of the bulk of Jews in the world? Because Zionism, alone of the Judaisms of the nineteenth and twentieth centuries, possessed the potential of accurately assessing the power of anti-Semitism and its ultimate destiny. Zionism turns out to have selected the right problem and given the right solution (at least, so it now seems) to that problem.

The cheerful prognostications of world brotherhood, characteristic of Reform Judaism and socialism alike, perished; and the Reform Judaism of the nineteenth century lost its hold on even the heirs of the movement. But Zionism faced reality and explained it and offered a program, inclusive of a world view and a way of life, that worked. The power of the Zionist theory of the Jews' existence came to expression not only at the end of the Second World War, when Zionism offered world Jewry the sole meaningful explanation of how to endure; it led at least some Zionists to realize as early as 1940 what Hitler's Germany was going to do. At a meeting in December 1940, Berl Katznelson, an architect of socialist Zionism in the Jewish community of Palestine before the creation of the State of Israel, announced that European Jewry was finished:

> The essence of Zionist awareness must be that what existed in Vienna will never return, what existed in Berlin will never return, nor in Prague, and what we had in Warsaw and Lodz is finished, and we must realize this! . . . Why don't we understand that what Hitler has done, and this war is a kind of Rubicon, an outer limit, and what existed before will never exist again. . . . And I declare that the fate of European Jewry is sealed.[21]

Zionism, in the person of Katznelson, even before the systematic mass murder got under way, grasped that, after the Second World War, Jews would not wish to return to Europe, certainly not to those places where they had flourished for a thousand years; and Zionism offered the alternative: the building, outside of Europe, of the Jewish state.

So Zionism took a position of prophecy and found its prophecy fulfilled. Its fundamental dogma about the character of the Diaspora as Exile was verified in the destruction of European Jewry. And Zionism's further claim to point the way forward proved to be Israel's salvation in the formation of the State of Israel on the other side of the Holocaust. So Katznelson maintained: "If Zionism wanted to be the future force of the Jewish people, it must prepare to solve the Jewish question in all its scope."[22] The secret of the power of Zionism lay in its power to make sense of the world and to propose a program to solve the problems of the age. In its context, brief though it turned out to be, Zionism formed the counterpart, as to power and success and self-evidence, to the Judaism of the dual Torah of the fourth through the nineteenth centuries.

The power of self-evidence of the Zionist system to overcome actualities near at hand is expressed in Amos Elon's remarkable description of the opening days of the first Zionist congress in Basel in 1897:

> The narrow streets of Basel were alive with a strange assortment of people. Students from Kiev, Stockholm, Montepellier, and Berlin, with proud duel slashes across their cheeks. Pious, bearded rabbinical scholars with earlocks mingled with scions of long-assimilated or even baptized families of the West and publishers of obscure little newspapers appearing in Warsaw and Odessa. Neurotic Hebrew poets, who wrote for audiences of a few hundred readers, or spent their lives translating Shakespeare, Goethe, and Homer into Hebrew, came in the hope of reviving their ancient national tongue. There were Romanian and Hungarian businessmen, university professors from Hei-

delberg and Sofia, a Kiev oculist, doctors, engineers, a small sallow Polish shopkeeper, a yellow-bearded Swede, a bespectacled French intellectual, a stiff Dutch banker, a courtly Viennese lawyer, and many journalists from all over the Jewish world, for whom Zionism was the great and sacred work of their lives. . . . All were wearing small blue, seven-cornered shields embossed with twelve red and gold stars and bearing the legend, in German, "The only solution to the Jewish question is the establishment of a Jewish state."[23]

To see these diverse people as "a people, one people" required a vision not of what was, but of what—to be believed—to begin with had to be self-evident. And the power of Zionism was to take that vision and transform it into fact. The whole was given urgency by the emphasis on the reality of anti-Semitism; so Herzl at Basel: "From time immemorial the world has been misinformed about us. That clannishness for which we have been reproached so often and so bitterly was in the process of disintegration just as we were attacked by Anti-Semitism."[24] So, as Elon says, Zionism came into being through a "congress [that] was the first authoritative assembly of the Jewish people since their dispersion under the Roman Empire."[25] The power of Zionism as both system of thought and program of action lay in its capacity to explain events that cried out for explanation.

Anti-Semitism in the early part of the twentieth century, yielding mass murder in the middle—these facts confronted Israel, the Jewish people, with a self-evidence of their own. The strength of Zionism lay in its confronting these preponderant facts of Jewish existence as effectively and as persuasively as the Judaism of the dual Torah had taken up and sorted out the facts of Christian paramountcy through the fifteen hundred preceding centuries. And that is the reason Zionism would dictate the setting in which other Judaisms of the age would work out their systems, in one way or another. History proved Zionism right—

history, not historians. Things that really happened made all the difference—actual events, not scholars' idle and self-indulgent speculation on the meanings and endings of events. In the full light of day, Zionism presented self-evident truth, the one genuinely successful and enduring Judaism in the age of evanescent self-evidence—alas!

CHAPTER 7

THE AMERICAN JUDAISM OF HOLOCAUST AND REDEMPTION

American Judaism, the system of Holocaust and Redemption, encompasses Nazi Germany's murder of six million Jewish children, women, and men between 1933 and 1945, and the creation of the State of Israel in 1948. This Judaic system flourishes in the United States and forms the principal force in the lives of American Jews. The world view stresses the unique character of the murder of European Jews, the providential and redemptive meaning of the creation of the State of Israel. The way of life requires active work in raising money and political support for the State of Israel. Different from Zionism, which held that Jews should live in a Jewish state, this system serves, in particular, to give Jews living in America a reason and an explanation for being Jewish. The complementary experiences of mid-twentieth-century Jewry—the mass murder in death factories of six million of the Jews of Europe and the creation of the State of Israel three years after the end of the massacre—are together seen as providential. The system as a whole presents an encompassing myth, linking one event to the other as an instructive pattern, and moves Jews to follow a particular set of actions, rather than others, as it tells them why they should be Jewish.

Diverse Judaic systems flourish in America. Reform, Conservative Orthodox Judaism, Zionism, the system of the dual Torah in its received and self-evident formulation—all have made their way. Remnants even of Jewish socialism and yiddishism endure. All, by definition, constitute Judaisms in America. But the distinctively *American* Judaism of Holocaust and Redemption is the one that exercises enormous power over the minds and imagination of Jewish Americans.* This distinctively American Judaism further tells them who they are, why they should be Jewish Americans, what they should do because of that mode of identification, and, it goes without saying, who the Jewish group is and how that group should relate to the rest of the world and to history.

By the mid-1980s, a distinctively American expression of Judaism has come to full realization: that is, a set of Judaic systems has come to definition in this country; and those

* A counterpart system of Holocaust and Redemption forms an important component of Israeli nationalism, but it serves a different purpose, explains a different set of facts, answers questions particular to the Israeli context. So that corresponding system, while interesting, makes no contribution to systemic description. Comparison among systems, of course, will have to consider the two species of the common genus at hand.

who have defined them clearly have found effective ways of transmitting, to a fourth and a fifth and a sixth generation, a rooted and ongoing Judaism made in America. Why that fact is noteworthy has now to be spelled out. The first generation (1890–1920), completing its migration and settling down in the 1920s, took for granted that its ways would not continue—as we know because they did not try to preserve Yiddish. As Ruth Wisse has pointed out, the ideology of yiddishism proved transient and unappealing to the children of the Yiddish-speaking immigrants in the United States.[1] The Yiddish language within the first generation gave way to English, often in the home, and with Yiddish went much else that had seemed definitively Jewish in the central and eastern European setting. With the notion that Jews (like other immigrants) must become American, the immigrant generation tended to accept—not always benignly, to be sure—what it perceived as the de-Judaization of its children. The parents kept the dietary taboos; the children did not. The parents practiced distinctively Jewish occupations, dominating only a few fields and absent from most others. The children spread out, so far as they could in the prevailing climate of anti-Semitism and exclusion.

It follows, therefore, that the founding generation of Judaism in America did not define a system of Judaism, let alone a set of such systems, that it imagined it could transmit to the next generation. While that generation contributed in rich and important ways to what the coming generation would inherit and utilize, it defined nothing, except by negative example: the second generation (1920–50) wanted to be American, therefore not Jewish. Judaism as an inherited religious tradition with rich theological insights and a demanding, enduring way of life bore little relevance to the American children of those Europeans who had walked on that path to God and lived by that mode of sanctification. And the immigrants took that fact for granted.

256

The second generation, for its part, accepted more from the founders than it planned. For while explicitly opting for "America" and against "Judaism," it implicitly defined life as a set of contrasts between the Jewish datum of life, on the one side, and everything else, on the other. Being Jewish was what defined existence for the second generation. That fact of life was so pervasive as not to demand articulation, let alone specific and concrete expression. The upshot was that the second generation organized bowling leagues and athletic clubs, rather than prayer circles and study groups. But everyone in the bowling league would be Jewish, as well as being neighbors and friends. The cultural distinctiveness that had characterized the first generation gave way to a Jewishness by association for the second. The associations, whether political or recreational or philanthropic, took for granted that the goal was nonsectarian. Little that proved definitively Jewish would mark the group's collective life. But how nonsectarian could an association become, when all its members lived in pretty much the same neighborhood, pursued the same lines of work, and came from Yiddish-speaking parents? In fact, the community life constructed on the basis of association characteristic of the second generation constituted as a social fact a deeply Jewish mode—if not a Judaic system. It took for granted exactly what the first generation had handed down: that is, the basic and definitive character of being Jewish, whatever that might come to mean for the new generation. The founding generation could not, and rarely tried to, articulate what being Jewish meant. But it imparted exactly the imprint of being Jewish that had become its hope to leave behind. The second generation was American and remained Jewish. More than that the first generation could not imagine.

The second generation did little to found camps, youth programs, schools beyond a perfunctory sort. The institu-

257

tions of the second generation recognized no need to make explicit, through either substantive or symbolic means, their Jewish character. There were few Jewish parochial schools. Jewish community centers did not regard themselves as "community agencies." Jewish philanthropic agencies maintained a high wall of separation between "church (= synagogue)" and "state (= Jewish community)." The result was that little public Jewish money went into Judaic activities of any kind. A great deal went into fighting anti-Semitism and maintaining nonsectarian hospitals. Proof of these contrasting modes of Judaic life is readily seen. Nearly all of the Judaizing programs and activities of the third generation, now received as the norm and permanent, date back only to the decades after the Second World War. Most of the earliest summer camps of Judaic character come from that period, especially camps under religious auspices (as distinct from Zionist and Hebrew ones). The several youth movements got under way in the late 1940s. The Jewish Federations and Welfare Funds in the 1960s fought the battle for a policy of investment in distinctively Jewish programs and activities. They undertook to treat as stylish anything markedly Judaic only from the 1970s. These and equivalent facts point to the passage from the second to the third generation as the age of decisive redefinition.

The factors that account for the shifts between generations begin in one simple, negative fact. The second generation did not need schools or youth groups in order to explain what being Jewish meant. It could rely on two more effective educational instruments: memory and experience. The second generation remembered things that the third generation could scarcely imagine: for example, genuinely pious parents; mothers and fathers who believed God revealed the Torah to Moses at Mount Sinai. But, as I noted earlier, the second generation also came to maturity in an

258

age when America turned against the newest Americans, children of the immigrant wave of 1880 to 1920 (as well as against the oldest Americans, the blacks, who from the mid-1890s suffered the wave of bigotry that would sweep over other Americans a generation afterward). Universities that had been open to Jews before the First World War now imposed rigid quotas against them. More important, entire industries declared themselves off limits to Jewish employment. The fact that the climate of bigotry and exclusion affected others just as much as Jews, so that the excluded minorities comprised a majority of Americans, did little to help excluded Jews.

Far more profound than the experience of personal exclusion was the impact of the rise of political, organized anti-Semitism as an instrument of national policy in Germany, Hungary, Rumania, Poland, and other European countries, with its parallel movements of Jew hatred in the Western democracies. Thus, exclusion from a country club or an executive suite became still more ominous, as the world at large took up the war against the Jews. Jewish immigration was barred when people fled for their lives. In such a setting, Jews scarcely needed to find reasons to associate with each other; the world forced them together. They did not lack lessons on how and why to be Jewish, or on what being Jewish meant. The world defined and taught those lessons with stern and tragic effect. All of the instrumentalities for explaining and propagating Jewishness, created for the third generation—and, in time, by the third generation—would earlier have proved superfluous.

The contrast, then, between the second and the third generations sets up the encounter with a hostile and threatening world, on the one side, against the experience of an essentially neutral and benign one, on the other. For, as I said, the third generation underwent few of the experiences of anti-Semitism—exclusion, vilification, pariahship—that had defined what "being Jewish" meant to the second generation. Yet that contrast between a hostile and a neutral or even benign circumstance proves somewhat misleading. For three other facts contributed to the renaissance of the highly articulated and self-conscious Judaism of Holocaust and Redemption among third-generation Americans of Jewish descent.

The first was the rise of the State of Israel. The second was the discovery not of the murder of nearly six million Jews in Europe but of the "Holocaust." The third was the re-ethnicization of American life: that is to say, the resurgence of ethnic identification among the grandchildren of the immigrant generations, on the one side, and among blacks and other excluded groups that long ago had become American by force, on the other.

That movement of rediscovery of difference responded to the completion of the work of assimilation to American civilization and its norms. Once people spoke English without a foreign accent, they could think about learning Polish or Yiddish or Norwegian once more. It then became safe and charming. My father had the Jewish name Shiyya but bore the American name Samuel. He, of the second generation, called his third-generation son (fourth on the mother's side) Jacob but meant Jack. That was more American—never Jake! The third-generation son named his son Samuel but called him by the Hebrew Shmuel. And that made all the difference (if not to the hapless sons, always bearing a name a generation out of date). Just as the Jewish third generation tried to remember what the second generation had wanted to forget, so the same pattern was exhibited elsewhere. Just as when black students demanded what they deemed ethnically characteristic food, so Jewish students discovered they wanted kosher food, too. Later I will examine the reasons for the self-evidence of the system of Holocaust and Redemption and will return to this matter: the three factors that imparted to the system an absolute facticity. Now we come to the moment when the Judaic system of Holocaust and Redemption came into sharp focus, with its answers to unavoidable questions: Who are we? Why should we be Jewish? What does it mean to be Jewish? How do we relate to Jews in other times and places? What is "Israel," meaning the State of Israel, to us, and what are we to it? Who are we in American society? These and other questions form the agenda for American Judaism.

In order to understand the power and importance of that system, we have to focus upon American Jews of the third generation (1950–80). That generation, no less than the first and second, has continued to see themselves as Jews, to regard that fact as central to their very being, and to persist in that choice. They have held strong convictions about how they would continue to be Jews. Most of them have hoped their children would marry within the Jewish community. Most of them have joined synagogues because they wanted their children to grow up as Jews. Above all, most of them have regarded the fact of being Jewish as of great significance. So American Jews of the third generation have continued to see everyday life in terms different from their gentile neighbors, beginning with the fact that to them, if not to their neighbors, being Jewish has seemed an immensely important fact of life. The words they used to explain that fact, the symbols by which they expressed it, are quite different from those of the Judaism of the dual Torah and its continuators. American Jews spoke, for example, of Jewishness, not of Torah. They were obsessed with a crisis of identity, rather than with the tasks and responsibilities of "Israel." They are deeply concerned with the opinion of gentiles.

In all, they were eager to be Jewish—but not too much so, not so much that they could not also take their place within the undifferentiated humanity of which they fantasized. They confronted a crisis not merely of identity but of commitment, for they did not choose to resolve the dilemma of separateness within an open society. In preferring separateness, they seemed entirely within the archaic realm; in dreaming of an open society, they evidently aspired to a true accomplishment of the early promise of political emancipation (which accounts for the enormous influence of Reform and Conservative Judaisms). The underlying problem was understanding what the ambiguous adjective *Jewish* is supposed to mean when the noun *Judaism* in its received meanings has been abandoned. It was the system of Holocaust and Redemption that answered that question: Who are you? What should you do? What do you make of the other?

The task of analyzing that Judaism now requires a brief exposition in the (by now) usual four steps. First, we need to ask about the context of that Judaism: Where, when, how did it come into being? Second, we require a description of the world view at hand; and, third, we want an account of the way of life as well: What do people do because of the world view that motivates them? Finally, we ask about the basis for my allegation that the system at hand enjoys the status of a Judaism of self-evidence.[2]

The Judaism of Holocaust and Redemption is a creation of the third and fourth generations of Jewish Americans— that is, the grandchildren and great grandchildren of the wave of immigrants who came to the United States in the great migration between 1880 and 1914. The immigrants produced diverse Judaisms. These included socialism and yiddishism, Zionism, a re-expression of that milieu piety I have called, following Katzburg, unselfconscious traditionalism. The boatloads of immigrants of the later nineteenth and early twentieth centuries (between 1880 and 1920, more than three and a half million Jews came to the United States from Russia, Poland, Rumania, Hungary, and Austria) spoke Yiddish all their lives. They pursued a limited range of occupations. They lived mainly in the crowded Jewish neighborhoods of a few great cities. The facts of language, occupation, and residence reinforced their separateness. Their several Judaisms then explained it. In this period, moreover, other immigrant groups, together with their churches, likewise came to constitute tight enclaves of the old country in the new.

The children of the immigrants—that is, the second generation in America—adopted the American language and American ways of life. This generation's Judaisms included Conservative Judaism, which thrived in the areas where the second generation moved, as well as Reform Judaism, which the children of the immigrants vastly changed in character and definition. Zionism exercised a great attraction for a portion of that generation as well. The second generation grew up and lived in a period of severe anti-Semitism at home and in Europe, especially in the 1930s and 1940s. While trying to forget the immigrant heritage, the second generation found the world a school for Jewish consciousness, and that of a distinctively negative sort. They did not have to go to class to learn what it meant to be a Jew. Excluded, vilified, placed in a pariah caste (among many pariah castes of the time), Jews learned their lessons in the streets and marketplaces. Coming to maturity in the Great Depression and the Second World War, the second generation did not have to decide whether to "be Jewish," nor were many decisions about what "being Jewish" demanded of them.

That set of decisions, amounting to the framing of a situation of genuine free choice, awaited the third generation, reaching its maturity after the war. This generation found little psychological pressure, such as had faced its predecessors, in favor of "being Jewish." Surveys of anti-Semitic opinion turned up progressively diminishing levels of Jew hatred. More important, while the second generation had strong memories of Yiddish-speaking parents and lives of a distinctively Jewish character, the third generation in the main had not. For in line with the Wisconsin historian Marcus Lee Hanson's law, which says that the third generation wants to remember what the second generation tried to forget,[3] the second generation made a vigorous effort to forget what it knew. The third generation had to make a decision to learn what it did not know—indeed, what it had no natural reason, in upbringing and family heritage, to know.

American Judaism as we know it today is the creation of that third generation, the result of its conscientious effort to remember what its parents equally deliberately forgot. The decision was made in a free society and represented free and uncoerced choice. So the third generation forms the first generation of Judaism in a long sequence of centuries to have the right to decide in an open society whether to be Jewish. More interesting, it is the first generation to define for itself what "being Jewish" would consist of, and how Judaism, as an inherited and received religious tradition, would be taken over as part of this definition. Its Judaism is the system of Holocaust and Redemption. But the questions to which the Judaic system of Holocaust and Redemption provided self-evidently valid answers proved urgent and ineluctable to third- and fourth-generation American Jews, speaking to the world as they experienced it, answering the questions they could not avoid.

To show how the third generation of American Jews defined for itself a distinctive and fresh Judaic system—that is, a world view and a way of life serving a distinct social group or class—we must recall a striking contrast: that is, between the state of Judaism at the point when the second generation (1920–50) had defined matters, with the equivalent condition of Judaism for the third generation (1950–80) thirty years later; hence, the Judaism of the 1940s and

1950s with the Judaism of the 1970s and 1980s. By the end of the Second World War, the second generation had left a sizable set of community institutions, but these tended to emphasize the nonsectarian and to neglect the Judaic. So the hospitals were strong; the Jewish schools, weak. There were few Jewish parochial schools. Jewish youth movements were just getting under way. The second generation did not think it had to perpetuate Judaism (whatever it can have meant by the word) in schools and youth programs. By the 1970s and 1980s, there had evolved a vast network of educational activities in Judaism, both formal and informal. There are, for example, camps devoted to the use of the Hebrew language in both prayer and everyday activities, youth groups, programs of Judaic interest in Jewish community centers. A system of Judaic schooling based on afternoon and Sunday sessions now competes with the more intensive all-day schooling of Jewish parochial schools, many under Orthodox, some under Conservative, auspices. The third generation clearly relies on education and wishes to develop a distinctive and markedly Judaic character for itself (whatever the indicators of "Judaic" may be).

The organized Jewish community in its philanthropic activities invests sizable sums in Judaic activities, youth programs, camps, and formal schooling. The religious observances of classical Judaism in Orthodox, Conservative, and Reform modes reach beyond the synagogue into the home, on the one side, and into formal community programs, on the other. Important historical events, such as the destruction of the Jews of Europe (the "Holocaust," in English; *Shoah*, in Hebrew), receive massive community attention and commemoration. Even through a program of quasi-religious pilgrimage, in the form of study trips to the Holy Land, the State of Israel attracts sizable proportions of the community, old and young. Jewish organizations of an

265

other-than-religious orientation (it is difficult to regard them as wholly secular) undertake these travel programs, generally imparting to them a strong religious-educational aspect. These same supposedly secular organizations include in their programs decidedly religious study sessions, in which the Hebrew Scriptures and other Judaic texts or events of sacred history play an important role. Surveys of religious observance confirm a fairly broad level of popular participation in at least some Judaic rites—for example, the Passover Seder—though many other rites have become mere curiosities.

Finally, alongside the neo-Judaic activism of the third generation has come the foundation, in the American Jewish community, of a quite distinct generation: a new first generation, made up of survivors of the European catastrophe who came to the United States in the late 1940s and early 1950s, with yet more recent immigrants from the State of Israel and Oriental countries, on the one side, and the Soviet Union, on the other. This new first generation, beginning with its own history, has founded a broad range of vigorously Orthodox institutions and created a separate life for itself, in which Judaism as a classical religion defines the affairs of culture and society in every detail. The new first generation has had a deep impact on the orthodoxy of the third generation. This brings us to the substance of the Judaism at hand—first, the world view; then, the way of life.

The World View of Holocaust and Redemption Judaism

A Judaism may bear its world view in the form not of theological propositions but of myth, a mode of conveying deep truth and abiding meaning in the form of a story. Let me recount the salvific story of Holocaust and Redemption as it is nearly universally perceived by American Jews. I refer to the reading of the experience of the community as a whole: that is, to how the myth sees things. But the power of the myth, the story at hand, profoundly grips not those about whom the story is told, but those for whom the story has meaning. So we speak of a long past, but mean the present. (I tell it in the masculine gender, but women could rightly add yet other dimensions of exclusion and alienation—from normal education and careers, for example.) But here is how the story goes:

Once upon a time, when I was a young man, I felt helpless before the world. I was a Jew, when being Jewish was a bad thing. As a child, I saw my old Jewish parents, speaking a foreign language and alien in countless ways, isolated from America. And I saw America—dimly perceived, to be sure—exciting and promising, but hostile to me as a Jew. I could not get into a good college. I could not aspire to medical school. I could not become an architect or an engineer. I could not even work for an electric utility.

When I took my vacation, I could not go just anywhere, but had to ask whether Jews would be welcome, tolerated, embarrassed, or thrown out. Being Jewish was uncomfortable. Yet I could not give it up. My mother and my father had made me what I was. I could hide, but could not wholly deny, not to myself even if to others, that I was a Jew. And I could not afford the price in diminished self-esteem of opportunity denied, aspiration deferred, and insult endured. Above all, I saw myself as

267

weak and pitiful. I could not do anything about being a Jew nor could I do much to improve my lot as a Jew.

Then came Hitler and I saw that what was my private lot was the dismal fate of every Jew. Everywhere Jew hatred was raised from the gutter to the heights. Not from Germany alone, but from people I might meet at work or in the streets I feared that being Jewish was a metaphysical evil. "The Jews" were not accepted, but debated. Friends would claim we were not all bad. Enemies said we were. And we had nothing to say at all.

As I approached maturity, a still more frightening fact confronted me. People guilty of no crime but Jewish birth were forced to flee their homeland, and no one would accept them. Ships filled with ordinary men, women, and children searched the oceans for a safe harbor. And I and they had nothing in common but one fact, and that fact made all else inconsequential. Had I been there, I should have been among them. I, too, should not have been saved at the sea.

Then came the war and, in its aftermath, the revelation of the shame and horror of holocaust, the decay and corrosive hopelessness of the displaced-person camps, the contempt of the nations who would neither accept nor help the saved remnants of hell.

At the darkest hour came the dawn. The State of Israel saved the remnant and gave meaning and significance to the inferno. After the dawn, the great light: Jews no longer helpless, weak, unable to decide their own fate, but strong, confident, decisive.

And then came the corrupting doubt: If I were there, I should have died in hell, but now has come redemption and I am here, not there.

How much security in knowing that if it should happen again I shall not be lost. But how great a debt paid in guilt for being where I am and who I am!

This story gives meaning and transcendence to the petty lives of ordinary people. The story recapitulates the most profound traits of myths capable of nearly universal appeal. It forms a Judaic example of the myth of the darkness followed by the light; of passage through the netherworld and past the gates of hell; then, purified by suffering and by blood, into the new age. The myth conforms to the supernatural structure of the classic myths of salvific religions from time immemorial.

And well it might, for a salvific myth has to tell the story of sin and redemption, disaster and salvation, the old being and the new, a vanquishing of death and mourning, crying and pain, the passing away of former things. This is the myth—the narrative expression of the world view—that shapes the mind and imagination of American Jewry, supplies the correct interpretation and denotes the true significance of everyday events, and turns workaday people into saints. This is the myth that transforms commonplace affairs into history, makes writing a check into a sacred act. So the generations that lived through disaster and triumph, darkness and light, understand the world in terms of a salvific myth. The generations that have merely heard about the darkness but have daily lived in the light take for granted the very redemption that lies at the heart of the salvific myth.

So much for the Holocaust, transformed from the mundane murders of millions into a tale about cosmic evil, unique and beyond all comparing. We come to the other half, the Redemption, which is symbolized by the use of the word *Israel*, the State of Israel, the Jewish state. The Holocaust formed the question; Redemption in the form of the creation of the State of Israel, the answer. It is that simple.

Nearly all American Jews identify with the State of Israel and regard its welfare as more than a secular good—a metaphysical necessity: the other chapter of the Holocaust. Nearly all American Jews are not only supporters of the State of Israel but also regard their own "being Jewish" as inextricably bound up with the meaning they impute to the Jewish state. I do not mean to suggest that American Judaism constitutes a version of Zionism. Zionism maintains that Jews who do not live in the Jewish state are in exile.

There is no escaping that simple allegation, which must call into question that facile affirmation of Zionism central to American Judaism. Zionism further declares that Jews who do not live in the State of Israel must aspire to migrate to that nation or, at the very least, raise their children as potential emigrants. On that position, American Judaism chokes. Zionism, moreover, holds that all Jews must concede—indeed, affirm—the centrality of Jerusalem, and of the State of Israel, in the life of Jews throughout the world. Zionism draws the necessary consequence that Jews who live outside the State of Israel are in significant ways less "good Jews" than those who live there. Now all of these positions—commonplace in Israeli Zionism and certainly accepted, in benign verbal formulations to be sure, by American Jews—contradict the simple facts of the situation of American Jews and their Judaism. First, they do not think that they are in exile: Their Judaism makes no concession on that point. Second, they do not have the remotest thought of emigrating from America to the State of Israel— even though on ceremonial occasions they may not protest when Israelis declare that to be their duty. Third, they may similarly make a ritual obeisance to the corollary that the Diaspora in general, and the mighty community of American Jews in particular, are peripheral and unimportant.

But scarcely a single important component of Zionism in its own systemic formulation is critical of the way of life of the system of American Judaism. American Judaism absorbs and reworks for its own systemic purposes the creation of the State of Israel. American Judaism is not a Zionism. For Zionism always insisted, and the State of Israel today maintains, that immigration to the State of Israel forms the highest goal—indeed, the necessary condition— for true Zionism. And nearly six million American Jews, including a great many deeply engaged by the Judaic system at hand, presently exhibit not the slightest intention of migrating anywhere, though they may gladly pay visits. But that is not Zionism. So what way of life does give substance to the doctrine? And how does a story of a tragedy of incalculable sorrow on one continent, finding a happy ending in the creation of a new nation on a second continent, find so deep a meaning for Jews living two oceans away, on yet a third continent? That seems to me the analytical fulcrum of the Judaism of Holocaust and Redemption: Why the formation of Jewish Americans? Whence the power of self-evidence to people utterly alien—in their personal lives—to the experiences by which they interpret their existence?

The Way of Life of Holocaust and Redemption Judaism

Let me begin once again with an individual and ask what he or she does to carry out in everyday life the expectations of the world view at hand. This is a Judaism that makes an ample place for women, so we take account (at last) of that fact. American Judaism is the first Judaic system that consistently accords to women a place of prominence.

Before us stands the president of a federation or a synagogue or a Hadassah chapter. He or she has devoted most of his or her spare time—and much time that could not be spared—to raising funds for these and similar good causes for twenty years or more. If a woman, she has given up many afternoons and nights to the business of her organization, attended conferences of states, of regions, and of "national," badgered speakers to speak for nothing and merchants to contribute to rummage sales, and all for the good cause. If a man, he has patiently moved through the chairs

271

of the communal structure, on the board of this client agency, president of that one, then onward and upward to lead a "division" of a "campaign," then to head a campaign, to sit on the board. Above all, both men and women have found for their lives transcendent meaning in the raising of funds for Jewish causes.

Mr. President, Madam Chairman—both have exhibited not only selflessness but also iron determination. They have enjoyed the good conscience of those for whom the holy end justifies all legitimate secular means. They have worked for a salvation of which they were certain—a salvation that was, despite appearances, not of this world. The makers of American Judaism have seen a vision and kept alive its memory. They have dedicated their lives to the realization of their holy vision, just as much as the students of Torah in another place and time gave their lives to the study of Torah—for all, a salvific enterprise, an exercise in the realized eschaton, in heaven on earth. They did not see their lives as trivial, their works as unimportant, because their lives were spent on significant things. Not for them the beaches of Florida, the gambling tables of Nevada. Their works were for a sacred goal. Superficially, these claims seem extravagant. What transcendent importance is to be located in the eleemosynary activities of the mattress makers' division of the local Federation of Jewish Philanthropies, devoted to raising money for the State of Israel and domestic Jewish purposes as well? Of what salvific consequence the leisure-time activities of a pants manufacturer in Hoboken? What great goals are perceived by men who spend their lives filling holes in teeth, litigating negligence claims, or running a store? How has Madam Chairman attained the end of days merely by meeting her quota? These are the four questions confronting an interpretation of the Judaism of Holocaust and Redemption.

What do devotees of the Judaic system of American Judaism actually do to deserve my commendation as people who do things that save the world? Well, for one thing they engage in a life of organizing for the accomplishment of good works. They raise vast sums of money for domestic and overseas support. For one example, in addition to their work of sustaining their community here at home and also a myriad of philanthropic activities in Jewish communities abroad and in the State of Israel, they select particular poor neighborhoods in Israeli towns: these they make their own, through visits and personal concern. Again, since political action forms a vital part of support for the State of Israel, they work hard in political affairs, seeking friends for the Jewish community and the State of Israel. In so doing, they undertake selfless commitments that demand much of their energy and time: they are women and men who live for others. That I think to be the measure of a transcendent goal, a life devoted to improving that part of the human condition for which they feel responsibility. And the great goal is to preserve the safe place for Jews to live out their lives—if they need it. In many ways, these Jews every day of their lives relive the terror-filled years when European Jews were wiped out—*and every day they do something about it.* It is as if people spent their lives trying to live out a cosmic myth and, through rites of expiation and regeneration, accomplished the goal of purification and renewal. Highfalutin language for humble deeds? True. But appropriate words as well.

The participants in American Judaism rightly claim to have helped improve the world. But they themselves claim to be more than merely good and useful people. They see themselves as engaged in serving a cause of salvific valence, whose righteousness confers upon them enviable certainty, a sense of worth beyond doubt or measure. These saints are as certain of their vision of the world—a vision of the work of redemption following the near-victory of evil—as were the sages of the olden days. Enjoying the certainty of a self-validating vision of the world, possessed of the security derived from the right understanding of perceived history, illuminated by an all-encompassing view of Jewish realities, these men and women are the saved. What characterizes group life in modern times is the development of specialists for various tasks, the organization of society for the accomplishment of tasks once performed individually and in an amateur way, the growth of professionalism, the reliance upon large institutions. So, as I said in the prologue to part III, it is not surprising that the way of life of Zionism, socialism and yiddishism, and American Judaism should have in common a single type of activity. The way of life of American Judaism, like that of the other Judaisms of the twentieth century, requires joining and supporting organizations—thus what is called the "culture of organizations."

The Self-Evidence of Holocaust and Redemption Judaism as a Judaism

The world view and the way of life of Holocaust and Redemption Judaism persuade participants prior to, and without, sustained argument. The world view so closely corresponds to, and yet so magically transforms and elevates, reality that people take vision and interpretation for fact. They do not need to believe in or affirm the myth, for they know it to be true. In that they are confident of the exact correspondence between reality and the story that explains reality: they are the saved, the saints, the witnesses to the end of days. "We know this is how things really were and what they really meant."

274

Among the Jews, three factors reinforced one another in turning the Judaism of Holocaust and Redemption into a set of self-evident and descriptive facts, truths beyond all argument: the Six Day War of 1967, the re-ethnicization of American life, and the transformation of the mass murder of European Jews into an event of mythic and world-destroying proportions.

Why date the birth of the Judaism of Holocaust and Redemption so precisely at the 1967 war? People take as routine the importance of the State of Israel in American Jewish consciousness. But in the 1940s and 1950s, American Jewry had yet to translate its deep sympathy for the Jewish state into political activity, on the one side, and the shaping element for local cultural activity and sentiment, on the other. So, too, the memory of the destruction of European Jewry did not right away become "the Holocaust," as a formative event in contemporary Jewish consciousness. In fact, the re-ethnicization of the Jews could not have taken the form it did—a powerful identification with the State of Israel as the answer to the question of the Holocaust—without a single, catalytic event.

That event was the 1967 war between the State of Israel and its Arab neighbors. When, on 5 June, after a long period of threat, the dreaded war of "all against one" began, American Jews feared the worst. Six days later, they confronted an unimagined outcome, with the State of Israel standing on the Jordan River, the Nile, and the outskirts of Damascus. The trauma of the weeks preceding the war, when the Arabs promised to drive the Jews into the sea and no other power intervened or promised help, renewed for the third generation the nightmare of the second. Once more the streets and newspapers became the school for being Jewish. On that account, the Judaism in formation took up a program of urgent questions—and answered them.

In the trying weeks before 5 June 1967, American Jewry

275

relived the experience of the second generation and the third. In the 1930s and 1940s, the age of Hitler's Germany and the murder of the European Jews in death factories, each day's newspaper brought lessons of Jewish history. Each Jewish man and woman knew that were he or she in Europe, death would be the sentence on account of the crime of Jewish birth. And the world was then indifferent. No avenues of escape were opened to the Jews who wanted to flee, and many roads to life were deliberately blocked by anti-Semitic foreign-service officials. In 1967, the Arab states were threatening to destroy the State of Israel and murder its citizens. Again the Israelis turned to the world. The world again ignored Jewish suffering, and a new "Holocaust" impended. But now the outcome was quite different. The entire history of the century came under a new light. A moment of powerful and salvific weight placed into a fresh perspective everything that had happened from the beginning to the present.

The third generation now had found its memory and its hope, as much as Zionism had invented a usable past, as socialism in its Jewish formulation a viable future. This generation could now confront the murder of the Jews of Europe, along with its parents' and its own experience of exclusion and bigotry. No longer was it necessary to avoid painful, intolerable memories. Now what had happened had to be remembered, because it bore within itself the entire message of the new day in Judaism: that is to say, putting together the murder of nearly six million Jews of Europe with the creation of the State of Israel transformed both events. One became the "Holocaust," the purest statement of evil in all of human history. The other became salvation in the form of the "first appearance of our redemption" (as the language of the Jewish prayer for the State of Israel has it). Accordingly, a moment of stark epiphany captured the entire experience of the age and imparted to it that meaning and order that a religious system has the power to express as self-evident. The self-evident system of American Judaism, then, for the third generation encompassed a salvific myth deeply and personally relevant to its devotees. That myth made sense at a single instant equally of both the world and the self, of what the newspapers had to say, and of what the individual understood in personal life.

The distinctively American form of Judaism described here clearly connects to the Judaism of the dual Torah, but is not at all continuous with it. American Judaism draws upon some of the received religious tradition and claims to take up the whole of it. But in its stress upon the realization, in the here and now, of ultimate evil and salvation, and in its mythicization of contemporary history, American Judaism offers a distinctively American—therefore, a new and unprecedented—reading of the received tradition. This is so by definition. For when Jews have come to speak of fully realized salvation and an end of history, the result has commonly proved to be a new religion, connected to, but not continuous with, the received religion of Judaism. So when we ask why the Holocaust plays so provocative a role in the imaginative and social life of American Judaism, and what the importance accorded to that corpus of symbols and stories reveals to us about the character of American Judaism and Jews, the answer is clear.

Specifically, we ask what urgent questions find their answers in the system at hand. To answer, we have to turn back, once more, to an earlier period, prior to the public recognition of the self-evidence of the Judaism of Holocaust and Redemption. From 1945 to about 1965, the Holocaust was subsumed under the "problem of evil." The dominant theological voices of the time did not address themselves to "radical evil" and did not claim that something had happened to change the classical theological perspective of Judaism. The theologians of the day wrote not as if nothing had happened, but as if nothing had happened to impose a new perspective on the whole past of Jewish religious experience. To be sure, the liberal, world-affirming optimism of the old theological left was shaken. But the Holocaust was part, not the whole, of the problem. The evil of humanity in conventional rhetoric came to realization in more than that one way. Indeed, few called to mind the murder of European Jewry, and the Holocaust did not yet exist.

Clearly, between the end of the 1950s and the beginning of the 1970s, an experience had happened so fundamental as to impart to the massacre of European Jewry a symbolic meaning, self-evident importance, and mythic quality. What happened, I think, was a sequence of events, some general, some particular to the Jews: the assassination of President Kennedy in 1963, the disheartening war in Southeast Asia in the 1960s and early 1970s, and a renewed questioning of the foundations of religious and social polity. "Auschwitz" became a Jewish code word for all the things everyone was talking about, a kind of Judaic key word for the common cause. People found certain problems: the tragic murders of political leaders—John and Robert Kennedy and Martin Luther King in particular—the unwanted war in Vietnam, unrest in the black ghettos, a whole host of national disappointments added up to a malaise. "Auschwitz" stood for everything troubling everybody, but made it all particular to the Jews. That—and nothing more. The Jewish theologians who claim that from Holocaust events one must draw conclusions essentially different from those reached after the destruction of the Second Temple, or after other tragic moments, posit that "our sorrow is unlike any other, our memories more searing." But they say so in response not to the events of which they speak, but through those events, to a quite different situation—their own.

278

What turned a historical event into a powerful symbol of contemporary social action and imagination was a searing shared experience. As I said, for millions of Jews, the dreadful weeks before the 1967 war gave a new vitality to the historical record of the years from 1933 to 1945—the war and its result. But the story of the extermination of European Jewry could not serve as the foundation for a usable myth of "Holocaust" without one further component. No myth is serviceable if people cannot make it their own and through it explain their own lives; no story of a life can end in gruesome death. A corollary of "Holocaust" had, therefore, to be redemption. The extermination of European Jewry could become *the* Holocaust only on 9 June when, in the aftermath of a remarkable victory, the State of Israel celebrated the return of the people of Israel to the ancient wall of the Temple of Jerusalem. On that day the extermination of European Jewry attained the—if not happy, at least viable—ending that served to transform events into a myth, and to endow a symbol with a single, ineluctable meaning.

But this is still only part of the story. For, once the myth of the Holocaust had taken shape, its suitability for the purpose of the social imagination still had to be fully exposed. It had to explain more than itself; it had to speak to more people, about more things, than it had at the outset. Certainly American Jews and Israeli Jews could not interpret the Holocaust in the same way and for the same purpose without doing violence to the distinctive context in which each group makes its life. As is now clear, the Judaism of Holocaust and Redemption falls into the category of the public, civil religion of American Jews. It serves the same function in the State of Israel, but there is an important difference: context and congruence. And when we address that difference, we see the basis for the self-evidence of the Judaism before us.

Let us start with the Israeli side, which shows the particularity of the Judaism of Holocaust and Redemption to Jewish Americans and their world. The place of "the Holocaust" in the civil religion of the State of Israel is easy to understand: it forms a critical element in the public explanation of why there must be a State of Israel, why it must be of its present character and not some other, and why every citizen must be prepared to support the state in peacetime and to fight for it in war. The state, then, forms the complement of the Holocaust, completing and rendering whole that sundered, pained consciousness represented by the humiliation and degradation of the event itself. For Israelis, the myth of "Holocaust and Redemption" provides that core of common truth on the foundation of which a society can be built. That to Israelis it is self-evidently a true myth goes without saying.

For American Jews, then, the myth of "Holocaust and Redemption" must prove puzzling. They have not drawn the parallel conclusion—that America is that refuge and hope the European Jews should have had—because America was there in the 1930s and 1940s and yet offered no refuge and no hope. They could not declare this country to have contributed a fundamentally new chapter to the history of the Jewish people—at least not in the way in which Israelis declared the foundation of the State of Israel to have inaugurated a new and wholly fresh era. Insofar as the myth of "Holocaust and Redemption" enters into the self-understanding of American Jewry, it has to answer different questions from those posed by the creation of a state and the sustenance of a society.

As is clear from my reference to the murder of President Kennedy and his brother, the tragedy of Southeast Asia, and the unrest in the United States that marked the 1960s and early 1970s, I am inclined to see the questions answered by American Judaism as two separate and distinct ones: the first addressed to the particular world of the Jews; the second, to the world at large. The first question is, Why should I be different; why should I be Jewish? The second is, How should I relate to the world at large? The Judaism of Holocaust and Redemption made available a powerful and critical experience in answer to the question of why be Jewish: because you have no choice. That same Judaism explained that "Israel" should relate to the world at large in its own state and nation overseas—and in its distinctive and distinct communities at home. So the two questions answered by American Judaism speak to the inner world and to the policy toward the outer world as well.

But the two questions are not unrelated: both of them emerge from the special circumstances of the American of Jewish origin whose grandparents or great-grandparents immigrated to this country. For that American Jew, there is no common and acknowledged core of religious experience by which "being Jewish" may be explained and interpreted. Because anti-Semitism as a perceived social experience has become less common than it was from the 1920s through the early 1950s, there is also no common core of social alienation to account for the distinctive character of the group and explain why it continues, and must continue, to endure. Indeed, many American Jews, though they continue to affirm their Jewishness, have no clear notion of how they are Jewish, or what their Jewish heritage demands of them. Judaism is, for this critical part of the American Jewish population, merely a reference point, one fact among many. For ideologists of the Jewish community, the most certain answer to the question of the third generation must be: "There is no real choice." And the Holocaust provides that answer: "Hitler knew you were Jewish."

The formative experiences of the Holocaust are now immediately accessible through emotions unmediated by sentiment or sensibility. No person can encounter the events of 1933 to 1945 without entering into them in imagination.

281

It is better to understate the matter. The experience of the Holocaust did not end in 1945: it ends when I wake up in the morning, and is renewed when I go to sleep. And so it is for all of us. These "Judaizing experiences," then, take the place of Sinai in nurturing an inner and distinctive consciousness of "being Jewish." So the first of the two questions before us, the inner one, is the question of who we are, and why we are what we are and not something else. "The Holocaust" is made to answer that question.

The second is a social question. Let me phrase it in the discourse of the people who participate: Who are we in relationship to everybody else? The utility of the Holocaust in this context is not difficult to see. For example, the television counterpart to the movie *Holocaust* was *Roots*. It follows that, for American Jews, the Holocaust is that ethnic identity that is available to a group of people so far removed from culturally and socially distinctive characteristics as to be otherwise wholly "assimilated." The Holocaust is the Jews' special thing: it is what sets them apart from others while giving them a claim upon those others. That is why Jews insist on the "uniqueness of the Holocaust." If blacks on campus have soul food, the Jews will have kosher meals—even if they do not keep the dietary laws under ordinary circumstances. Unstated in the simple equation *Roots* = *Holocaust* is the idea that being Jewish is an ethnic, not primarily a religious, category. For nearly a century, American Jews have persuaded themselves and their neighbors that they fall into the religious—and therefore acceptable—category of being "different," and not into the ethnic—and therefore crippling and unwanted—category of being "different." Now that American Jews have no Jewish accent, they are willing to be ethnic.

So a profound inner dilemma and a difficult matter of social differentiation and identification work themselves out within the myth of "Holocaust." As to the "Redemption" chapter of the story, the State of Israel tells the same truths to American as it does to Israeli Jews. But since American Jews do not, and cannot, infer the same consequences from that story of redemption that Israeli Jews must infer, a certain incongruence has arisen between the two versions. After all, it is difficult to speak much about a redemption that we do not really wish to experience. A salvation that works for others and not for oneself is, in the end, not of much value. Thus the Holocaust part of the myth tends to play a larger part in this country than it does in the State of Israel.

The human dimension of the Judaic system of Holocaust and Redemption finds its measure in the America of the 1960s, 1970s, and 1980s. Third-generation American Jews found in the continuator Judaisms of the synagogue something conventional and irrelevant. To make of those Judaisms the model for viable life—an explanation of the world, an account of how to live—Jews found that they had to give what they did not have. They required either memories that few possessed, or the effort to locate a road back which few found the will to invest. The world of the everyday did not provide access to so subtle and alien a world view as that of the Judaism of the dual Torah and its conception of humanity and of Israel, let alone to the way of life formed within that world view. Another generation would have to pass before the age of reversionary Judaisms, those that form the bridge to the twenty-first century, would arrive. How then to engage the emotions without the mediation of learning in the Torah? And how to define a way of life that imparted distinction without much material difference? To state matters in a homely way, what distinctively Judaic way of life would allow devotees to eat whatever they wanted anyhow? The answer to the questions—how to gain access to the life of feeling and experience, how to find the way of life that made one distinctive without leaving the person terribly different from everybody else—emerged in the Ju-

283

daic system of Holocaust and Redemption. This system presented an immediately accessible message, cast in extreme emotions of terror and triumph, its round of endless activity demanding only spare time. In all, the system of American Judaism realized in a poignant way the conflicting demands of Jewish Americans to be intensely Jewish, but only once in a while, and not exacting much of a cost in meaningful difference from others.

NEW AND OLD IN THE MYTHIC IDEOLOGIES OF BEING JEWISH

The two traits common to the twentieth-century Judaisms contradict one another: first is the power to persuade by a logic deemed self-evident, and second is the inability to last very long. The half-life of a Judaism in this century appears to encompass not much more than a generation. True, institutions, long in dying, preserve the detritus of self-evident truth of a "long ago," so confusing us about the vitality of what is, in fact, a corpse. Does this mean that the problems that precipitate rethinking the world and the way to live

285

reach solution? Some do—"the Jewish problem" in its political definition, for example (though not solved as anyone in darkest nightmare anticipated); some do not—the issue of Jewish difference in America's open society remaining open, for instance. Jewish Americans still sort out the conflicting claims of segregation and integration.

The cultural issues addressed, and solved, by Jewish socialism and yiddishism—the Jews form a distinctive sector of the international working class, and Yiddish marks the point of acceptable difference—passed in a cataclysm of migration and mass murder. Millions of Yiddish-speaking workers left for America and the West; millions of others were murdered; and within the Communist world, still other millions were swallowed up and lost all but the most attenuated connection to their Jewish origins: a name on an internal passport, yielding a life condemned to degradation for a distinction that, outside the context of pathological hatred of Jews, makes no material difference. So when we observe that Judaisms prove transient, the reason is not always the same.

Yet I see a single factor that accounts for the impermanence of the Judaic systems of the twentieth century. The ideological Judaisms have addressed transient moments and treated as particular and unique what are structural, permanent problems. As a result, none of the Judaisms before us exhibits stability, all of them presently appearing to serve, for a generation or two, as the explanation in cosmic terms of rather humble circumstances. For not more than three generations, Zionism thrived as an ideal for life and a solution to urgent problems. It essentially solved the meager "Jewish problem" that was left by the Second World War to be solved, and that, with the creation of the State of Israel, passed on into institutional continuations bereft of all ideological interest. Socialism and yiddishism turn out to have expressed the ideals of exactly that sector of Jewry to which they spoke, the Yiddish-speaking workers. When the vast Yiddish-speaking populations were murdered, between 1941 and 1945, yiddishism lost its natural constituency. Jewish socialism in the United States thrived for that one generation, the immigrant one, that worked in factories; the Jewish unions then folded into the larger amalgam of unionism and lost their distinctive ethnic character; the Jewish voters, originally socialist or radical, found a comfortable home in New Deal Democracy in America. The Jewish Communists of Poland and Soviet Russia in Stalin's time only with difficulty survived their revolution's success. Disqualified by perfect faith in what they were doing, most of them lost out to the bureaucrats who made the new order permanent. So, in all, the Judaic systems of the morning of the century, eager in the light of day to exhibit their promise of a renewed Judaic world view and way of life— one to bring a rebirth to "all humanity, not just the Jews"— turned in the harsh light of afternoon wrinkled faces and tottering gait. Not without reason do Israeli teenagers say, "When we get old, we'll talk in Yiddish."

Let me dwell on the odd contradiction between the self-evidence of the ideology and the transience of its appeal and heuristic power. Of American Judaism we may scarcely speak; it is the birth of a single generation. Its power to mediate between a generation out of touch with its roots and a society willing to affirm ethnic difference—on carefully defined and limited bases to be sure—remains to be tested. I shall presently address the beginnings of the Judaisms of the century beyond, but for the moment may only affirm that the system at hand presently functions as does a Judaism and presents a structure conforming with the systemic requirements of a Judaism. Whether it will turn out to form more than an effect of a sociological shift and a political ripple, only time will tell. The self-evidence has yet to wane. Ours is not a task of predicting currents in public

287

opinion, or even of measuring them, but only of trying to discern the inner workings of the ideas that for groups of like-minded Jews—phalanxes of generations, for example—coalesce to generate opinion and justify it.

Socialism, yiddishism, and Zionism, for their part, share in common a transient character. Each came into existence for a generation that found itself in the middle, unable to continue what it had inherited, unable to hand on what it created. As Wisse has pointed out for yiddishism (see chapter 5), so Anita Shapira tells us about the founders of Zionism, the ones who made the Judaism at hand:

> Theirs was the generation of the great leap; their parental homes were pervaded with religion, with innocent faith and hallowed custom; the homes of their children were detached from Jewish tradition, rooted in a secular life style and alienated from the Jewish past. They themselves were affected by the ambivalence which comes from being bred in a small society and living in another. Wherever they went and whatever they did, they were influenced . . . by the society from which they emerged. . . . All . . . cast off the burden of Jewish religion at an early age.[1]

The way of life defined by Judaic systems of the twentieth century differed in yet a second way from the way of life of the Judaic systems of the nineteenth century. A devotee of a Judaism of the nineteenth century would do deeds that differed in quality and character from those done by a devotee of another system altogether—for example, either a Christian or a Socialist one. The way of life in definition (not merely *by* definition) differed from any other; the categories were distinctive to the system. The ways of life of the twentieth-century movements—whether essentially political, as in Zionism, or fundamentally economic, as in the Jewish labor unions of Jewish socialism, or in category basically ethnic and cultural, as in American Judaism—all produced a culture of organizations, each such culture fitting comfortably into the category that encompassed all of them. So when I try to describe the way of life of a given system, I find it difficult to do more than specify the name of the organization one joined because of adherence to that system.

What the one who joined then did was pretty much what he or she would have done in any other organization: The flags had different colors, but the flagpoles were all made of the same wood. It is difficult to identify the *systemically distinctive* ways of life among the Judaic systems at hand. All of them call for actions of a single kind: the building of organizations, institutions, bureaucracies, institutions of collective action. The contribution of the individual is to the support of the bureaucracy.

Every way of life requires action of the same order as every other way of life, and each system treats the devotee as a specialist in the doing of some few deeds. None any longer is a generalist, doing everything on his or her own. The labor of the individual in one system therefore hardly differs from the role of the individual in another. Ordinarily what is asked for by all systems is the same thing: money, attendance at meetings, repeating the viewpoint of the system. Yet that description misses the point, because it treats as trivial what to the participants meant life. In attending meetings, in giving money, people gave what, in the circumstances, they had to give. They went to meetings because they believed their presence mattered, to others and to themselves, as much as in attending services in worship of God pious people considered their presence important— holy. Paying dues marked identification not with the organization but with the ideal and goal of the organization. So the way of life bore that same weight of profound commitment that the holy way of life had earlier sustained.

Besides evanescence and a certain uniformity of activity definitive of the way of life, all three Judaisms share a third trait as well. They each take up a position on the matter of historicism, appealing to facts of history in the formation and defense of the faith. Zionism, Reform, and, later, Conservative Judaism all constructed their positions on the foundation of that same conception of the facticity of history and of its power, furthermore, to dictate, out of facts, the values and truths of not one time but all time.

We may then place into perspective the half-dozen Judaisms subject to analysis here by asking how each identified facts. Two sources of facts served: the past, for Zionism; and everyday, acutely contemporary experience, for Jewish socialism and yiddishism as well as American Judaism. Zionism found for itself links to a remote past, leaping over distasteful (and contradictory) facts near at hand. History would supply the two things a Judaism required: first, acceptable models for a Jewish politics; second, a powerful link to the chosen land. The selective reconstruction of history, parallel to the selective piety of Orthodoxy, produced a well-composed ideology—indeed, one based on the obvious, the factual, the self-evident. But how different a claim did the other approaches present for themselves? For in place of the facts of history, they appealed to the facts of everyday life, of the streets and factories (for Jewish socialism and yiddishism), of the exclusion, actual and perceived, from the imagined society of undifferentiated America, joined with the (contradictory) quest for a distinct, if not wholly distinctive, place (for American Judaism). So the mode of thought—appeal to felt facts of life—proved uniform for the three ideologies.

And the basis for the power of these facts to make a difference is clear. The several Judaisms in common share enormously emotional appeals to the (self-evidently probative) experiences of history, meaning what is happening today. Each framed a grievance for itself, a doctrine of resentment. For Zionism, statelessness; for Jewish socialism and yiddishism, economic deprivation; and for American Judaism, a sense of alienation expressed that grievance, bringing to words the underlying feeling of resentment. The ideologies of the twentieth-century Judaisms came after the fact of experience and emotion and explained the fact, rather than transforming feeling into sensibility and sentiment into an intellectual explanation of the world. The systems in common appeal to a self-evidence deriving from a visceral response to intolerable experience, near at hand. Unemployment and starvation made entirely credible the world view and explanation of Jewish socialism, made compelling the program of activity, the way of life, demanded thereby. Zionism formed into a single whole the experiences of remarkably diverse people living in widely separated places, showing that all those experiences formed a single fact, the experience of a single sort—exclusion, victimization, anti-Semitism—which Zionism could confront. American Judaism linked to an inchoate past the aspirations of a third and fourth generation of Jews who wanted desperately to be Jewish but in its own experience and intellectual resources could find slight access to something to be called "Jewish."

Emotion—the emotion of resentment in particular—for all formed the road within: strong feeling about suffering and redemption, for American Judaism; powerful appeal to concrete deed in the here and now by people who thought themselves helpless, for Zionism; outlet for the rage of the dispossessed, for the suffering workers of czarist Russia and turn-of-the-century America alike. So the power and appeal of the three ideological systems, all of them enjoying self-evidence for those for whom they answered basic questions, proved not only uniform but also apt. For the problems taken up for solution—political, cultural, social, economic—raised for deep reflection the everyday and the factitious. What, after all, preoccupied the Jews in the twentieth century? Politics, economics, the crumbling of connection to a thousand-year-old culture, the Yiddish one, and a fifteen-hundred-year-old way of life and world view, the Judaism of the dual Torah. These were, as a matter of fact, things the most sanguine person could not ignore—experiences of the hour, education in the streets.

PART IV
From Self-Evidence to Self-Consciousness

TOWARD THE TWENTY-FIRST CENTURY

What distinguishes the Judaic system of the dual Torah from its continuators and competition in the nineteenth and twentieth centuries is a simple trait. The Judaism of the dual Torah encompassed the whole of the existence of the Jews who found its truth self-evident, its definition of life ineluctable. In the way of life of that system, a Jew was not simply always a Jew; he or she was *only* a Jew. The other Judaisms acknowledged the former: Jews never stopped being Jews. The world would not let them, even if they wanted to stop. But the Judaism of the dual Torah made slight provision for Jews to be anything but Jews: the holy people had no other vocation, no alternative, to its holiness.

Its history as a people different in kind from other peoples, its destiny at the end of time—these matched its distinctive holy way of life in the here and now. So Israel was always Israel *and only Israel.* But in modern times Israel became one of several things that Jews would be: also Americans, also workers, also Israelis, among the twentieth-century Judaisms, but never only Israel, God's people. And that theory of Israel matches in social terms the conception of the individual person as well. For in the received Torah, Israel, the Jew, lived out life in the rhythm of sanctification of the here and now, realizing in concrete deeds the Torah's words, once more, not only always but also Israel. It was not a brief romance; it was a lasting marriage. It was for all time, not for part of the time, and it was strict monogamy: a Jew always, and a Jew only—nothing else.

The conception of Israel once more presents us with the key to interpreting a system. From antiquity forward, the Judaism of the dual Torah saw Israel as solely Israel. But from the eighteenth century on, Judaic systems took shape that saw Israel as something less than the whole of the Jews' existence. They differed on the question, What more? They took issue, further, on the range of permissible difference, on issues of segregation versus integration. But all concurred that, in some ways, Jews would integrate. That concurrence by itself distinguished all modern Judaic systems from the received system of the dual Torah. In the systems of continuation of the nineteenth century, for instance, the Jew was a citizen as well as a Jew. Thus, being a Jew required reframing: a new theory of Israel, demanding also a fresh conception of the way of life of that Israel and, it would follow, also a new world view to explain that way of life and situate it among the received texts. The mythic Judaisms of the twentieth century, for their part, accepted as given the multiple dimensions that took the measure of the Jew: individual; member of diverse groups, of which one was Jewish. So the Jewish Socialist was a Socialist, too; and between Zionism and Jews' other worlds, or between American Judaism and Jewish Americans' other concerns, competition for commitment could scarcely come to resolution. For in modern and contemporary times, the Jews concerned themselves with many things, even though, from the viewpoint of the world, a Jew might be only a Jew.

What this meant in practice we have seen in both the nineteenth- and the twentieth-century systems: a redefinition not only of the range of difference but also of the degree of commitment. A Jew in eastern Europe, within the received system, wore Jewish clothes and talked a Jewish language and in it said thoughts he or she took for granted were uniquely Jewish. Jews in Germany, Britain, and America did none of these. Zionism in its Israeli realization produced Jews whose commitment to profession—state building, army building, institution building—in no way demanded particularly Judaic (in context, Zionist) action and activity. True, the state builders would say that everything they did was by definition Zionist action, and so it was. But in other contexts, as we have repeatedly noticed, others did the same action and, by definition, were not Zionists.

Now as this century draws to its close, the divisions within a human existence, setting apart the Jewish from the not-Jewish, have yielded two curious modes of Judaic existence. For a small minority, on whom I shall concentrate, "being Jewish" in the partial definitions of available systems has left dissatisfaction. This small minority has determined to find a mode of "being Jewish"—in my terms, a Judaic system—that would encompass not part but the whole of life. They have wished not a protracted romance, however ardent, but a marriage: a permanent relationship, whole, enduring, and complete.

For larger numbers, typified in this survey by the devotees of American Judaism, "being Jewish" has represented a kind of ongoing romantic attachment—episodic but intense. American Judaism, as I have noted, has left Jews free to be many things—some of them Jewish (or, in my terms, Judaic); others not—and therein has lain its appeal. No permanent and encompassing commitment has required American Jews to be only or mainly Jewish (that is, in my language, devotees of the American Judaic system). But the romantic attachment has meant that, when these Jewish Americans have chosen to "be Jewish," they have entered into an intense and exhausting encounter. And when they have not chosen to be Jewish, they did not have to be. The emotional appeal of Holocaust and Redemption should not be missed: it allows ready access to deep feelings, direct encounter with transcendental experience. But it does not demand, or even make provision for, protracted feelings and lasting encounter with that transcendent moment of redemption. When carrying out the critical act within the American Judaic way of life of visiting the State of Israel, American Judaists have ended up not as pilgrims, come to celebrate and stay, but as tourists. They have gone home and re-entered those other dimensions of human experience that they share with others in the same time and place: undifferentiated Americans. So it might be said that, as to the diverse Judaic systems of the modern age, what they have in common is a certain transient intensity—romance, not marriage. Deep, enduring commitment for about fifteen minutes is what people have been prepared to give. As I have said, the twenty-first-century movements of reversion show the alternative—the sixty-minute Judaic hour, so to speak.

In analyzing the system of reversion, I want—but only by the way—to show how the system at hand relates to the received system of the dual Torah. To participants, the relationship is clear: they are coming home, and home is what

298

it always was. But reversioners have never known what the home was like, and those who claim to inform them live not in the fifth or tenth century but today. Tradition is what people make of it, what they declare it to be; and, when all ties of continuity are broken, we cannot concede the givenness of what anyone proposes to hand over to us as binding. So it is necessary to learn what the first generation of reversion makes out of the received system, since that system, to them, scarcely forms a given. It by definition is new, and they renew it: a new Judaism, which may, of course, become the old one in a generation or two. In fact, as we shall see, quite objective indicators may tell us what is old, linear, incremental, and what is new and the product of fresh initiative, of acutely contemporary consciousness.

We clearly confront, in this generation of new beginnings, self-conscious decision, so we fairly wonder about the definition of the world view, the form and shape of the way of life, the identity of the Israel subject to address, that all together form the system of (to the participants) regaining the tradition, and (to others) rebirth and renewal from without. So, the question, stated simply, is: Do Judaisms of reversion constitute linear developments on an incremental course? Or are they something essentially new, made out of something very old indeed? Since the participants in reversion cannot claim to be born to the Judaism they claim to recover, we may dismiss as uninteresting the fact that, in context, they are reborn. That is not at issue. It is to what are they *now* born. And that requires us to know what is at stake in reversion, and that in two parts: the push, the pull. For, as I shall explain, religion recapitulates resentment, and a generation that reaches the decision to change expresses resentment of its immediate setting, as much as it proposes to commit itself to something better. The urgent question yields its ineluctable answer: Resentment produces resolution.

By the end of the twentieth century, some want in; and, so far as new and vigorous efforts at system building take place, they find their power and vitality in the magnetism of the received Judaism, not in its Orthodox form as a well-explained and well-considered world, but in its version as a self-evidently valid statement of how things "really" are. The road from outside to inside, of course, can never open again, for as the medieval Muslim philosopher Al Ghazali has said, "There is no hope in returning to a traditional faith after it has once been abandoned, since the essential condition in the holder of a traditional faith is that he should not know he is a traditionalist."[1] So the systems of reversionary Judaism by definition mark new beginnings, not mere re-entry into the tradition. But these systems, as I shall stress, last only a lifetime. For the children of reversioners do not know that they are traditionalists. They do not carry forward a reversionary Judaism. They find a datum in their lives: the given of the Judaism of the dual Torah. They are raised in that received way of life, absorb the world view rather than adopting it, and, in all, regain connection and take up a place in a chain they scarcely know has been snapped. On that account, the reversioners to the received Judaism of the dual Torah, paramount in the system building of the day, rightly point to themselves as the single important and influential Judaism of the day. Theirs is the energy, theirs the power of renewal, and theirs the Judaism that, at this moment, appear to enjoy the richest promise in the twenty-first century.

CHAPTER 8

REVERSION IN CONTEMPORARY TIMES: INVENTION AS DISCOVERY

Once upon a time, there was a Jewish boy in West Hartford, Connecticut, who grew up in the Reform temple and so admired his father, publisher of a Jewish newspaper for the Jews of the Connecticut valley, and his rabbi that he planned to become a Reform rabbi. But as the years passed, he came to believe that Reform Judaism offered less Judaism than he wanted: he wanted more than his father and mother practiced. Anyhow, it was a good way to rebel. So he began to keep the dietary laws, to observe the Sabbath,

301

and, in other ways as well, to live by the tradition. In that third generation that tried to remember what the second generation had wanted to forget, his remembering meant more religion, for the parents had none. They were "just Jewish," something they could not define or explain; and he wanted something to believe in. If the tradition was to be for him more than Reform Judaism, it would be Conservative Judaism; he decided therefore to become a Conservative rabbi and to go to the seminary of that Judaism, rather than to the Reform one.

"Reversion" to the tradition in his context meant a move one chair over. Had he grown up in a Conservative synagogue and reached a similar decision, he would have gone to an Orthodox yeshiva instead of the Conservative seminary. And if his parents had brought him up in an Orthodox synagogue, he would have rejected the mainstream Orthodox seminary, Yeshiva University, with its combination of religious and secular education, and chosen to study at a yeshiva that rejected Western secular education altogether. As may be obvious, I am that Reform boy from West Hartford; and, looking back thirty-five years, I realize that I and others like me stood at the beginning of what would become a considerable movement toward religiosity, greater observance of Judaic religious requirements, and commitment to the way of life of the received Judaism(s). At the time this step was a sensation. My class at the Jewish Theological Seminary of America was the first to comprise more alumni of Harvard College than of Yeshiva University. Afterward there were many, including even alumni of truly gentile Yale. The grandchildren of the immigrants were "coming home." But it was to a house they themselves had built.

Reversion both marks a movement and also defines a particular Judaic system. Extant Judaisms of the last third of the twentieth century all bear the marks of reversion, for the reason I have given: When people have wished to find their way home, they generally have moved over one chair. But a particular reversionary system has also taken shape, the one that has led utterly secular, but searching young Jews into one or another of the Orthodox-Judaic systems of the age, both in America and in the State of Israel. Let me speak first of the movement, which has imparted a style of its own to existing Judaisms, all of which, in the end of the twentieth century, see themselves as more traditional than they were earlier.

While reversion to Judaism began with the third generation, it reached its height with the fourth and beyond. That movement I call "reversion" uses the language of "return": that is, reversion to the Judaic way of life and world view in a religious rather than a secular formulation. I stress "return" because the world view of reversionary Judaisms sees Israel as God's people, who by nature and by definition should keep the Torah. All Jews who do not keep it ought to return to their true calling and character as the people of the Torah. So the title of the movement expresses its world view and its theory of who is Israel and of what it is natural for Israel to become. The world view of the movement perceives the Jews as alienated from the tradition to which they must "return." The way of life, on the surface, is simply that mode of behavior prescribed by the tradition for whatever chair the reversioner chooses to occupy.

But let me define, in more neutral language, the reversionary movement, away from assimilation and back to Torah, or tradition. For the charged words *return, Torah,* and *tradition* permit little analysis and so do not lead to understanding. The Judaic system of reversion encompasses large numbers of Jews who have moved from an essentially secular and naturalist to a profoundly religious and supernatural view of Israel, God's people, and of themselves as well and so have adopted the way of life of the received Judaism

303

of the dual Torah or of one of its continuators, whether Reform, Orthodox, or Conservative systems of Judaism. We may wonder why Jews growing up in secular circumstances opt for a religious Judaism, and—more important—how that tendency on the part of individuals became a movement and generated a Judaism, the Judaic system(s) of return—indeed, the one fresh Judaism that we see as we turn toward the twenty-first century.

To answer these questions, I have first of all to revert to the story of American Judaism. (Israeli young people, as I shall shortly discuss, explored the same path for the same reasons.) We recall that this system provided a mode of "being Jewish" when one wanted to be Jewish, and of being part of an undifferentiated society when one wanted not to be, in particular, Jewish. It involved essentially secular activity—fund raising, political organizing—and left untouched the inner life and values of the participants. But the success of American Judaism had an unexpected effect. People took seriously the powerful emotions elicited by rehearsals of the Holocaust and by engagement with the ongoing crises of the State of Israel. As the 1970s unfolded, the stress on the community at large of a high pitch of emotion, joined to only occasional activity and then activity of an essentially neutral character, affected younger people in a curious way. Some of the children wanted that same "more" that I had wanted as a young man. That is to say, people sold on the centrality of "being Jewish" in their lives required modes of expression that affected their lives more deeply, and in more ways, than the rather limited way of life offered by American Judaism. In search, once more, for values, rejecting what they deemed the superficial, merely public Jewish activities of their parents, they resolved that tension between being Jewish and not being too Jewish generated, for the third generation, by American Judaism. They were sold on "being Jewish" and looked not for

304

activity but for community, not for an occasional emotional binge but for an enduring place and partnership: a
covenant.

The life of activity in fund raising divorced from the inner disciplines of the faith, the inner pleasures of the way
of life, the deeper insights of the traditions of learning—
that life palled. At that same time—in the later 1960s and
1970s—a broader youth movement of rejection of parents'
values, deemed materialistic, and a quest for a deeper spiritual life characterized a segment of an entire generation of
young people. So we move from the precursors, the now
middle-aged returnees of the mid-1950s through the 1970s,
and come to the mainstream of reversion, those who in the
late 1970s and 1980s made familiar and routine what earlier had been the experiment in a religious Judaism conducted by a few intellectuals.

While secular Jews may convert to the Judaism of the
dual Torah in any of the versions just now outlined, I treat
them as uniform. In America, reversioners have come from
Reform or secular backgrounds, from Conservative or Orthodox ones. It hardly matters which. Each case involves a
conversion process, a taking up of a totally new way of life
and a rejection of the inherited one, the parents' way of life.
In the State of Israel, reversioners derive from three different sources of Jews: America, Israelis of European background, and Israelis of Asian or African origin.[1] The movement of reversion dates from the mid-1960s and begins in
a rejection of Western culture.

This brings us to reversion not as a mode but as a particular system, a Judaism on its own. The definitive chronicle
of the matter, by Janet Aviad (whom I shall cite at length),
provides not only a systematic picture of the ideology and
way of life but a synoptic portrait of the movement as a
whole. Still, enough is in hand to generalize. The movement's American component derived, she says, from the

youth rebellion of the 1960s: "Protesting a war they regarded as immoral, a situation that permitted terrible injustices to ethnic minorities, what appeared as a wasteful directionless use of technology, youth struck out in various directions. One direction was toward new forms of a religious life." Involved was a rejection of the "tradition of skeptical, secular intellectuality which has served as the prime vehicle for three hundred years of scientific and technical work in the West." The reversioners described here had earlier in the 1960s experimented with diverse matters, including drugs, poetry, and religion. And, among the religions, some Jews tried out Judaism. The quest involved travel, and Judaism "was often only the end station of a long search." Coming to Judaism came about by chance meetings with rabbis or religious Jews, but staying there was because of the yeshivas that received the reversioners. Yet another group of reversioners derived from Reform and Conservative synagogues; they came to improve their knowledge and raise their level of practical observance of piety. A further group, Israelis of Western background, compared, over all, with this second group. They had seen themselves as secular but sought to become, in Israeli terms, religious. Their search for meaning brought them to the yeshivas ready to receive them. The final group Aviad surveys were Israelis of poorer and Asian or African origin; and to them, too, reversion represented a religious conversion, from life "experienced as empty or meaningless to one experienced as fully, whole, and holy."[2]

In all, this is a Jewish expression of a common, international youth culture of the 1970s and 1980s, just as American Judaism was a version, in a Judaic idiom, of a larger cultural development in American life of the 1960s and early 1970s. These were the children of the "baby boom" following the Second World War—a generation that grew up in prosperity; a generation also in search, in a shared

306

quest for something to transcend the ("merely") material achievements. Children of successful parents had the leisure and resources to "try to find themselves," in the language of the day: some turned to drugs; others, to social concerns; still others, to a search for a faith that would demand more than the (to them shallow, compromising) religiosity of their parents. Whether Roman Catholic Pentecostalism, Protestant Biblical affirmation (called "fundamentalism"), Judaic reversion, Islamic renewal from Malaya to Morocco (also called "fundamentalism" or "extremism"), the international youth movement exhibits strikingly uniform traits: young people in rebellion against the parents' ways, in search of something more exacting and rigorous. If the Judaism of the dual Torah insisted that Jews are not only Jews all the time but never anything else, then we may characterize the movement of reversion as a return to that theory of Israel—but only in that sense. For as an acutely contemporary movement, part of a broad rejection of the secular, humanistic, and liberal values of a generation concerned to live an affable and affluent life, the reversion to Judaism presented much that was fresh, unprecedented, and, above all, selective.

These reversioners formed thus part of a world movement, a youth movement of resentment of the parents' generation and affirmation of the childrens'—a Jewish equivalent of the Cultural Revolution in far-off China. The reversioners expressed in the Judaic idiom an international message and viewpoint, no less than had Jewish socialism, yiddishism, Zionism, and, each in its own way, the Reform, Orthodox, and Conservative Judaisms—all constituting Judaic systems composed within categories available, so to speak, in the larger world of humanity.

The system of reversion drew its categories, its values, its goals from a larger setting as well. These it then adapted to the Judaic circumstance: a totally fresh, totally new, totally autonomous Judaic system. A Judaism invented or discovered? Both, to begin with, invented. In her description of reversion in the State of Israel, Janet Aviad uses such language as: "who turned outward . . . who noticed a change in the spiritual climate." That, I think, is a mark of invention. But then, assuredly, it was also a Judaism discovered and recovered: "The traditional world of Judaism contains all truth."[3] So the idiom, as Aviad says, may have proved new, but the content was more than welcome: it was what the reversioners had brought with them. The world view of reversionism in its present form constitutes a Judaic statement of what a great many people were saying, all of them in the language and categories of their own.

Let me make this picture of the return to Judaism more concrete. When, as happens not uncommonly, Jews in America make a decision to observe the dietary laws and the Sabbath, to say prayers every day, and to identify with a Torah-study circle in a yeshiva, they adopt a way of life and a world view new to them. For the generality of American Jews have defined their lives in other terms. Reversion marks the entry of Jews not born and brought up within the Judaic system of the dual Torah into the way of life defined by the dual Torah and the adoption of the viewpoint and values of that same Torah. Reversioners enter into the Israel to whom the dual Torah speaks: that is, into an intense social life lived in a round of daily and Sabbath prayers, study sessions, celebrations. Leaving Judaic systems that favor or accommodate integration, they choose a Judaic system that, in effect if not in articulated policy, creates a life of segregation. The shift from world to world brings one into a stunningly powerful Judaic system.

Reversion by itself presents no surprises. Throughout the nineteenth century and into our own day, stories accumulate of Jews who found their way "back." That route of return may pass from Reform Judaism to Orthodoxy, or from a situation of complete indifference to a commitment to the Jews as a group and even to the formation of a new Judaic system to carry out that commitment. Theodor Herzl, founder of Zionism, retraced a path to Jewish concern after a career of indifference to Jewish matters. So, too, did Zhitlowsky and Medem with socialism and yiddishism. Jews' testimonies to the effect of the Six Day War tell the same story. So the diverse Judaic systems of the nineteenth and twentieth centuries bear the power to attract to themselves persons of Jewish origin but with no involvement. So by itself the process of conversion, by Jews, to Judaism hardly constitutes a system. What is special about contemporary reversion is that it forms an *ism*, coalescing in a world view and a way of life attractive to a group of Jews, who bond themselves into a community and present a Judaism. They would fairly claim that their Judaism *is* Judaism: that is, that they are reverting to the Judaism of the dual Torah and recognize no other. And that claim, at face value, demands a hearing. So when we consider reversion to Judaism, a powerful force in contemporary Judaic affairs, we take up from yet another perspective the issue of systemic analysis. We want to know specifically whether this sense of homecoming is return or mere self-deluded reverie, whether the Judaism being expressed is rediscovered and renewed or made up for the occasion.

I have first of all to sort out certain aspects of reversion to the Judaism of the dual Torah. It takes place in both American Jewry and the State of Israel. It is expressed in a broad variety of institutions that receive reversioners. All of them, uniformly and rightly, claim to preserve and embody the Judaism of the dual Torah: (just) Judaism. So the direction of reversion presents no issue. It is possible at the outset to stipulate that the system to which reversioners come is not a discovery but "authentic"—that is to say, quite unselfconscious. To the proprietors of the institutions that receive reversioners, the Judaism of the dual Torah presents a self-evidently true composition: a world view; a way of life, realized in an Israel very near at hand; the institution itself, the community; the circle of the faithful.

Some well-established institutions, Orthodox in every way, center around Yeshiva University in America and equivalent centers of Orthodoxy in Britain, Australia, South Africa, and even the State of Israel (in Bar Ilan University). The premise there is the same as Hirsch's: One acquires a secular and a Torah education at one and the same time and lives in both worlds. A second sort of institution is made up of yeshivas, centers of classical Judaic learning conducted in exactly the patterns familiar for centuries: study of the canon in the accepted and familiar manner. These schools, constituting also synagogue communities, absorb the adherents and take up a sizable part of their lives with activities of prayer and study. They do not concede that secular learning deserves the time it demands; all energy belongs to Torah study. Secular education needed to earn a living may to be sure go forward, but Torah study (mainly in talmudic texts and commentaries) takes priority to the near exclusion of all else. Yet a third sort is composed of religious communities organized around the personality and charisma of their leaders, holy men called *rebbes.* The communities lay stress on pretty much the same activities of prayer and study as the rest of the Orthodox and the traditional worlds, but add doctrines entirely distinctive to themselves, mostly concerning the centrality, in the holy realm, of their *rebbes.* These institutions, called Hassidic, also take up the better part of their participants' existence, even providing guidance on correct clothing and on the use of the bulk of one's leisure time. In the many other types of institution that receive reversioners, the picture does not materially differ. All institutions of reversion and perpetu-

310

ation of the Judaism of the dual Torah, except for Orthodoxy in its familiar form, adopt a single policy as to society.
They opt for a life not of integration but of isolation, social
autonomy and separation, preferring not to relate to the
common society, whether of the United States, involving
gentiles, or of the State of Israel, involving Jews not similar
to themselves. In this regard, the larger number of institutions that receive reversioners have adopted a policy of separation that would have surprised, and dismayed, not only
the founders of Orthodoxy but even more all other Judaic
systems of the nineteenth and twentieth centuries.*

My special interest in these institutions does not focus
upon their system, however, since it may be taken for
granted as fact that that system conforms in all ways to the
Judaic system of the dual Torah. I simply stipulate in advance that the reversioners' understanding of themselves as
the natural continuators of the unchanged Torah corresponds to the facts. For the problem is not the systems of
those who allege they simply do what everyone before them
did, but the systems of those who do not do what everyone
before them did. Reversioners in their context represent
new, not traditional choices. The reversioners do undertake
to redefine—for themselves, but they are exemplary—that
way of life and world view that they received as traditional
from their parents. But that was *not* the received system of
the dual Torah, its world view, its way of life. So to the
reversioners the new is what (they say) is old, even as what
was old is new to them. Accordingly, this analysis requires
us to treat as fresh not the received system but the way the
reversioners receive it: a system of reversion is fresh, even
though that to which people return draws them (in its own
terms) upward to Sinai.

* Whether that same policy characterized the received system of the
dual Torah does not concern us, being an issue relevant only to an evaluation of the claim of the communities at hand to carry forward unbroken
the received Judaism.

Contemporary Reversion in Israeli Orthodoxy

The movement of reversion flourishes throughout the Jewish world. It attains realization as a system, however, in the yeshivas—the centers for full-time study of Torah, comparable to monasteries in providing for a holy way of life for all participants. The yeshivas in the State of Israel lead the movement of reversion and give full expression to its world view and way of life. But the yeshivas that succeed in embodying the ideals of reversion derive not from Israeli Orthodox rabbis but from American ones living in Jerusalem. It was American Orthodox rabbis trained in yeshivas who saw the opportunity and the issue. They understood as self-evident, of course, that all Jews should live by the Torah and study it; but they had the wit to recognize a generation of young Jews who were prepared to revert to that way of life and world view. And these rabbis further undertook to give form and full expression to the system of reversion. The yeshivas that received the newcomers came into being because of American rabbis settled in Jerusalem: "They discerned a new openness to religion. . . . They felt strongly that Orthodox Judaism would appeal to the young Jews being drawn to non-Jewish religious groups. . . . the problem seemed merely technical: how to make young people aware of orthodox values and beliefs as a way of life."[4] What these rabbis found points to the freshness of the movement at hand; for, in fact, the established yeshivas took no interest at all in the possibilities and did not think that they could absorb the types of student coming their way. So the rabbis founded autonomous schools.

That fact alerts us to the presence of an innovative system. A system that, to begin with, finds itself rejected and ignored by another system of the same family will have

312

difficulty claiming to be an incremental outcome of the system whose institutions prove—by their own word—utterly incompatible. So Aviad underlines the originality of the institutions of the reversioners in Jerusalem:

> If one looks carefully at the beit midrash [study hall] in Ohr Sameah, certainly highly distinctive features are evident that distinguish it from the beit midrash of a standard yeshivah. . . . One sees a rather strange mix of figures in a variety of fashions. . . . Their [the students'] gestures seem uncertain and even straining. . . . They still lack the confidence and naturalness of those who are truly at home in a study hall and truly comfortable in black suits and hats.[5]

The heroes of the system are those who have accomplished a true and lasting reversion. The newcomers' scale of values places a high premium on successful conversion, with the result that people who are not recognized scholars gain prominence in the movement.

Here, too, there has been a shift in the scale of values. In the Judaism of the dual Torah, achievements in learning find recognition, and absence of such achievement also is noted. Here, on the other hand, there is a transvaluation of that critical value: gifts of the spirit take priority and endow the gifted with status out of all relationship to his—or her—intellectual attainment. The addition of "or her" provides another signal of a system aborning, for the familiar yeshiva world makes slight provision for women's participation in its Judaism.

Yet a third point of stress—the importance of accomplishing the reversion when in the State of Israel, particularly in Jerusalem—distinguishes this system from the familiar formation of the dual Torah. For yeshivas flourish wherever Jews live freely. But reversioner yeshivas concentrate in Jerusalem. The reversioners naturally need a supportive environment, a large number of persons who affirm their conversion as natural and normal and right. The Judaism of the dual Torah rooted in lives flourished, by definition, wherever its devotees chose to live. Now the transience of the reversioner system comes to the fore. For within a generation the successful reversioner finds his or her place in the existing community and its system. The reversioner yeshiva takes as a principal task leading the reversioner into the existing community, a policy comparable to that of socialism, both Jewish and Zionist, which claimed to lead Jewry into the normal economic structure of nations and to form a stage in the onward progress of the Socialist drama.

What about the world view? If reversion is a sport of the existing system, then its basic ideas, in detail and in structure, should form a simple recapitulation of those of the long-time system. But if there is an emphasis particular to the group at hand, then the world view has to take a position on its own and not as a restatement of an established one. Of course, it does not suffice to classify as a single system all systems that refer to the same documents. All continuator Judaisms, after all, cite not only the written but also the oral Torah. So to call all expressions of the received system "Orthodox" would bring a measure of confusion to our analysis. Aviad in this regard makes the striking point that between the choices—integration with separation, exemplified by Hirsch, and utter isolation, exemplified by Hirsch's critics—the world view of reversionism selects complete segregation from the gentile world. At the same time, she notes, in an abstract that contains the main message for analysis:

> Despite the fundamental inward-turning of the ultraorthodox posture, it was the rabbis from ultraorthodox [in our categories, "isolationist"] yeshivot in the United States, and later in Israel, who turned outward toward the potential "returnees." It was these men who noticed a change in the spiritual climate

... and who were prepared to consider new ways to act in order to channel the new interest in religion toward Orthodox Judaism. The ideological position of the yeshivot for baalei teshuvah [reversioners] is consistent with that of the community with which they are linked. Thus, in those yeshivot dominated by rabbis whose fundamental orientation is ultraorthodox, a basic negation of the value of Western culture is not only expressed, it is also enunciated outright. . . . Western culture is alien to Jews and . . . assimilation to Western culture is a betrayal of Judaism. The traditional world of Judaism contains all truth . . . and traditional Jews are the saving remnant of the Jewish people. It is precisely this message, both parts, that resonates loudly and positively for the majority of baalei teshuvah who are protesting the cultural values of the societies from which they have emerged. The idiom used to express the protest may be new to the baalei teshuvah, but the content of the message is apparently welcome to them. The West is portrayed as the source of confusion and false ideologies. Absolutely no value is accorded secular values or achievements. . . . The West is depicted as overrun by drugs, crime, degenerate sexual mores, spiritual ignorance. In this view, assimilation to the West is personal suicide, a condemning of oneself to a valueless and meaningless existence.[6]

Aviad here provides a striking portrait of something old, something new, something borrowed—therefore a new union of value, viewpoint, deed and duty: something profoundly at home only in a context of its own.

That this is a system distinct from the one constituted by avatars of the dual Torah proves self-evident. The established system made slight provision for reversioners and did not find, in its available world view, the motivation to accommodate them. I may add a personal observation. When I came to Jerusalem in 1957, as a precursor of the generation of reversion that would follow, I found in the yeshiva world no comprehension whatsoever—either among students or among rabbinical masters—of the approaches of an unapologetic son of a Reform Temple, a

315

proud student of the Conservative Seminary and of the Hebrew University Talmud faculty. What a mishmash of heresies—and I innocently affirmed them all! I in my person violated more than any individual's share of taboos, personal and intellectual alike. Eating a meal of a ham sandwich with a glass of milk on the Day of Atonement would scarcely compete. I fell into a category beyond their comprehension (as, if truth be told, they did for me).

What provides solid evidence that a new system is under way is what is fresh here. The total negation of Western culture that forms the centerpiece of the reversionist world view finds no ample precedent in the received dual Torah, which felt itself entirely at home in diverse circumstances and drew both deliberately and unselfconsciously on the world in which it flourished. I need hardly point to obvious precedents for a policy of selecting what was appropriate. The policy of rejecting the entire world beyond that Aviad outlines finds few precedents and, on balance, presents an egregious exception to a long history not of integration but of mediation. But another wellspring for the world view at hand is readily discernible. The world view of reversion, resting on the principle of total rejection of Western culture, in fact, as I have said, corresponds point by point with the world view of comparable movements of its time and circumstance: the youth revolution of the 1960s.

So to conclude: the view that reversion is a homecoming, that the values of reversionism simply replicate, for the occasion, the theology of the Judaic system of the dual Torah, contradicts the particular structure and points of value and emphasis of reversionism. The questions at hand come from circumstance; the answers then derive from a process of selection and arrangement of proof-texts provided by the canonical writings, on the one side, and by (if truth be told) the everyday way of life of the Judaic system of the dual Torah, on the other. The whole, then, compares with other

316

wholes, other Judaic systems: a work of selection along lines already determined, a system dictated by its own inventive framers to answer questions urgent to themselves in particular—Judaism.

The movement of reversion bears comparison to the twentieth-century systems of Jewish socialism and Zionism in being, by definition, a system for a particular circumstance, as I have already noted, and, also by definition, in succeeding or failing in a single generation. The reversioner finds a place within the community of the faithful or goes on to other matters entirely. For a particular moment a system does come into being: with its world view, one that responds to the system of the dual Torah but reshapes that system for the occasion; and with its way of life, one of persistent and highly self-conscious experimentation with received forms. Nothing could so totally contradict the received system of the dual Torah as the attitude of experimentation and questioning: the principal definitive trait of a system that has endured for fifteen hundred years is givenness, not trial and testing.

Contemporary Reversion in American Yeshivas

In the Israeli version of reversionism, Jews go through the established patterns but with fresh attitudes. Reversionary Judaism constitutes a distinct system because the world view is fresh, though the way of life is essentially familiar. In American reversionism, while the attitudes accord, over all, with the world view of the received system, the actions do not. Jews say the right words but do the deeds uncertainly and oafishly. I refer specifically to the critical

317

act of the received system: Torah study. I treat that paramount act as indicative of the character of the larger pattern of actions. The word for "Torah study" in Yiddish is *lernen*, meaning spiritual meditation on Jewish books of a certain character. Students "learned" full time; and many, some of the time. Now the important fact is that *lernen* in Talmud Torah involves something more than the mere acquisition of facts. It is a mistake to assume that when Jews express piety through study of the Torah, they come for information only or mainly.

To discuss Torah study in a Judaism in America, I turn to a brilliant work of ethnography by Samuel Heilman. He tells how he set out to write a book about Jews who study Torah, or "learn," as an avocation. These uniformly encompass the reversioners; no adept would treat the matter as a hobby, even if such a person did not do it full time. In noticing that the issue was not merely the acquisition of knowledge but something else, he makes an important observation:

> From early on I realized that, for many of the Jews I was observing, this experience was more than simply the assimilation of knowledge. For one thing, many of those I watched had been lernen for years, but still seemed to be unable to review the texts on their own or recall very much of the content in front of them. For another, even those who had *lernt* a lot and displayed an erudite familiarity with the texts took apparent great pleasure in repeating what they had already studied rather than looking for the new and as yet unknown. The best lernen, it seemed, was the sort which reiterated what everyone already knew. The best questions to ask were those the texts themselves asked; and the best if not the only true answers were those already written on the pages open before one. Finally, while the members of the study circles I observed ostensibly gathered in the house of study to get the wisdom of Judaism from the books into their minds, they often spent more time in class getting their feelings about Judaisms off their chests. Clearly much more than learn-

ing or the accumulation of information about Jewish texts was going on. I wanted to find out what that something more was.[7]

Heilman's reflections on his many years of observing the process of study of Torah provide insight into the issue. As I have said, in *lernen*, the ultimate goal is sanctification; and while what is learned may appear to be secular facts, the source of what is learned, which is Torah, and the intent of the ones who do the learning, which is to study Torah, reshape the intellectual act into a religious quest, a holy event.

Now when Heilman states that among hobbyists he observed "more than simply the assimilation of knowledge," he points toward what distinguishes the act of study of Torah from all other acts of learning, the setting of the study house and the circle of rabbi and disciples from all other situations of intellect, and the process of teaching and studying Torah from all other processes by which people enlarge their intellects and enhance their knowledge. In this regard, the scenes Heilman describes conform to those portrayed in the canonical literature of the dual Torah. But the act remains the same: the use of the mind; the formation of a social group—it is always a social group—for the acquisition of knowledge; and the improvement of one's status. So how does this act of learning differ from all other acts of learning, this Talmud Torah, this realm of *lernen*? The verbal explanation invokes language and image not routinely associated with schooling and study. But the act itself—use of the mind—remains what it is. A great deal of class time is spent in free-associating, expressing how people feel, chatting about this and that—all under the auspices of God and revealed Torah. As Heilman says, among the hobbyists whom he studied "much more than learning . . . was going on." But in his book he demonstrates that a great deal less than learning also was going on: experience, not intellect; emotion, not disciplined speculation and

319

imagination; transactions of a private and individual character, not a public exchange of reasoned and well-constructed argument. Jews who come to class to get "their feelings about Judaism off their chests" do not come to learn at all.

Heilman's ethnography describes a group that cannot be replicated in the canonical writings. He writes about people concerned more with feeling than with knowing, and engaged in a ritual of learning that contains no sizable component of the acquisition of knowledge even of the holy books. But that hardly conforms to the character of Torah study in the received system of the dual Torah. So far as Heilman's characterization of the something more—and the something less—of Talmud Torah, or *lernen*, proves accurate, therefore, the learning of reversioners addresses issues other than did and does the *lernen* of those who stand upon solid foundations within the received Torah. For *lernen* as Heilman portrays it, and Talmud Torah as the classic texts of Judaism portray it, bear slight resemblance to one another. *Lernen* solves problems other than those of learning with the hope of sanctification. Heilman's picture leaves a single impression. People who come together to study Torah are looking for an excuse to get together. But the sort of excuse they seek must connote more than joining a pinochle club.

Return to Judaism in the Secular Kibbutz

A brief review of what reversion produces when piety does not accompany profession of something very like the "faith" allows us to grasp more amply the nature of the reversionary transformation of the continuator Judaisms—Conservative, Orthodox, and Reform—that have been affected by the common impulse. Militantly secular, the collective farming communities, called "kibbutzim," in recent times have undertaken a re-engagement with religion—a re-engagement called by its chronicler Shalom Lilker "a new tradition in the making."[8] An account of the system as it emerged allows a comparison of two or more reversionary Judaisms.

The components of the world view of the kibbutz movement, as Lilker describes them, begin with a trust in man: "concern for the soul of each member. . . . Unless the kibbutz is worthy of man and is built for man, its future holds little promise." Lilker reports that the kibbutz members regard themselves as secular, Socialist humanists, most of them explicitly atheists. The way of life at hand is "aimed at lifting the individual beyond his material concerns into the realm of values."[9] But this humanism draws upon the Judaic canon; and, Lilker reports, that interest in the canon grows. But the competing values—asceticism, the work ethic, for example—draw equally upon other sources entirely. What makes the Judaic canon important is the movement of reversion, and it draws our attention to the kibbutz system. Lilker describes the world view of reversion in the idiom of the kibbutz in these terms:

> For this generation the central problems are in its relationship to Jewish history, the Jewish people, Jewish literature, Jewish identity, Jewish fate. The God dimension is absent from their religious quest. Their interest in ritual is negligible. The absence of theological questions results from a lack of knowledge of religious and philosophical thought of the West. . . . Religious symbols have become a major means of expressing the emergence of a greater sense of social-national belonging.[10]

What is left after the removal of the "God dimension,"

321

"ritual," and theology is not entirely clear. The articulated view that reversion of the kibbutz sort forms a Judaism emerges in the following statement of a kibbutz member, cited by Lilkin: "The kibbutz is more religious than Reform Judaism. If we put aside the question of God for a moment and see Jewish religion as a relationship to Jewish values, ethical values, Jewish history, Jewish festivals and customs, then the average kibbutz is more religious than the average Reform congregation." In this reversionary Judaism, only the forms, and not the substance, of values, history, customs are attended to. But the conception that one can form a "relationship" to "values" and "history" leaves open the critical questions of secular religion: What transforms events into history, or Jewish History, and what imparts to "values" that status of religious duties, not to say the specificity of requirements for concrete actions? In Lilkin's view, this is a Judaism:

> The kibbutz has succeeded in achieving one of Judaism's prime values—maximum mutuality. Because the kibbutz was established to cultivate brotherly relations and could not survive if they deteriorated, the creation of community feeling is more than just an observance of a prime Jewish value. It is a matter of life and death. Its purpose and character dictate the deep feeling of responsibility among and toward its members that Judaism has so steadfastly urged upon all Jews.[11]

Perhaps Lilkin represents, in English, conceptions that in Hebrew bear more substantial meaning. In English I hear baloney. The sense of "maximum mutuality," the substance of "brotherly relations," yield little more than the notion that in a kibbutz people are supposed to be nice to each other. How a rather generalized attitude of mutual accommodation may turn into a "value" and add up to a "religion" I cannot say, and thus I feel that the reversion in the kibbutz movement presents somewhat less than meets the eye. By contrast, the intense spirituality of the reversioners described by Aviad, the sense of a historic opportunity for national religious regeneration exhibited by the American rabbis in Jerusalem, point out the difference between an allusive rhetoric and the perceived reality of God's presence, of rebirth of the Torah in two media. Whether or not one can go home again, the kibbutz reversion does not show the way. For while one may invent a usable past, one cannot invent a religious system. That is not how religions arise, at least not in the generation of Judaic systems. Reviewing Lilkin's picture, I find difficult the identification of the urgent questions, the self-evidently valid answers, that all together form a Judaism. Maximum mutuality hardly serves as antidote to that profound resentment that elsewhere serves as catalyst: the feeling that things cannot go in a particular way.

The mode of argument, of course, alerts us to the processes of invention. We identify an important trait and go in search of proof-texts to find roots for that trait in "Judaism." Lilkin performs a primitive ethnography, so my comparison between the reversion of some sort of Judaic religion in the kibbutz movement and the reversion to the Judaism of the dual Torah accomplished in the yeshiva world may prove awry. Still, the comparison may offer some illumination. Reversion in the kibbutz version deals with a way of life well defined, with a world view wholly derivative of the existing Socialist one that forms a whole Judaic system—the Socialist-Zionist one in its kibbutz formulation. So the reversion in the secular kibbutz teaches little about system formation in the present and coming centuries, because so far it constitutes little more than an inchoate and scarcely articulate chapter in the ongoing system at hand. None doubts that the kibbutz is a Judaic system: a world view, a way of life, addressed to a specified Israel. But in the study of contemporary and coming reversion, the kibbutz system as yet plays no part. That conclusion teaches us how considerable and fresh a Judaism is the reversion to the Judaic system of the dual Torah—and warns us not to regard anyone who invokes religious rhetoric as the framer of a Judaism of reversion, or of a Judaism at all.

The "Last Jew on Earth" Syndrome

So far I have considered reversionary Judaism in its theological and institutional dimensions; but the reversioners are diverse, and the "Orthodoxy" they encounter is equally so. The quest of the reversioner cannot find its full measure in the public space of politics. There is an inner quest rich in private, even idiosyncratic detail. What the reversioner seeks and what he or she finds do not often correspond. One of the most thoughtful reversioners—who passed through Orthodoxy and out the other side—states in all honesty, "By 'the Orthodoxy I believed in' I meant a sort of fantasy-religion world, a place where people somehow could rise above all the faults attendant to being human, a place where people thought of nothing but God and Judaism and each other's feelings all day long." The reversioners, Michael Graubart Levin reports, have to clear hurdles. They have to adapt themselves to Judaism in its classical mode. But they must also find a place for themselves in Orthodox Jewish society, and that society exhibits what Levin calls "neutral to negative feelings": "Nothing in yeshiva prepared me for the suspicion and lack of acceptance I encountered." The birthright Orthodox suspect the Orthodoxy of the reversioners, whom they dismiss "as people who could not handle their responsibilities and had turned to Orthodoxy for relief the way other people turn to drugs or alcohol."[12] Any conception that, in the rediscovery of Judaism in its classical form, we witness mere Orthodoxy proves insufficient. What we have is an age of experimentation, a return not to yesterday but to tomorrow.

For if I had to point to a single given that characterizes all Judaic systems at their nascent stages, it is the conviction that things cannot go on this way. Speaking for those whose urgent questions find no answers in the available Judaisms, I would phrase matters simply: "Change or perish." And no one proposes to perish, for those who have wished to stop "being Jewish" have always managed to succeed. They have defined themselves as the last Jews of their line. The founders and framers of systems, by contrast, saw themselves as the last Jews on earth—and wanted to make sure that they would not mark the end of the line. Reversionary movements and the Judaic system of reversion in particular mark the rejection of what the participants see as "assimilation," the "dejudaization of the Jews," and draw enormous energy from their participants' fear of being the last Jews on earth.

So let me examine what I call the "last Jew on earth syndrome": "With me 'the tradition' must not die." The first two or three generations of Reform, Orthodoxy, and the Historical School reacted against something, as much as they went in quest of something else. Zionism confronted head on the political powerlessness of scattered, weak Jews and turned them into Israel, the Jewish people, a political entity before its nation had attained realization. Jewish socialism faced squarely and honestly the economic crisis affecting (among others) the Jews of eastern Europe and the immigrants of America, and offered the doctrine of the united working class in search of its rights before the unions had gained the power that would make things change. Along these same lines, as we have seen, the testaments to reversion repeatedly invoke rejection of the old

325

before they confess to affirmation of the new. So it may be said, first of all, that religion recapitulates resentment.

But what does reversion recapitulate? Let me draw once more on the memories of a third-generation American Jew, sympathetic to all Judaisms, empathetic with none of them. When that boy in West Hartford entered seventh grade, his father allowed him to go to afternoon Hebrew classes at a nearby Orthodox synagogue. It was only for that year; after becoming a bar mitzvah, at the beginning of the next year, the boy worked in his father's newspaper office every day after school, as well as on Saturday mornings, through the end of high school. But in that prepubescent year the boy met, for the first and only time before his mature years, that realm of the Torah that he would later find defined his being. One day while walking to Hebrew class, which he vastly enjoyed, he began to wonder what would happen when his father died, when "his" rabbi died (he meant the Reform rabbi who talked endlessly in lovely words; only later did the boy realize that that rabbi had absolutely nothing to say to anyone), when he would be the last Jew on earth—he and maybe his best friend, Eddy. "It must not be that way. I shall not let it. I shall become a rabbi." From then to now a straight line stretched forward. "Let me not be the last Jew on earth. I shall replace my father—but be a better Jew than he was: *I will know things.*" And the boy did. But not what his father knew—different things.

That vision turns out to be broadly shared among the third and fourth and fifth generations of Jews in America, though it takes diverse form, to be sure: The "Jews are dying out, and I do not want that to happen. So I must do this or that"—whatever this or that may be. This "last Jew on earth" syndrome forms a powerful motif in the discourse of Jews as they move toward the twenty-first century, and draws their attention once more to the one thing they know has endured through time: the Torah. For as

326

Jews look back on the interesting centuries from the American Constitution and the French Revolution to the present, they see only change—sequences of Judaisms, each with its half-life of a generation, marking, in the life of the imagination, that outer change that touched all Israel, all at once. Whether migration for the living or mass murder, whether state building or (for Jews in the Soviet Empire) systematic deracination, Jews experience worrisome and unsettling change. Few can look back on family histories of more than three generations in one place, and most cannot look back that far at all.

Whether it is the great grandfather who came to America or the grandfather who came to Tel Aviv, someone in the near past marks the end of family memory. Just as the past consists of a near-at-hand terminus, so can the future: "Shall I be the last Jew on earth?" "Are we the final generation?" True, the question itself reaches back to the very beginnings of the mythic beginnings of Israel: "But Abram said, 'O Lord God, what will you give me, for I continue childless, and the heir of my house is Eliezer of Damascus?' "(Gen. 15:2). And the fear of forming the final generation at the outset found its match in faith: "And he brought him outside and said, 'Look toward heaven and number the stars . . . so shall your descendants be.' And he believed the Lord, and he reckoned it to him as righteousness"(15:5–6). That kind of faith in the face of fear for the future is indeed to be reckoned righteousness, there being so little foundation in fact. The Jews, in the elegant phrase of the Brandeis University philosopher Simon Rawidowicz (1897–1957) have been "the ever-dying people,"[13] because they feared always for their future. And they were always right to fear, but always right to persist.

The reversionary Judaisms begin, I think, in that fear, a mix of resentment of a social present with a right and natural reflection on an awful, near-at-hand past. The reversion to the dual Torah marked the generations following the murder of the Jews of Europe, facing the demographic loss. It affected the generations that made the State of Israel, addressing the perpetual insecurity of the bastion-become-beleaguered-fortress. It touched deeply the great-grandchildren of the immigrants who formed American Jewry, the children of the framers of American Judaism, looking backward at integration fully realized and forward toward what they feared would be no future at all. No family was untouched by outmarriage (however demographically advantageous); many families were framed out of all relationship with distinctively Judaic or even culturally Jewish activity (however defined)—no wonder that some could imagine themselves the last Jews on earth. Every generation is the last but for the next, the one that it creates; and the generations that face the twenty-first century—the fourth and the fifth and the sixth beyond mass murder and migration—have sound reason to wonder, "What will you give me, for I continue childless?" In that setting, the power to believe does stand for righteousness, or so I think. And that brings me to the final systemic development that can be presently identified, to the reversionary ones, the last, the least expected, the most effective for the moment. The resentment flows from deep fears for the group's final dissolution: "I shall be a stranger in the land, a Cain, with no one to talk to." Expressed in rejection of the values of the West—beginning with those, of course, of the father and the mother—the resentment reaches resolution in Judaisms of return. For the few, return is to the dual Torah. For the many, it is to a destination not yet defined. For all, it is not to romance but to marriage, if only they can get to the marriage canopy, the altar formed of the vault of heaven.

As far as what I call the "systemopoeic" power—the power to create Judaic systems to address difficult and demanding problems (see chapter 9)—residing in the Jews at all, presently that power flows from the reversioners. I see no other group of Jews attempting to construct an encompassing account for themselves of who they are and what they must do, where they are heading and who joins them in the journey: a Judaism. The reversion to Judaism within the kibbutz movement, consisting as it does of a flow of empty words, validates that judgment. There is no yes, only a maybe. The reversionary systems, for their part, say no to two hundred years of Judaic system building. They reject the premises and the programs not only of the Judaic systems of an essentially economic and political character—socialism and American Judaism, for example—but also the ones that affirm religious viewpoints and ways of life. Since these systems by definition have come into being as the creation of children—great-great-grandchildren, really—of the nineteenth-century reformers, they mark the conclusion of the age of modernization.

The pressing problem they address seems to me clear. The Jews en route to the Torah in its dual statement once more address profound and pressing human problems. They want to know the answers to such questions as, Why do I live? What do I do to serve God? What should I do with my life? No wonder Orthodoxy cannot cope with these Jews. The reversioners come to study Torah as God's word, not as a source of historical facts. They take up a way of life quite alien to what they knew from their parents, and they take it up as an act of conversion to God, not as a means of expressing or preserving their Jewishness. They repudiate, yes—but only to affirm. If I had to explain in a single sentence the remarkable power of reversionary Judaisms—whether to Reform or to Israeli Yeshiva-Orthodoxy—I would invoke a single consideration. The one question ignored by the former Judaic systems, the human question, found its answer here; and, after two hundred years of change, the final turning of the wheel brought up the original issue afresh.

For what questions had the Judaic system of the dual To-

329

rah set at the center of discourse if not the ones of living a holy and a good life? The Jews for those long centuries in which Christianity defined the frame of reference for all Western society understood that that question pressed, its answers demanded attention. The Judaism of the dual Torah addressed that Jew who was always a Jew and only a Jew, delivering the uncompromising lesson that God demanded the human heart, and that Israel was meant to be a kingdom of priests and a holy people, and that the critical issues of life concerned conduct with God, the other, and the self. That piety that explained from day to day what it meant to be a *Mensch*, a decent human being, answered the question that through the Christian centuries the West understood as critical: How shall I live so as to die decently?

The issues of modern times shifted from the human questions framed by humanity in God's image and in God's likeness to an altogether different set of urgent concerns, having to do with politics and economics. The received Torah echoed with the question: Adam, where are you? The Torahs of the nineteenth century answered the question: Jew, what else can you become? For millennia, Jews had not wanted to be more than they were; and now the Jewish question, asked by gentiles and Jews alike, rested on the premise that to be Jewish did not suffice. Now Jews wished not totally to integrate, but also not entirely to segregate themselves. They no longer had in mind a place in a people that dwells alone. The Judaic systems of the twentieth century, with their stress on politics for professionals, ephemeral enthusiasm for everybody else, reconstituted the people that dwells alone—for fifteen minutes at a time. No wonder then that, at the end of two hundred years, the heirs of a set of partial systems would go in search of a whole and complete one: one that provided what all the established ones did not, that same sense of center and of the whole that, for so long, was precisely what Jews did not want for

330

themselves. The protracted love affair over, some Jews re-engaged the received Torah, the one in two parts, in a long-term union. Not many, not experienced, sometimes awkward, often forced and unnatural, they in time would find their path—and, in ways they could not imagine or approve, lead the Jewish world.

These Judaisms of reversion have begun in self-awareness and, in doctrine (for Israeli reversionism) and deed (for American reversionism), give powerful testimony to the capacity of Judaic systems to come to grips with the acutely contemporary issues of Jews' lives. That forms the source of their remarkable power to change lives, to bring about what, in secular terms, one would call conversion and, in Judaic terms, return. The reversionary Judaisms—and they include Reform, Orthodoxy, Conservatism, each in its many formulations—take up today's concerns and draw them into the framework of an enduring program of life and reflection. That capacity to form a relationship between the individual here and now and the social entity, Israel, in the far reaches of time takes the measure of Judaic systems. By that criterion, the systems of reversion, however limited their actual effect in numbers and even moral authority, enjoy remarkable success. I discern only one source of that success: the Judaic system of the dual Torah, its enduring power to address the human condition in God's name. "And he believed the Lord, and he reckoned it to him as righteousness."

CHAPTER 9

CONTINUITY AND NEW CREATION: JUDAIC SYSTEMS FOR THE TWENTY-FIRST CENTURY

The End of "Systemopoeia" (System Formation)

The destruction of most of the Jews of Europe, the end of the possibility of a distinctive community life of the Jews of the Soviet Union, the creation of the State of Israel, the advent of a powerful and assertive Jewry in America—none of these extraordinary events has generated a new and substantial Judaic system. The current systems claim merely to rehearse what has happened and dwell on the past (though, of course, that is not what they really do) or merely to repeat the holy words and recapitulate the sacred deeds. The Judaisms of Holocaust and Redemption and of reversion, by their own word, offer no counterpart to the originality and fresh perspective of Reform, Orthodoxy, Zionism, or Jewish socialism. For all of those Judaisms stepped essentially outside the framework of the day, making original use of all that had gone before in the composition of a system of stunning originality. Zionism asked utterly new questions. Jewish socialism addressed the fundamental issues of economic life and class structure, issues that had never found public recognition as categories of thought at all. Reform Judaism, surely the most subtle and fecund of all Judaisms born after the death of the self-evidence of the received system, took up the unthinkable and thought through its givens.* The Judaism of Holocaust and Redemption, for its part, obsessively rehearses—in an awful sense, one might even say "celebrates"—the past but bears little message for the future and offers no program beyond the repetition of the truths of a politics of dying. Beyond its equivalent negativism, in the utter rejection of the values of Western civilization, the set of Judaisms of reversion likewise has found little to say, proving incapable of taking up and answering urgent questions of a social and political character. As we have seen, that set of Judaisms centers on the individual and teaches a personal salvation for people abstracted from the larger Judaic world. Jews in the reversionary systems not without justification bear the title "reborn," aptly borrowed from the Protestant experience of individual salvation, and so testify to the opposite of that "authenticity" to

---

* That is the reason Reform Judaism defined the agenda of all Judaisms of the nineteenth century.

333

the true Judaism—that mere, that pure reversion they claim to realize.

The twentieth century, in fact, produced no Judaic systems for seventy-five years. Except for the Judaic system of Holocaust and Redemption, all of the systems we have surveyed derive from the nineteenth century. Let us look backward and see how things really worked themselves out. From after the beginning of Reform Judaism at the start of the nineteenth century to the later twentieth century, we identify three periods of enormous system building—or *systemopoeia*. In each of these, the manufacture of Judaic systems came into sharp focus: 1850–60, for the systems of Orthodoxy and the Positive Historical School; 1890–1900, for Jewish socialism and Zionism (I am less clear on appropriate dates for yiddishism); and 1967–73, for the systems of American Judaism and American and Israeli reversionism. That fact requires that we reconsider our earlier view of matters.

Within a span of one hundred years, from somewhat before 1800 to somewhat after 1900, all but one of the Judaic systems of the nineteenth and twentieth centuries reached articulated statement, each with a clear picture of its required deeds and doctrines and definition of the Israel it wished to address. One wonders how it was that one period produced a range, only some of which I have surveyed, of Judaic systems of depth and enormous breadth, which attracted mass support and persuaded many of the meaning of their lives, while the next three quarters of a century produced but one. What requires explanation is the end, not the beginning and fruition, of Judaic systemopoeia.

We may eliminate answers deriving from mere accidents of political change. Even important shifts in the political circumstances of Israel, the Jewish people, have not necessarily led to exercises in symbolic redefinition to accommodate social change. Take, for example, the State of Israel.

The creation of the first Jewish state in two thousand years yielded nothing more interesting than a flag and a rather domestic politics, not a world view and a way of life such as the founders of the American republic, Madison and Hamilton, enunciated, and such as their contemporaries, Washington and Jefferson, imagined that they were constructing. State building need not yield large visions and revisioning of everyday life and how it should be lived; in most cases, it has not done so, though in the United States it did. But not in the state of Israel. No Judaic systems have emerged there; instead, there have been only rehearsals and representations of European ones. (Israeli nationalism is not a Judaic system, as I explain in the appendix.) The rise of the State of Israel destroyed a system, the Zionist one, but replaced it with nothing pertinent to Jewry at large.

American Jewry presents the same picture. Wars and dislocations, migration and relocation—these in the past stimulated those large reconsiderations that generated and sustained system building in Jews' societies. The political changes affecting Jews in America, who became Jewish Americans in ways in which Jews did not become Jewish Germans or Jewish Frenchmen or Jewish Englishmen or women, yielded no encompassing system. The Judaic system of Holocaust and Redemption leaves unaffected the larger dimensions of human existence of Jewish Americans—and that is part of that system's power. When we consider the strength, in the Judaisms of America, of Reform, Orthodoxy, and Historical or Conservative Judaism, each in its German formulation, we see the reality. The Judaic systems of the nineteenth century have endured in America, none of them facing significant competition of scale. In other words, millions of people have moved from one world to another, changed in language, occupation, and virtually every other significant social and cultural indicator—and produced nothing more than a set of recapitula-

335

tions of systems serviceable under utterly different, and not necessarily appropriate, circumstances. The failure of Israeli Jewry to generate system building finds its match in the still more startling unproductivity of American Jewry. Nothing much has happened in either of the two massive communities of Israel in the twentieth century.

Where political change should have precipitated fresh thought and experiment, and Judaic systems should have come forth, change of an unprecedented order has yielded a rehearsal of ideas familiar only from other contexts. Israeli nationalism as a Jewish version of Third World nationalism, American Judaism as a Jewish version of a national cultural malaise on account of a lost war—these set forth a set of altogether stale notions. Let me now recapitulate the question, before proceeding to my answer: Why no system building for seventy-five years or so? And we come, then, to the reason for what is, in my judgment, the simple fact that, since the First World War, Judaic system building (with the possible exception of the system of Judaic reversion) has come to an end.

I believe that three factors are pertinent to why no vital Judaic system has come forth since the end of the nineteenth century: the Holocaust, the demise of intellect, and the dominance of large organizations. While I do not claim that these factors—demographic, cultural, institutional and bureaucratic—are the only reasons, I think they can help to answer the question before us.

The Effect of the Holocaust

First of all, the demographic factor. Judaic systems in all their variety emerged in Europe—not in America or in what was then Palestine and is now the State of Israel—and, within Europe, came from central and eastern European Jewry. The systemopoeia of central and eastern European Jews may be accounted for in two ways: first, the Jews in the East, in particular, formed a vast population, with enormous learning and diverse interests; second, the systems of the nineteenth and twentieth centuries arose out of a vast population that lived in self-aware circumstances, not scattered and individual but composed and bonded. The Jews who perished in the Holocaust formed enormous and self-conscious communities of vast intellectual riches.

To them, being Jewish constituted a collective enterprise, not an individual predilection. In the West, the prevailing attitude of mind identifies religion with belief, to the near exclusion of behavior; and since religion tends to identify itself with faith, religion is understood as a personal state of mind or as an individual's personal and private attitude. So the Judaic systems that took shape after 1900 exhibit that same Western bias not for society but self, not for culture and community but conscience and character. Under such circumstances, systemopoeia hardly flourishes, for systems speak of communities and create worlds of meaning, answer pressing public questions, and produce broadly self-evident answers. The contrast makes the point, between the circumstance of reversionary systems of Judaisms—involving individuals "coming home" one by one—with the context of the ideological Judaic systems, all of them, in fact, mass movements and Jewish idiomatic statements of still larger mass movements. The demographic fact then speaks for itself. Whether one can specify a particular demographic (and not merely intellectual) base necessary for the foundation of a given Judaic system I do not know. As I said, the reversionary systems demand a demographic base of one person, but Zionist and Socialist systems demanded one of millions—millions provided by the mass populations of central and eastern Europe, which everyone who has traced the history of Judaic systems in modern times has found to be the point of origin of nearly all systems. And then from the 1930s to the mid-1940s this most productive segment of world Jewry died in the Holocaust, and with it, Judaic systemopoeia. Stated as naked truth, not only too many (one is too many!) but the wrong Jews died. The impact of the destruction of European Jewry cannot, then, be underestimated. The destruction of European Jewry in eastern and central Europe brought to an end the great age of Judaic system construction and explains the paralysis of imagination and will that has left the Jews to forage in the detritus of an earlier age: rehearsing other peoples' answers to other peoples' questions. Indeed, I maintain that until Judaic system builders come to grips with the full extent of the effects of the Holocaust, they will do little more than recapitulate a world now gone. For the systems before us answered the questions urgent to European Jewry in the nineteenth and early twentieth centuries—those questions, not others.

Yet the demographic issue by itself cannot suffice. For today's Jewish populations produce massive communities—three hundred thousand here, half a million there, and, after all, both American Judaism and Israeli nationalism testify to the possibilities of system building even beyond the mass murder of European Jewry. When we consider, moreover, the strikingly unproductive character of large populations of Jews, the inert and passive character of ideology (such as it is) in the Jewries of France, Britain, South Africa, and the Soviet Union (where, so far as the world knows, no Judaic system has come forth—no world view joined to a definition of a way of life capable of sustaining an Israel, a society), the picture becomes clear. Even where there are populations capable of generating and sustaining distinctive Judaic systems, none is in sight. So there is yet another factor, which proves correlative with the first—the loss of European Jewry.

The Demise of Intellect

The utter indifference of the Judaic systems of the twentieth century to the received writings of the Judaism of the dual Torah calls attention to the second explanation for the end of systemopoeia. That is the unappreciated factor of sheer ignorance, the profound pathos of Jews' illiteracy in all books but the book of the streets and marketplaces of the day. This second factor, the loss of access to that permanent treasury of the human experience of Jewry preserved and handed on in the canonical Torah, began even before the nineteenth century: the extant raw materials of system building now prove barren and leached.

People nowadays resort mainly to the immediately accessible experiences of emotions and politics. We recall that the systems of the nineteenth and twentieth centuries made constant reference to the Judaism of the dual Torah—at first, intimate; later, merely by way of allusion and rejection. The nineteenth-century systems drew depth and breadth of vision from the received Judaism of the dual Torah, out of which they produced—in their own words—variations and continuations. So the received system and its continuators realized not only the world of perceived experience at hand. The repertoire of human experience in the Judaism of the dual Torah presents as human options the opposite of the banal, the one-dimensional, the immediate. Jews received and used the heritage of human experience captured, as in amber, in the words of the dual Torah. So they did not have to make things up fresh every morning or rely only on that small sector of the range of human experience immediately accessible and near at hand.

By contrast, Israeli nationalism and American Judaism—the two most influential systems that move Jews to action in the world today—scarcely concern themselves with that Judaism. They find themselves left only with what is near at hand. They work with the raw materials made available by contemporary experience—emotions on the one side, politics on the other. Access to realms beyond requires learning in literature, the only resource for human experience beyond the immediate. But the Judaic systems of the twentieth century, except for the reversionary Judaisms, do not resort to the reading of books as a principal act of their way of life, in the way in which the Judaism of the dual Torah and its continuators did and do. The consequence is a strikingly abbreviated agenda of issues, a remarkably one-dimensional program of urgent questions.

In this regard, the reversionary systems point toward a renewed engagement with the canon and system of the dual Torah; but—in consequence, I think—those systems prove (quite properly) transitory and preparatory—ways back to Sinai. So their definitive characteristic points toward what has not happened: that is, a systematic exploitation, by system builders working out an original and urgent program of questions and answers, of the received Judaism of the dual Torah. The reason for neglect is the self-evident fact that the Jews of the world today—especially in France and elsewhere in western Europe, the Soviet Union, and the United States, but also in Canada, Australia, South Africa, Argentina, Brazil, and other areas of sizable Jewish populations—have lost all access to writings of the Judaism of the dual Torah that sustained fifteen centuries of Jews before now. The appeal to contemporary experience, whether in emotions or in politics, draws upon a relatively poor treasury of reflection and response to the human condition. And the utter failure of imagination, the poverty of contemporary system building where it takes place at all, shows the result. From a mansion Israel has moved into a hovel. Jews in the European, African, and Australian worlds no longer regard "being Jewish" as a matter of intellect; and so far as they frame a world view for themselves, it bears few points of intersection with the Judaic canon.

One reason that Judaic systems did not emerge in the American Judaic setting derives from the astounding failure of education to transmit to the bulk of Jewry in America the received system in any accessible form. In the processes of settling down in the United States, American Jewry denied itself access to the resources on which other communities had drawn—that is, the canon of the Judaism of the dual Torah. Recognizing too late what had already happened—the deracination of the Jews—the third generation then attempted to create a domestic Judaism resting on experiences no one had undergone or would want to undergo. So American Jewry forms a community of Jews with little interest in books, with virtually no religious school system for fully half its children. Jewish Americans have, in the main, neither studied Torah nor, in light of the written human experience of Jews through the ages, closely reflected on their own lives as the first Jews to live in a free society. They work out their lives as not the last Jews on earth, but as the first and only Jews who ever lived.

They have, therefore, opted for neither the worst of one world nor the best of another: that is, they focus such imaginative energies as they have generated upon the Holocaust as myth, and center their eschatological fantasies on "the beginning of our redemption" in the State of Israel. But they have not gone through the one nor chosen to participate in the other. Not having lived through the mass murder of European Jewry, American Jews restated the problem of evil in unanswerable form—the Holocaust is beyond all speech—and then transformed that problem into an obsession. Not choosing to settle in the State of Israel, moreover, American Jews further defined redemption, the resolution of the problem of evil, in terms remote from their world. One need not look far to find the limitations of the system

of American Judaism: its stress on a world other than the
one in which the devotees in fact are living. As to the reversionary Judaisms of the hour, it is too soon to tell what they
yield or how they will endure. By nature transient, by doctrine alien to the canonical system they allege they merely
recapitulate, by program of deed separate from the world
to which they allegedly propose to gain access, they have
yet to show us how, and whether, they will last. That is
what I mean by failure of intellect.

The Dominance of Large Organizations

Third and distinct from the other two factors in the
dearth of new Judaic systems is the bureaucratization of
Jewry in consequence of the tasks it has rightly identified
as urgent. To meet the problems Jews find self-evidently
urgent, they have had to adopt a way of life of building and
maintaining and working through vast organizations and
institutions. The contemporary class structure of Jewry,
therefore, places in positions of influence Jews who place
slight value on matters of intellect and learning, and that
same system accords no sustained hearing to Jews who
strive to reflect. The tasks are other, and they call forth
other gifts than those of heart and mind. The exemplary
experiences of those who exercise influence derives from
politics, through law; from economic activity, through
business; from institutional careers, through government,
industry, and the like. As the gifts of establishing routine
take precedence over the endowments of charisma of an
intellectual order, the experiences people know and understand—politics, easy emotions—serve also for the raw materials of Judaic system building. Experiences that, in a Judaic context, people scarcely know, do not so serve. This I

take to be yet another consequence of the ineluctable tasks of the twentieth century: the building of large organizations to solve large problems. Organizations, by their very nature, require specialization. The difference between the classes that produce systemic change today and those who created systems in the nineteenth and early twentieth centuries then proves striking. What brought that difference about, if not the great war conducted against the Jews, beginning not in 1933 but earlier, from the 1880s on, with the organization of political anti-Semitism joined to economic exclusion? So, in a profound sense, the type of structure now characteristic of Jewry is one of the uncounted costs of the Holocaust.

Intellectuals create systems. Administrators do not; and thus when they need ideas, they call for propaganda and hire publicists and journalists. When we remember that all of the Judaic systems of the nineteenth and early twentieth centuries derived from intellectuals, we realize what has changed. Herzl was a journalist, for instance, and the Jews who organized Jewish socialism and brought yiddishism all wrote books. The founders of the system of Reform Judaism were mainly scholars, rabbis, writers, dreamers, and other intellectuals. It is not because they were lawyers that the framers of the Historical School produced their historicistic system. The emphases of Hirsch and other creators of Orthodoxy lay on doctrine, and all of them wrote important books and articles of a reflective and even philosophical character. So much for Reform, Orthodox, Conservative, socialist-yiddishist, and Zionist systems: the work of intellectuals, one and all.

The contrast with American Judaism and Israeli nationalism demands only a brief observation. While writers bring to expression the main themes of these two systems, the priests of the systems of American Judaism and Israeli nationalism, those who conduct the rites and dictate the pat-

343

tern of observances, find qualification other than in the books they have written—or even read. And I need not dwell on the virulent anti-intellectualism recorded by Aviad in her portrait of Israeli reversionism and by Heilman in his portrait of the American. So, in all, the institutions of American Judaism and Israeli nationalism bring to influence as well as to power (which, in the perspective of systems, makes less difference) people who do, but do not find engaging, the tasks of abstract and speculative thought.

These three factors—demographic, cultural, institutional and bureaucratic—scarcely exhaust the potential explanation for the long span of time in which Jews have brought forth few Judaic systems, relying instead on those formed in a prior and different age and circumstance. But I do think that all of the systems will figure in any rigorous account of what has happened, and not happened, in the present century. And they point directly or indirectly to the extraordinary price yet to be exacted from Jewry on account of the murder of six million Jews in Europe.

I have to justify the correlation between mass murder and an exemplary leadership of lawyers and businessmen and politicians and generals. Because of the crisis presented by the German nation's war against the Jews, the latter had to make every effort to constitute themselves into a political entity capable of mass action; and Jewish leaders responded to that requirement of the twentieth century. Administrators, not intellectuals, bureaucrats, not charismatic thinkers, formed the cadre of the hour. In an age in which, to survive at all, Jews had to address the issues of politics and economics, and build a state (in the State of Israel) and a massive and effective set of organizations capable of collective political action (in the United States), not sages but *politicians* in the deepest sense of the word—namely, those able to do the work of the polity—alone could do what had to be done. And they did come forward. They did their task, as well as could have been hoped, in a time that demanded gifts other than those prized by intellectuals. And the correlation between mass murder and a culture of organizations proves exact: the war against the Jews called forth, from the Jews, people capable of building institutions to protect the collectivity of Israel, so far as anyone could be saved. Consequently much was saved. But much was lost.

Celebrating the victory of survival, we should not lose sight of the cost. Determining the full cost of the murder of the six million Jews of Europe will require a long time. The end of the remarkable age of Judaic systemopoeia may prove a more serious charge against the future, a more calamitous cost of the destruction of European Jewry, than anyone has yet realized. More suffocated than Jews in gas chambers; spirit, too, perished. The banality of survival forms a counterpoint to the banality of evil represented by the factories built to manufacture dead Jews in an age of the common and routine atrocity.

People draw upon only their experience of emotions, inside, and of politics, without. Then they treat themselves as the paradigm of humanity. What they are, they think, is all they can become. That they think so is not surprising. Who does otherwise, except those with eyes upon a long past, a distant future—a vision? The system builders, the intellectuals, book readers, book writers, truth tellers— these are the ones who appeal to the experience of the ages as precedent for the hour, and who produced out of the death of the received system all the Judaic systems born in the death of that received one: whether Reform theologians invoked the precedent of change; or Orthodox, of Sinai. Today there are no system builders, so we can scarcely ask for the rich perspectives, the striking initiatives, that yield compelling systems of life and thought.

Judaic Systems: The Corporate Model

We do not have, therefore, to wonder whence come the nullities that have taken the place of the system builders. The ready answer brings us to the end of the story of the death and birth of Judaism. The twentieth century presented to Jews the necessity to create large bureaucracies to deal with large problems. It is no accident that system building came to an end in an age of large Jewish organizations: armies and governments, in the State of Israel; and enormous instruments of fund raising and politics, in America. So let me dwell on this matter of the building by specialists of large organizations. Specialization in modern times has meant that systems require their elite, the specialists, and relegate all other people to a life essentially at the fringes of the system. Every Judaist in a Judaic system of the dual Torah said prayers on his own (women were not given the same task). But, for example, Zionists who attended meetings did not do the same thing as did Zionists who built the land. Specialization as part of the construction of a rational system, a calling that came to expression in a particularity of work characterizes organization—that is, collective action—in modern times. And all the Judaic systems of the twentieth century conformed to the requirements of organization in that age: all formed, as I said, systems of organization, meaning specialization for all but the doing of the distinctive work of the system by only a few. The specialized work of organizations demanded from each renunciation of a role in the general scheme of the system.

In so stating, I draw upon the image of the "iron cage" of Max Weber*—an image he alludes to in the following

* My entire intellectual life, from my dissertation on, has addressed the program of Max Weber; and my entire notion of systemic analysis and the comparison of systems within Judaism, worked out most fully and in

famous passage: "The care for external goods should only lie on the shoulders of the saint like a light cloak, which can be thrown aside at any moment, but fate decreed that the cloak should become an iron cage." What Weber says about economic action applies equally to the sort of broad systemic, existential behavior that I mean when I speak of a Judaism:

> Where the fulfilment of the calling cannot directly be related to the highest spiritual and cultural values . . . the individual generally abandons the attempt to justify it at all. . . . No one knows who will live in this cage in the future. . . . For of the last stage of this cultural development, it might well be truly said: 'Specialists without spirit, sensualists without heart; this nullity imagines that it has attained a level of civilization never before achieved.'[1]

The point of intersection with organizations in the twentieth century I locate at the reference to "specialists without spirit." The division of labor that has rendered a mockery of the category of a way of life joined to a world view demonstrates why we cannot define a distinctive way of life associated with a given world view.

When I describe the world view of a movement in the nineteenth century, I allude to an encompassing theory that explains a life of actions in a given and particular pattern. When I speak of the world view of a movement of the twentieth century, I refer to the explanation of why people, in a given, distinctive circumstance, should do pretty much what everyone is doing somewhere, under some equivalent circumstance: an army is an army anywhere, but study of Torah is unique to Israel. Anyone can join a union, and why invoke a Judaic world view to explain why to join a Jewish union? I know only that Judaic world views did offer such

---

acute detail in the study of the Judaic systems of late antiquity, simply applies in detail his main perspectives.

an explanation and made a great difference to those to whom that explanation answered an urgent question. What has changed? Once more I find the answer in the history of Western civilization. The processes that shaped the Judaic systems of modern and contemporary times form part of the larger movement of humanity—a distinctive and therefore exemplary part, to be sure. Let me specify what I think has made all the difference.

The critical Judaic component of the Christian civilization of the West spoke of God and God's will for humanity, of what it meant to live in God's image, after God's likeness. So said the Judaism of the dual Torah; so said Christianity in its worship of God made flesh. That message of humanity in God's image, of a people seeking to conform to God's will, echoed in the Christian world as well: both components of the world—the Christian dough, the Judaic yeast—bore a single message about humanity. The first century after the end of the Christian formulation of the West—that is, the twentieth century—spoke of class and nation, not of one humanity in the image of one God. Calling for heroes, the century demanded sacrifice not for God but for state. When asked what it meant to live with irreconcilable difference, the century responded with total war on civilians in their homes, made foxholes. Asked to celebrate the image of humanity, the twentieth century created an improbable likeness of humanity: mountains of corpses, the dead of the Somme in the First World War and of Auschwitz in the Second, and all the other victims of the state that took the place of church and synagogue, even up to the third of the population of the Khmer killed by their own government, and the half of the world's Armenians by what, alas, was their government—and the Jews, and the Jews, and the Jews.

The first century found its enduring memory in one man on a hill, on a cross; the twentieth, in six million men, women, and children making up a Golgotha—a hill of skulls—of their own. No wonder that the Judaisms of the age struggled heroically to frame a Judaic system appropriate to the issues of the age. No wonder that they failed. Who would want to succeed in framing a world view congruent to such an age, a way of life to be lived in an age of death? And no wonder again—if I may render my opinion—that the Judaisms of the age proved transient and evanescent. I like to think that no Judaic system could ever have found an enduring fit with an age such as the one that now draws to a close. The age of reversionary Judaisms, dawning at the first light of the century beyond, forms the right, the hopeful, epitaph on the Judaisms of the dying century. They had formed Judaisms that, to Israel, the Jewish people, struggled to speak of hope and of life in the valley of the darkest shadows. But they had to fail, and their failure forms their vindication. For the Jews are a people that never could find a home in the twentieth century. That, in the aspect of eternity, may prove the highest tribute God will pay to those whom God among humanity first chose.

A NOTE ON THE COMPARISON OF SYSTEMS

To compare Judaisms with one another, I return to my point of departure: the enduring system, the Judaism of the dual Torah. The Judaism of the dual Torah took up a long perspective, situating Israel in the entire cosmos of creation and in the majestic unfolding of human history, a vast and noble vision. The Judaisms born from the death of the self-evidence of the system of the dual Torah ask smaller questions. The great tradition of old overshadows the smaller ones of the age. Contrast the humble agenda in the Judaisms of the twentieth and (as it would now appear) the twenty-first centuries with the turning point of late antiquity. The one unfolded out of a crisis of conscience and of

351

confidence, but scarcely of culture and of politics; the other, out of a calamity of political economy. The one asked, Given what has happened, what should the Jews do? The other, Given what is happening, what should someone—Jew, gentile—do with the Jews?

The questions of the formative age of the Judaism of the dual Torah addressed the meaning and end of history. The issue was how to make sense of what was happening, viewed as part of a divine plan. Through typology, which compared Israel of the day to the Israel described in the book of Genesis, the sages answered that question: the meaning of events now derives from the story of the patriarchs and matriarchs of long ago. The definition of Israel called into question the standing and status of the Jews, since Christians maintained that they were the new Israel. The answer, worked out through genealogy, posited that the Jews now were the family, in a perfectly physical sense, of Abraham, Isaac, and Jacob. The Christians' ineluctable claim that Jesus had been, and now is, Christ was countered by the Jews with the doctrine that the Messiah would come at the end of days, and that the Messiah would be a sage. Now these issues invoked deep and farsighted questions of human history from creation to redemption. They were framed in response to the conflict between Scripture's promises to Israel and history's disappointments for Israel. So these questions responded not to the hour, though they were precipitated by a critical moment. They turned the evanescent occasion into a moment in eternity, taking a long view of things. That perspective, I think, forms part of the power to abide and endure that can be discerned in the Judaic system of the dual Torah.

The smaller questions asked by modern Judaic systems yield commensurately modest answers. Indeed, the issues of the Judaism of the dual Torah and the agenda of the present day are jarringly discrepant. The issues, though matters of life and death, seem less in dimension; so, too, do the answers: political answers to political questions, economic and social responses to a crisis of European society in its political economy. The Judaism of the dual Torah invoked heaven and earth to do battle for the soul of disappointed Israel. The systems of the twentieth century call into being a culture of organizations and create not theologies but, as I said in chapter 9, bureaucracies instead.

If we ask the source for the remarkable depth of vision of the Judaic system of the dual Torah, we do well to turn to Scripture, which shaped that vision. Constant reference to Scripture and tradition produced that reading that yielded Judaism in the system of the dual Torah. The questions derived from the world of imagination and sensibility, and so did the answers. The pressing issues of the age of Constantine and the birth of Christianity concerned not the Jews' political standing within the Roman empire, nor their economic and social position. These remained essentially what they had been: subordinated, but so was everyone within the empire; on the whole, satisfactory, as, in the region, most lived lives they found acceptable. The agenda took up eternal issues, reaching back to creation and forward to the end of time. Those issues proved perennial; and, for a long time, so did the responses.

In the nineteenth century, close to the received system, the continuator Judaisms, thriving in an age we now perceive as benign, dealt with questions of the same sort and answered them in essentially the same canonical way—that is, by reference to the dual Torah. But the twentieth century—so it appears at its end—was different. And the Judaisms of reversion, pointing toward the twenty-first century, are different yet again. So at the surface, we see a radical break—not in 1789, with the American Constitution and the French Revolution, but in 1897, with the founding of the Zionist Organization and the Jewish Workers Union,

353

the Bund. To extend the *jeu d'esprit*, we may say that Judaism in the received form took a century to die, and the newborn Judaisms came forth, in paradigm, in a single year.

Yet how pertinent, in all, is the comparison of the continuator Judaisms of the nineteenth century—the ones so long in dying, as I propose—and the new ideologies, framed out of the materials of the contemporary idiom of thought and politics, of the twentieth and twenty-first? The Judaic systems of a theological order, in full knowledge and self-consciousness, by self-aware decision in the nineteenth century created fresh systems out of available materials. The utterly new ideologies of the twentieth century formed ways of life and world views out of nothing particular to the Judaic systems that had gone before; instead, they formed a Jewish expression within a cosmopolitan and international idiom of sociology (class struggle), culture (linguistic basis for group life), and politics (nationalism). So how compare the one with the other at all, when we may have in hand not two species of a single genus but two genera?

Now the obvious objection—the point of continuity from century to century—derives from the Judaisms of reversion. Yet the claim to continuity of belief (in Israeli reversionism) and behavior (in the American kind) cloaks remarkable selectivity. For the theology of rejection of all that is secular and Western contradicts the perceptions of the continuator Judaisms that the received system presents no conflict between the West and the Torah. More to the point, that system, in its long history, managed quite comfortably to accommodate diverse worlds and to address Jews living in them. But that theology does conform in every substantive detail to the ideology of the very distinct moment at which it came to expression. It stated a no more distinctively Judaic viewpoint than did Jewish socialism or Zionism speaking only out of Judaic canonical writings and experience (world view, way of life).

So, to proceed with the argument, how appropriate the comparison? For we talk now, in the twentieth-century systems, of politics, scarcely of a world view; of sociology, migration, demography, and the movement of generations, hardly of a way of life. Rejection of everything in favor of a made-up "authentic tradition" turns out, too, to express a general malaise with modernity—a cliché of experience, a banality no more nuanced, no less shallow, than the unspeakable banalities of "kibbutz Judaism." We wonder, therefore, whether we are comparing things that sustain comparison and contrast, things of a single genus but different species. We ask ourselves whether the effect of a circumstance, a condition brought on from the outside and cleared off by external forces deserves analysis as a Judaic system in the way in which the received compositions of thought and programs of behavior addressed to an Israel do. In all, the wildly attractive ideologies of the twentieth century, with their power to move people through their statement of self-evident (if diverse and contradictory) truths, by morning sprout up and by evening wither.

So the question is, Were they ever Judaisms? And what do their successes and (up to now) abrupt demises teach us about a Judaism? The answer depends upon the purpose of asking the question. If we propose to form judgments upon questions of content, then we err in considering the ideologies at hand. For proving that they do not continue and build upon the received system of the dual Torah requires only that we cite their own ideologies. They, after all, said—over and over again, to audiences eager to hear exactly that message of liberation from an unwanted past— that they had done so. That past stood as a symbol for an unsatisfactory present. The treatment of the past as symbol and symbolization in no way differentiates any of the Judaisms before us, continuator and theological, or fresh and ideological, or reversionary alike. That mode of thought pervaded the world. Claiming that the ideologies of the twentieth century in no way grew out of an incremental process generated within the logic of the tradition itself, moreover, scarcely requires effort, except in the case of reversionism—and, then, not much effort. The move from (at least) proof-texts to (at most) pretexts finds nearly universal recognition. It is not something people debate any more, except, again, in regard to reversionism; and then the debate hardly generates much heat. So the essentially new and utterly unprecedented Judaic systems of the present century prove somewhat less than meets the eye, since the basic propositions—not a linear history, not an incremental process—find ample substantiation right on the surface.

But—to revert—were they ever Judaisms? And what do their success and abrupt demise teach us about a Judaism? I review: A Judaism is constituted by a world view, telling people who they are and why they must do what they have to do; by a way of life, defining everyday activities in the context of a pattern of meaning transcending the mundane, addressed to an Israel (or to "all Israel"). So of course the systems at hand all constituted Judaisms—why not? The aspect of perfect faith that characterizes the three Judaic systems of the twentieth century, and the ones of the twenty-first that I have considered, testifies to the systemic power of each one. The source of that power lies in the system's sorting out and answering the real questions. So much for success. It derives from the strength of a system to identify urgent problems, issues that have crossed the line separating the chronic from the acute considerations confronting Jews. Each of the twentieth-century systems succeeded in doing just that: Each answered extraordinarily pressing questions in a persuasive way. We learn, therefore, that a system succeeds—that is, attains the status of self-evidence—when it asks the right questions and proposes answers perceived, scarcely through argument, to work.

And what do we learn from the astounding instability of the systems at hand? It is that, given the character of society in this century, focus upon today guarantees nearly instant obsolescence, whether in machines or in the social constructs of humanity I call systems. Problems change, because the world changes; and a Judaism that selects as urgent a social or political problem gains for itself nearly immediate currency but certain, rapid devaluation, too— even defalcation of all value. Jewish socialism and yiddishism, after all, did not die because people disbelieved; they died because the Israel to whom they spoke had been murdered. Zionism did not perish because it failed but because it succeeded; the Jewish problem changed, and the success of Zionism itself created new problems for Jews. American Judaism thrives, so none can say where and how it will lose its presently supreme power of self-evidence. Doubtless Israeli and American reversionism has yet a way to run in its course. I can only maintain, with perfect certainty, that all Judaic systems are like Jonah's castor oil plant, that shade that saved Jonah from the heat. By dawn a worm will attack the plant, and it will wither. And none will be angry for the plant, for which none labored, which none made to grow, which came into being in a night and perished in a night. And so it is with Judaisms: come up in a night; pass in a night, whence and why and whither, no one knows.

So we may refer, for a probative analogy, to the taxonomy of botany: Are plants that perish in a night plants, too? Sure, why not? In our terms, we wonder how long a system has to survive to serve as a system. Doubtless they also serve who last but a brief generation, even form a system for a half-life of an hour. So that question proves trivial. But the consequent one does not: Which plants last and resist the worm and which do not, and what is the difference? In our terms, why does one system last and another perish quickly? Among the eight systems I have surveyed—counting the Judaic system of the dual Torah as well as its continuators in Reform, Orthodox, and Conservative Judaisms, as well as in its successors in Jewish socialism and yiddishism, Zionism, and American Judaism, and, finally, the Judaic system(s) of reversion—what points of differentiation present themselves?

First, a system that meets the definition at hand—world view, complemented by a way of life, addressed to a clearly denoted Israel—however long it lasts constitutes a system. No criterion of age or of longevity pertains. The reason is that a religious system presents a fact not of history but of immediacy, of the social present. The issue of survival by itself proves impertinent to the analysis of a system. A system is like a language. A language forms an example of language if it produces communication through rules of syntax and verbal arrangement. That paradigm serves full well, however many people speak the language, or however long the language serves. Two people who understand each other form a language community, even, or especially, if no one understands them.

So, too, by definition religions address the living, constitute societies, frame and compose cultures. For however long, at whatever moment in historic time, a religious system always grows up in the perpetual present, an artifact of its day, whether today or a long-ago time. The only appropriate tense for a religious system is the present. A religious system always *is*, whatever it was, whatever it will be. The reason is that its traits address a condition of humanity in society, a circumstance of an hour—however brief or protracted the hour and the circumstance.

When we ask that a religious composition speak to a society with a message of the *is* and the *ought* and with a meaning for the everyday, we focus the power of that system to hold the whole together: the society the system addresses, the individuals who compose the society, the ordinary lives they lead, in ascending order of consequence. And that system then forms a whole and well-composed structure. Yes, the structure stands somewhere, and the place where it stands will secure for the system either an extended or an ephemeral span of life. But the system, for however long it lasts, serves. And that focus on the eternal present justifies my interest in analyzing why a system works (the urgent agenda it successfully solves) when it does, and why it ceases to work (loses self-evidence, is bereft of its Israel, for example) when it no longer works. The hypotheses that present themselves to fulfill that interest in no way depend for verification on the accidents of mass murder or migration; on systemic success unprepared for, as with Zionism; or even on systemic exhaustion of undernourished intellects and overstrained emotions, as (I suspect) may yet afflict American Judaism. So the phrase "the *history* of a *system*" presents us with an oxymoron. Systems endure in that eternal present that they create. They evoke precedent, they do not have a history. A system relates to context but, as I have stressed, exists in an enduring moment (which, to be sure, changes all the time). We capture the system in a moment; the worm consumes it an hour later. That is the way of mortality, whether for us one by one, in all mortality, or for the works of humanity in society.

Then we wonder which system lasts and which does not and how we are to know the difference. The systems before us—seven acutely contemporary, one remarkable for its endurance—differ in one important way. The seven ask today's questions and answer them by appeal to facts and the claim of mere facticity. The one asks questions framed out of a long perspective, seeks the answers in the interstices of a vast and persistent canon of writings, makes provision for the active intellect and its ongoing labor of exegesis. The Judaism of the dual Torah appeals to the authority of sages and stimulates a permanent confrontation between them and the changing world at hand. The sages, for their part, sustained the system by mediating between the one and the other: the system and the world of change. The outcome is an exercise in harmonization within the system and of mediation between temporal change and eternal verity beyond the system. Change did not destroy, time did not attenuate, so long as the fundamental issues persisted. The issues, moreover, possessed an enduring urgency, for pretty much everyone in the world Jews knew asked the same questions and answered them by appeal to the same set of facts, however diversely construed.

And in the West the issues of the Judaism of the dual Torah registered somewhere between chronic and acute for so long as Christianity controlled the West's systems of social bonding, of world creating. Then the issues of a long perspective—a past to creation, a future to the end of time—impended every day but, for Judaism, came to resolution on the seventh day (so to speak).

The Israel of the Judaism of the dual Torah lived in a timeless world of the everyday, for the *now* of sanctification, and of the future redemption, for the *then* of salvation. And the larger circumstance of that system spoke of God's will in the now and plan for the then. So the system corresponded to the circumstance and lasted for that long. But when it collapsed, a century of continuators saved what they could (and it was a great deal). Then, a hundred years beyond, a set of systems, acutely exemplified by the three I have surveyed, composed new Judaisms, each out of the wherewithal of the world at hand. None of these systems in its day exhibited profound flaws of composition and construction, because each amply disposed of the urgent questions it, to begin with, had selected. To state matters in a less anthropomorphic way, the framers of each produced systems adequate to deal with the questions each set of framers thought urgent. The precipitating catalyst and the consequent solution served full well. But none of the theologies of continuation or the ideologies of the new age appealed to more than the facts at hand. And when the facts changed, so did Jews' minds.

This brings us back to the matter of what might have been: why some circumstances yielded the formation of new systems, and others did not. Let me expand on my remarks in chapter 9. In the three-quarters of a century since the First World War (with the stated exceptions) we look in vain for important and influential Judaic systems aborning. I can think of examples of what might have been—for example, in Reconstructionism, a this-worldly theology and handsomely articulated world view produced by Mordecai M. Kaplan but altogether derivative, as to way of life, from Conservative Judaism and lacking any considerable influence. Focused on the thought of a single individual, however noteworthy, a set of ideas hardly serves the composition of a system, and a philosophy is not a Judaism. But this is a trivial example. To take a stunning and important fact: I discern no Judaic system taking shape from the decade after the First World War to the decade after the Vietnam War (for the unfolding of Jewish Americans' Judaic existence) and after the Yom Kippur War (for Israelis)—not one. Considering the mass appeal and power of Zionism, we look in vain to Israeli life for evidence of the formation of Judaic systems of cogent composition and distinctive character. Only with the reversionary systems of the late twentieth century do we see what might have been. It seems a valid observation, therefore, that no systems came into being between the 1890s and the 1970s. We ask what might have been, and why what might have happened did not happen.

To answer the first question, we turn to Israeli nationalism, which can have constituted such a system but has thus far failed to do so. To be sure, perhaps it has done so, but it made no impression outside the country. True, an Israeli nationalism has framed a distinctive world view and way of life for a defined Israel. Its way of life? Doing whatever you want, within a prescribed set of national boundaries. Its world view? Citizenship in the Jewish state and the viewpoints connected with the duties of that citizenship. Its Israel? The question answers itself. That nationalism belongs in the classification of a Judaic system, no less than did Jewish socialism and yiddishism, on the one side, and Zionism, on the other. The fact, therefore, that that nationalism also falls into a genus in no way particular to Israel's taxonomic system is immaterial. A Judaic system that addresses only one segment of the Jews certainly does not suffer disqualification on that account.

But the definition of Israeli nationalism as a Judaic system produces one important flaw. For, by legal definition, Israeli nationalism—encompassing, after all, citizenship—presents a Judaic system that encompasses non-Jews, as, in the nature of things, Israeli nationalism must provide. This is a different matter, lacking all self-evident resolution. We can say that while Israelism—that is, a generalized sentiment of concern for the welfare of the State of Israel, joined to important activity to realize that sentiment—flourishes among nearly all Jews, Israelism scarcely explains the meaning of life to any sizable sector of world Jewry. Israelism, moreover, attracts non-Jews as well as Jews, and so does not have a clear address to an Israel. Moreover, in the nature of politics, Israelism scarcely absorbs a substantial part of the life of the devotee, as did, for example, Zionism or Orthodoxy or Jewish socialism and yiddishism. And neither does Israeli nationalism for that heterogeneous and diverse population. For a Judaic system must tell me what I, a Jew, am not, but also what I am and must become, why I must do what I must do, where I am heading and what my life means within the larger framework of Israel. Zionism answered those questions; Israeli nationalism for Israelis scarcely asks them. The country is too divided and diverse, the population too absorbed within its ordinary and mundane life, and such civil religion as any society puts forth to hold things together as a matter of national and state policy cannot serve also as a systemic structure. So, in all, no Judaic system here. Whether Israeli nationalism presents a species of the genus *civil religion* does not concern us.

Let me conclude these remarks on the comparison of systems with a systemic comparison—between the list of the systems at hand and the prior ones. The movements of reversion, in both the State of Israel and the United States as well as in other parts of the Diaspora, bring Jews to affirm what they think is the received system of the dual Torah. And that fact must present a surprise. Who, in 1897, could reasonably predict that Zionism would achieve its objectives, that Jewish socialism would not? And who, nearly a century ago, could have outlined the urgent problems of explaining the world that would preoccupy Jews in the final decade of the twentieth century? For the issue today that moves Jews to change and to do derives from the one question they thought they had dismissed a century ago: How to get back to the Judaism of the dual Torah? The Judaisms of continuation answered the opposite question: How far might one go from that received system? The twentieth-century Judaisms of an essentially original order ignored the received system as if it scarcely existed. Accordingly, all the mythopoeic—or really system-generating or system-opoeic—energies of the age derived from the question, How to get away from that Judaism?

Every system except Orthodoxy took as its premise a general alienation from that received Judaism; and Orthodoxy, for its part, proposed to attain a balance between separation from, and replication of, that system—this, not that. The

363

selective piety so brilliantly validated by Hirsch explained the answer. But the orbits of other systems derived energy from the reaction against the received system. The force that sent on their way six of the systems I have analyzed was the negative energy generated by the Judaism of the dual Torah. True, in each case, the issues of continuity and change required sorting out; in all cases, the matter of dealing with the precedent and authority of the received Judaism demanded much thought. But the simple fact is that from the eighteenth century forward all the makers of new Judaic systems did so because they wanted out. The self-evident question for two hundred years concerned integration. At the dawn of the twenty-first century, Jews fully at home in the West have opted for segregation.

That fact indicates how the centrifugal force of a hundred years ago has become a centripetal power today—a change of remarkable character, wholly beyond the imagination of anyone to predict. I do not mean to suggest that the Judaic systems of the two hundred years between the self-evidence of the Judaism of the dual Torah and the self-evidence of American Judaism exercised no centripetal power of their own. Quite to the contrary, we have seen how each one answered the question, How to get in? Zionism, for instance, attracted to its program and viewpoint Jews who formerly had slight interest in Judaic life in any form, Herzl being an outstanding example. We recall how the Jewish socialists and yiddishists came back to the Jewish people after a journey far away; they credited Jewish socialism and yiddishism with the power to draw them back. American Judaism gave access to vivid participation in a Judaic system to sizable numbers of people whose interest in the continuator Judaisms in the synagogue at best proved formal and conventional. And Reform Judaism opened a two-way road, on which many chose to travel backward into a Judaic system: its power to address the situation of Jews entirely remote in experience and upbringing found no match elsewhere. In all, therefore, the Judaisms at hand drew inward as much as they led outward. But, in every instance, the road back did not lead to the Judaism of the dual Torah. And today the single most interesting systemic development is precisely a reversion not to a generalized "Jewish identity"—that is, identification with Jewish things—but to a reappraisal of, a re-entry into, that Judaism of the dual Torah that had for so long repelled so many. This fact, above all, no one could have predicted.

NOTES

Preface

1. Jacob Neusner, *Foundations of Judaism: Method, Teleology, Doctrine* (Philadelphia: Fortress Press, 1983–85): vol. 1, *Midrash in Context: Exegesis in Formative Judaism;* vol. 2, *Messiah in Context: Israel's History and Destiny in Formative Judaism;* vol. 3, *Torah: From Scroll to Symbol in Formative Judaism.*

2. Rosemary Radford Ruether, *Sciences Religieuses/Studies in Religion* 2(1972):1–10.

3. Jacob Neusner, *Judaism in the Matrix of Christianity* (Philadelphia: Fortress Press, 1986).

4. Jacob Neusner, *Judaism and Christianity in the Age of Constantine: Issues of the Initial Confrontation* (Chicago: University of Chicago Press, 1987).

5. Jacob Neusner, *Self-Fulfilling Prophecy: Exile and Return in the History of Judaism* (Boston: Beacon Press, 1987).

Introduction: Religion, Theology, and Political Change

1. Jacob Neusner, *Judaism and Christianity in the Age of Constantine* (Chicago: University of Chicago Press, 1987); idem, *Judaism in the Matrix of Christianity* (Philadelphia: Fortress Press, 1986); and idem, *Foundations of Judaism* (Philadelphia: Fortress Press, 1985), 3 vols.

2. Jacob Neusner, *Self-Fulfilling Prophecy: Exile and Return in the History of Judaism* (Boston: Beacon Press, 1987).

3. Ibid.

Prologue to Part II: The Nineteenth Century and Its Theological Ideas

1. Benzion Dinur, "Emancipation," *Encyclopaedia Judaica* 6:696–718; quotation in col. 696. The *Encyclopaedia Judaica* was published in Jerusalem by Keter in 1971.

2. Ibid., col. 697.
3. Ibid., col. 699.

Chapter 2: Reform Judaism: History and Self-Evidence

1. Cited in Jakob J. Petuchowski, "Reform Judaism," *Encyclopaedia Judaica* 14:36.
2. Michael A. Meyer, *The Origins of the Modern Jew: Jewish Identity and European Culture in Germany, 1749–1824* (Detroit: Wayne State University Press, 1967), p. 48.
3. Petuchowski, "Reform Judaism," col. 25.
4. Ibid.
5. Max Wiener, *Abraham Geiger and Liberal Judaism: The Challenge of the Nineteenth Century* (New York: Jewish Publication Society of America, 1962), trans. Ernst J. Schlochauer.
6. Ibid., p. 11.
7. Ibid., p. 13.
8. Ibid., pp. 40, 42.
9. Ibid., p. 50.
10. Jacob Neusner, *Self-Fulfilling Prophecy: Exile and Return in the History of Judaism* (Boston: Beacon Press, 1987).
11. Wiener, *Abraham Geiger*, p. 51.
12. Abraham Cronbach, *Reform Movements in Judaism* (New York: Bookman, 1963), pp. 7–9.
13. Ibid., p. 132.
14. Cited in W. Gunther Plaut, *The Rise of Reform Judaism. A Sourcebook of Its European Origins* (New York: World Union for Progressive Judaism, 1963), p. 115.
15. Ibid., p. 119.
16. Petuchowski, "Reform Judaism," col. 26.

Chapter 3: Orthodoxy: Perfect Faith and Selective Piety

1. Nathaniel Katzburg and Walter S. Wurzburger, "Orthodoxy," *Encyclopaedia Judaica* 12:1486–93.
2. Ibid., col. 1487.
3. Ibid., col. 1488.
4. Ibid., col. 1490.
5. Moshe Shraga Samet, "Neo-Orthodoxy," *Encyclopaedia Judaica* 12:957.
6. Jacob Neusner, *The Way of Torah* (Belmont, Calif.: Wadsworth, 1979); idem, *The Life of Torah* (Belmont, Calif.: Wadsworth, 1974).
7. Samet, "Neo-Orthodoxy," 12:956–58.
8. Ibid., col. 957.
9. Simha Katz, "Samson (ben) Raphael Hirsch," *Encyclopaedia Judaica* 8:508–15.

10. Ibid., col. 512–13.
11. Ibid., col. 513.
12. Ibid., col. 514.
13. Samson Raphael Hirsch, *The Collected Writings*, 3 vols. (New York and Jerusalem: Philipp Feldheim, 1984), vol. 1, pp. 388–89.
14. Katzburg and Wurzburger, "Orthodoxy," col. 1489.
15. Ibid.
16. Hirsch, *Collected Writings*, vol. 3, pp. xiii–xiv.
17. Ibid.

Chapter 4: Conservative Judaism:
Orthopraxy and Anachronism

1. Arthur Hertzberg, "Conservative Judaism," *Encyclopaedia Judaica* 5:901–6.
2. Marshall Sklare, *Conservative Judaism* (New York: Schocken, 1955).
3. Ismar Schorsch, *Heinrich Graetz: The Structure of Jewish History and Other Essays* (New York: Jewish Theological Seminary of America, 1975), p. 48.
4. Ibid.
5. Joel Gereboff, "The Pioneer: Zecharias Frankel," in *The Modern Study of the Mishnah*, ed. Neusner (Leiden: E. J. Brill, 1973), pp. 59–75.
6. Schorsch, *Heinrich Graetz*, p. 48.
7. Ibid., pp. 61–62.
8. Alexander Marx, *Essays in Jewish Biography* (Philadelphia: Jewish Publication Society of America, 1948), p. vii.
9. Alexander Marx and Max L. Margolis, *History of the Jewish People* (Philadelphia: The Jewish Publication Society of America, 1927).
10. Arthur Hertzberg, "Louis Ginzberg," *Encyclopaedia Judaica* 7: 584–86.
11. Ibid., col. 584.
12. Louis Ginzberg, *The Legends of the Jews* (Philadelphia: Jewish Publication Society, 1909–38), vols. 1–7.
13. Louis Ginzberg, *The Significance of the Halakhah for Jewish History* (Jerusalem: Hebrew University, 1929).
14. Eli Ginzberg, *Keeper of the Law: Louis Ginzberg* (Philadelphia: Jewish Publication Society of America, 1966), pp. 145, 148.
15. Ibid., pp. 159–60.
16. Robert Gordis, *Understanding Conservative Judaism*, ed. Max Gelb (New York: Rabbinical Assembly, 1978), pp. 26–27.
17. Ibid., p. 26.
18. Ibid., pp. 39–40.

Chapter 5:   Socialism and Yiddishism as a Judaic System

1.   Quoted by Melech Epstein, *Profiles of Eleven: Profiles of Eleven Men Who Guided the Destiny of an Immigrant Society and Stimulated Social Consciousness among the American People* (Detroit: Wayne State University Press, 1965), p. 17.

2.   Ruth R. Wisse, "The Politics of Yiddish," *Commentary* 80(1 [1985]): 29–35; quotations on pp. 29, 30.

3.   Ibid., p. 31.

4.   Ibid., pp. 32, 33, 35.

5.   Ibid., p. 35.

6.   Schneier Zalman Levenberg, "Socialism," *Jewish Encyclopaedia* 15: 24–29, col. 25.

7.   Ezra Mendelsohn, "Socialism, Jewish," *Encyclopaedia Judaica* 15: 38–52; quotation in col. 38.

8.   Ibid.

9.   Ibid., col. 39.

10.   Ibid., col. 42.

11.   Chone Shmeruk, "Yiddish Literature," *Encyclopaedia Judaica* 16: 798–833; quotation in col. 811.

12.   Moshe Mishkinsky, "Vladimir Medem," *Encyclopaedia Judaica* 11:1175–76.

13.   Vladimir Medem, cited in Lucy S. Dawidowicz, ed., *The Golden Tradition: Jewish Life and Thought in Eastern Europe* (New York: Holt, Rinehart & Winston, 1967), pp. 432, 434.

14.   Ibid., p. 411.

15.   Chaim Zhitlowsky, cited in ibid., p. 412.

16.   Ibid., pp. 415, 421–22.

17.   Yerucham Tolkes, "Chaim Zhitlowsky," *Encyclopaedia Judaica* 16:1009–11.

18.   Melech Epstein, *Jewish Labor in U.S.A.: An Industrial, Political and Cultural History of the Jewish Labor Movement* (New York: Ktav Publishing, 1969), p. 275.

19.   Nora Levin, *While Messiah Tarried: Jewish Socialist Movements, 1871–1917* (New York: Schocken, 1977), pp. ix, x.

20.   Wisse, "Politics of Yiddish."

21.   Ibid.

22.   Ibid., pp. 29–30.

Chapter 6:   Zionism: Reversion to an Invented Past

1.   Walter Laqueur, *A History of Zionism* (New York: Holt, Rinehart & Winston, 1972), p. xiii.

2.   Arthur Hertzberg, ed., *The Zionist Idea: A Historical Analysis and Reader* (New York: Doubleday and Herzl Press, 1959), p. 15.

3. S. Ettinger, "Hibbat Zion," in "Zionism," *Encyclopaedia Judaica* 16:1031–78; Ettinger cited in col. 1041.

4. Arthur Hertzberg, "Ideological Evolution," in ibid., col. 1044–45.

5. Ber Borochov, cited in Hertzberg, ed., *Zionist Idea,* pp. 365–66.

6. Hertzberg, "Ideological Evolution," col. 1046.

7. Ibid., col. 1047.

8. Anita Shapira, *Berl: The Biography of a Socialist Zionist. Berl Katznelson 1887-1944* (Cambridge: Cambridge University Press, 1974), p. 137.

9. Ibid., p. 167.

10. Jacob Klatzkin, cited in Hertzberg, ed., *Zionist Idea,* pp. 317, 318, 319.

11. Ibid., p. 319.

12. These verses of Isaiah quoted from *The New English Bible* (New York: Oxford University Press, 1976), pp. 901–4.

13. Amos Elon, *The Israelis: Founders and Sons* (New York: Holt, Rinehart & Winston, 1971).

14. Raphael Mahler, *A History of Modern Jewry, 1780–1815* (New York: Schocken, 1971).

15. Elon, *Israelis,* p. 13.

16. Ibid.

17. Ibid., p. 38.

18. Ibid., pp. 99, 106.

19. Ibid., pp. 125, 141.

20. Ruth R. Wisse, "The Politics of Yiddish," *Commentary* 80(1 [1985]):29–35.

21. Shapira, *Berl,* p. 290.

22. Ibid.

23. Amos Elon, *Herzl* (New York: Holt, Rinehart & Winston, 1975), p. 235.

24. Theodor Herzl, cited in Elon, *Herzl,* p. 239.

25. Elon, *Herzl,* p. 239.

Chapter 7:   The American Judaism of Holocaust and Redemption

1. Ruth R. Wisse, "The Politics of Yiddish," *Commentary* 80(1 [1985]): 29–35.

2. I summarize and revise my discussion of these matters in the following books: *American Judaism: Adventure in Modernity,* 4th printing (New York: Ktav Publishing, 1978); *Understanding American Judaism: Toward the Description of a Modern Religion,* 2 vols. (New York: Ktav Publishing, 1975), which deals with the synagogue and the rabbi in America, as well as Reform, Orthodoxy, Conservatism, and Reconstructionism; and especially *Stranger at Home: Zionism, "The Holocaust," and American Judaism* (Chicago: University of Chicago Press, 1980), and *Israel in America: A Too-Comfortable Exile?* (Boston: Beacon Press, 1985).

3. Ibid.

Epilogue to Part III: New and Old in the Mythic Ideologies of Being Jewish

1. Anita Shapira, *Berl: The Biography of a Socialist Zionist. Berl Katznelson 1887–1944* (Cambridge: Cambridge University Press, 1974).

Prologue to Part IV: Toward the Twenty-First Century

1. I cited Al Ghazali in my *History and Torah* (New York: Schocken, 1965) but have since been unable to locate the source.

Chapter 8: Reversion in Contemporary Times: Invention as Discovery

1. Janet Aviad, *Return to Judaism: Religious Renewal in Israel* (Chicago: University of Chicago Press, 1983), p. ix.
2. Ibid., pp. 2, 4, 10.
3. Ibid., p. 10.
4. Ibid., p. 16.
5. Ibid., p. 24.
6. Ibid., p. 61.
7. Samuel Heilman, *The People of the Book: Drama, Fellowship, and Religion* (Chicago: University of Chicago Press, 1983), p. 2.
8. Shalom Lilker, *Kibbutz Judaism: A New Tradition in the Making* (New York: Herzl Press, 1982).
9. Ibid., pp. 48, 50.
10. Ibid., p. 66.
11. Ibid., p. 77.
12. Michael Graubart Levin, *Journey to Tradition: The Odyssey of a Born-Again Jew* (Hoboken, N. J.: Ktav Publishing, 1986), pp. 106, 114.
13. Simon Rawidowicz, "The Ever-Dying People," in *Studies in Jewish Thought*, ed. N. N. Glatzer (Philadelphia: Jewish Publication Society of America, 1974), pp. 210–24.

Chapter 9: Continuity and New Creation: Judaic Systems for the Twenty-First Century

1. Max Weber, *The Protestant Ethic and the Spirit of Capitalism*, trans. Talcott Parsons, with a foreword by R. H. Tawney (New York: Charles Scribner's, 1930), p. 182.

INDEX

80–81, 83; Talmud, as history of, 154–59, 163, 167–68; tradition, 151, 161, 163–64; unity of community in, 150; and Zionism, 150
Conservative Judaism (Marshall Sklare), 152
Constantine, age of: conversion and Christian policy, 3–4, 7, 27, 33–39, 42–43, 46
Creizenach, Michael, 111
Cronbach, Abraham, 106–9

Darkhé hammishnah ("Ways of the Mishnah") (Zechariah Frankel), 154
Dawidowicz, Lucy S., 216–17
Dinur, Benzion, 77–78, 80–81
Dreyfus, Alfred, 228
Dual Torah, 24–27; focus of, on history, 57–69; formulation of Judaism of, 33–44; Judaism of antiquity, 3–29; messianism and, 55–71; nineteenth-century Judaism and, 75–84; and Orthodox Judaism, 116–18, 123–26, 128–30, 132, 135, 145–46, and Reform Judaism, 86–87, 91, 94, 98, 104, 108–10; symbolism of, 49–55

Education: and American Judaism, 265; and Orthodox Judaic attitudes, 116, 119, 121–23, 131, 134–36

Eleazar: on dual Torah, 53
Eleazar of Modin: on Bar Kokhba War, 66–67
Elon, Amos, 243–46, 251–52
Emancipation, 119; of Jews and new Judaism, 76–78, 82; and Reform Judaism, 92–93; and Zionism, 225–53
Enlightenment: and emancipation of Jews, 78–79, 81
Epstein, Melech, 219
Essays in Jewish Biography (Alexander Marx), 162
Ethnicity: and American Judaism, 260; and birth of twentieth-century Judaisms, 189–97; and Conservative Judaism, 148–78

France: human rights in, 82
Frankel, Zachariah, 100, 146; and Conservative Judaism, 153–59, 164–66, 169, 172, 177

Geiger, Abraham, 154–55, 161, 165; and Orthodox Judaism, 135, 140; and Reform Judaism, 100–108
General Jewish Workers Union (Bund), 189, 198, 204, 209, 213–14
Gereboff, Joel, 155
Germany: human rights in, 78–80, 82; Orthodox Judaism in,

INDEX